# The Heart Rate Monitor Book for

# Cyclists

## Second Edition

Sally Edwards
and Sally Reed

VELO press

Boulder, Colorado

Printed in the United States of America

10  9  8  7  6  5

Distributed in the United States and Canada by Publishers Group West.

International Standard Book Number: 1-931382-04-2

Library of Congress Cataloging-in-Publication Data applied for.

VeloPress
1830 North 55th Street
Boulder, Colorado 80301-2700 USA
303/440-0601; Fax 303/444-6788; E-mail velopress@insideinc.com

To purchase additional copies of this book or other VeloPress books, call 800/234-8356 or visit us on the Web at velopress.com.

Cover and interior design by Susie Alvarez Perry.
Interior production by Kate Keady Hoffhine.

# Contents

*Sally Reed (left) and Sally Edwards at the Danskin Women's Triathlon awards ceremony in Seattle.*

# Acknowledgments

We co-authors, Sally Reed and Sally Edwards, would like to extend heartfelt thanks to the people who contributed to and helped develop this book.

On the Vietnam memorial in Sacramento, California, one plaque reads "Some Gave All, All Gave Some." The names of those who died fighting that war, those who gave all, are inscribed on its wall.

We are happy here that the following individuals gave some; none gave all:

Lyle Nelson, Olympian and author, and Marty Rudolf, for providing their retreat home in Oregon; Estelle Gray, owner of R & E Cycles in Seattle, Washington, gourmet chef, and our consultant and venue director; Scott Reed, our star heart zones trainer; Bellevue Club, Bellevue, Washington, for its support in the early development of this program; the people in the original Heart Zones Cycling class, who were willing participants in the Heart Zones Training Lab; Sue Matyas, fitness director at Bellevue Club, for listening to Sally Reed for four years about this project; Nancy Weninger from Marin County, California, for her cutting-and-pasting talents; Sue Dills of Seattle, Washington, for providing the Lake Union Waterworks retreat; Jack Dills of Mercer Island, Washington, our English professor extraordinaire; Betsy Herring of Seattle, Washington, for her attention to editing details; Carolyn Behse of Bellevue, Washington, for applying the science of Heart Zones Cycling with analysis and flair; Kathy Kent of Naperville, Illinois, for taking Heart Zones Cycling to the Midwest; Shawn Boom of Sacramento, California, for reading the original manuscript and teaching it; Carla Felsted of Austin, Texas, for being a role model and an inspiration; Dorey Schmidt of Wimberley, Texas, for assembling and compiling the rough draft; Ida May Norton of Wheat Ridge, Colorado, for finishing the final edit; Judy Moise of Seattle, Washington, for her sculpting and refining; and Gena Reebs and Aimee Bluhm, Publications Department, Bellevue Club, for their photography contributions.

# Introduction

This is the first easy-to-follow cycling program that uses technology—a heart rate monitor—to guide you through your training. A heart rate monitor is a way for the mind to see what the heart is saying. The program, Heart Zones Cycling, uses the heart muscle as the smart motor for you to get healthier and fitter on a bike. The book includes more than sixty indoor workouts and outdoor rides along with key information on heart zones training and tips on using your monitor for weight management, fitness testing, and fitness goals.

This is a training book. It does not include information on bike setup, maintenance, fit, handling and skills, or how to buy a bike. There are wonderful books on the market today about all of those topics. Rather, *The Heart Rate Monitor Book for Cyclists* is an entirely new way of training for cyclists, triathletes, cross-trainers, and anyone who trains indoors and outdoors.

Why did we write this book? There are two answers, just as there are two authors. Sally Reed's perspective is based on her experience after attending a seminar Sally Edwards first presented in summer 1996:

In the seminar, Sally Edwards encouraged us to take the material from her books on Heart Zones Training and apply it. Heart Zones Training seemed like a perfect fit for indoor cycling. She [Sally Edwards] was emphasizing training smarter and safer. I knew there must be a way for fitness professionals to apply what world-class athletes and exercise physiologists were telling us about training, and that these same training principles could apply to cyclists at all levels. With permission granted to be creative, the seminar inspired me to develop the Heart Zones Cycling program and ultimately this book.

*A Heart Zones Cycling class at the Bellevue Club. From left to right:*
*Wally Prestbo, Marilyn Caplan, Sally Edwards, and Mark Allison.*

The other viewpoint about why this book was written is from Sally Edwards. She blames it all on Sally Reed's incredible ability to motivate others:

As the athletic director of the Bellevue Club in Bellevue, Washington, Sally Reed has more than a full-time job. She took the initiative and decided to launch a heart rate monitor test program using an existing indoor cycling program. I admire Sally Reed. She follows one of the most basic tenets of heart zones training—it's personal and individualized, in the same way people have their own dreams, physiology, and finish lines. Just as she and I share the same first name, the two of us are one in our mission to help build a happier, heart-healthy society.

Before starting any exercise program, it's important to have a complete physical examination. Men over age forty and women over age fifty should have a medical examination and diagnostic exercise test before starting a vigorous exercise program, as should symptomatic men and women of any age. If in doubt, consult your physician for clearance.

—SALLY EDWARDS AND SALLY REED

# 1

# Your Maximum Heart Rate: The Anchor Point

*You notice the burn in your shoulder, like a single nerve tingling. You are feeling exhilarated and it's just the smallest sensation, so you push harder and faster as you gulp another mouthful of air. So it was for Sue, until her shoulder burn became unbearably painful and her daily swim workouts became mostly kick sets. The doctor ordered time off from swimming and weeks of rehab. I suggested indoor cycling with a heart rate monitor to maintain cardiovascular fitness and strengthen her legs. Sue agreed and began a four-year training program that not only got her back in the water and setting national records but also had her winning her age group in triathlons.*

*How did Sue progress from being a great swimmer to being a champion age-group triathlete? She learned how to train smarter by using a heart rate monitor, and she committed to the Heart Zones Cycling program, an indoor cycling class using all the concepts we write about in this book. I can't promise you the same success Sue had, but I can promise that you will be healthier, stronger, and fitter for cycling or any sport you choose.*

—Sally Reed

Getting healthier, getting fit, and getting your fittest: It all starts with getting on your bike. To tackle these goals, it helps to have a heart rate monitor (HRM). These watchlike devices use the electrical signal from the heart muscle to measure the number of beats per minute your heart contracts. An alternative technique if you don't yet have a heart rate monitor is to count your pulse rate with your fingers placed on your wrist or the side of your neck: Using a watch or clock with a second hand, count your pulse for six seconds, then multiply the number by ten (or add a zero to your count). This is your pulse rate in beats per minute (bpm). An HRM and your manual count will produce the same number.

The basic idea is to use your heart muscle to set the intensity for your personal training zones. Getting to know your response at each heart rate level is a first step. Ride according to heart rate, and use feeling, cadence, and speed as support information.

## DETERMINING 60 PERCENT OF YOUR MAXIMUM HEART RATE

It's time to get on your bike and ride to make your first self-assessment. The purpose is to determine your initial riding heart zone. A heart zone is a range of heartbeats. Each zone is 10 percent of your maximum heart rate, or 10 percent of the fastest your heart can beat for one minute. Co-author Sally Reed's maximum heart rate for cycling is 180 bpm; the chart shows her heart zones.

The anchor point is your maximum heart rate. There are four self-assessments to help determine 60 percent of your maximum heart rate:

1. Every two minutes cycle harder.
2. Use the highest number your HRM has shown (or you have counted manually).
3. Use your favorite workout ride to determine a rate.
4. Use a mathematical formula.

| Heart Zones Chart for Sally Reed | | |
|---|---|---|
| Zone | Percent Maximum Heart Rate | Beats per Minute |
| 5 | 90–100 | 162–180 |
| 4 | 80–90 | 144–162 |
| 3 | 70–80 | 126–144 |
| 2 | 60–70 | 108–126 |
| 1 | 50–60 | 90–108 |

*Stop!* Intermediate and advanced cyclists should go to Chapter 5, at the section "Submax Test for Cycling."

## 1: Every Two Minutes Cycle Harder

To begin a training program, you should set a starting point. This point should be based on heart rate information about you. The first and one of the simplest self-assessments is based on your subjective feeling of exercise intensity, called "perceived exertion," or RPE (rating of perceived exertion).

In the 1950s, a Swedish physiologist named Gunmar Borg correlated how hard someone exercised with the person's verbal description or feeling of that sensation. In 2001 Carl Foster, Ph.D., modified and improved this scale to reflect American idiomatic English. Both scales measure an individual's perceived exertion. We have chosen the Foster modified scale, where a 10 is maximum exertion and a 1 is barely moving. For example, if you were at rest and I asked for your exercise intensity, you would say zero. When you started to ride slowly, just warming up, you might call that a 3 and describe it as easy to moderate intensity. RPE is a number you assign to your personal feeling of how hard you're training (Foster 2001). As you cycle faster or ride up a hill, or as you increase the exercise resistance or load, your heart rate increases, and so does the number you perceive as your exertion level. For this simple assessment, you will ride two minutes at each number until you feel challenged or tired.

When you reach this level of exertion, slow down (or remove the resistance) and cool down. During the assessment, you should always be able to talk; never ride harder than that. Every two minutes record the number that best corresponds with that level of exercise intensity as you perceive it. Use a watch to measure the time. A heart rate monitor will make this test easier, or you can manually count your heart rate.

Here are some descriptions of how activity at each of the RPE numbers feels so you know what number to associate with the feeling:

| RPE Number | Description | Feeling | Zone |
|---|---|---|---|
| 1–2 | Very easy | Very little effort, very comfortable | 1 |
| 3–4 | Moderate to somewhat hard | Easy to talk; could keep up pace for a long time | 2 |
| 5–6 | Hard to #x*! hard | Feels hard, more challenging | 3 |
| 7–8 | Very hard to #x*!, #x*! hard | Tough, very challenging | 4 |
| 9–10 | #x*!, #x*!, #x*! hard to maximal | Uncomfortable, can't talk; ready to stop | 5 |

Now you have the information you need to start your self-assessment. Take adequate warm-up time before you begin. Use an easy gear or light to moderate resistance so that your leg muscles don't fatigue before the test is complete.

You can stop the workout when you reach RPE 4 in your feeling of exercise intensity. For most people the moderate-exercise heart zone falls between an RPE of 3 and 4.

| Minutes of Warm-up | Heart Rate in bpm Fewer Than 100 | Your Rating of Perceived Exertion (scale of 1–10) |
|---|---|---|
| 0–2 | 100–110 | _____ |
| 2–4 | 110–120 | _____ |
| 4–6 | 120–130 | _____ |
| 6–8 | 130–140 | _____ |
| 8–10 | 140–150 | _____ |

Write down your heart rate when you were at an RPE of 3: _____ bpm

Write down your heart rate when you were at an RPE of 4: _____ bpm

## 2: The Highest Number Your HRM Has Shown (or You Have Counted Manually)

This assessment is for those who are fit.

Think of a time when you were riding your hardest. Perhaps you were chasing someone, attempting to pass, or grinding up a steep mountain summit. You could hardly breathe, your legs were screaming, you had your foot on the gas pedal; in other words, you were "red-lining" (close to maximum heart rate, explained in Chapter 2). If you were wearing an HRM, it would have displayed the highest number you've ever seen. It's hard work to reach this point.

If you were counting your pulse manually (palpation), it would beat the fastest you've ever felt. Count for six seconds; you might be surprised that in a short six seconds your heart can beat fifteen to twenty contractions. Add a zero to this number to get beats per minute. (For example, a count of 15 equals 150 bpm.) This number is very close to your maximum heart rate.

Write down the highest heart rate number you have ever seen or counted: _____ bpm.

## 3: Use Your Favorite Workout Ride

You probably have a training ride you love. If you're like most of us, you choose that route or workout most often because it's easy, familiar, and fun. This time, you will collect information about your heart rate during that ride.

Strap on your heart rate monitor. Every two to three minutes during your ride, observe the monitor and ask yourself what RPE best fits that moment. Since you are trying to correlate heart rate to RPE, when your level feels like what Foster would call an RPE 4, note the heart rate number. If you were to describe that feeling you might say, "I could ride like this for a long time. It's very comfortable."

If you ride a stationary bike, follow the same procedure.

As you ride your favorite workout, count your pulse rate when you feel that the exercise intensity is moderate. You should be able to ride for a long period of time at that level.

Write down your heart rate number on your favorite ride when you are at an RPE of 3: _____ bpm.

Write down your heart rate number on your favorite ride when you are at an RPE of 4: _____ bpm.

## 4: Use a Mathematical Formula

You may have used a formula that determines your heart zones based on age. These formulas were first created in the 1930s when exercise research was in its infancy and measurement was far from precise. Using a mathematical formula is not as accurate as was previously thought; however, it can still help determine a training zone. If you've found a workable formula, use that. All these formulas approximate a maximum heart rate used to set your training heart zones.

We asked a colleague, Dan Heil, Ph.D., to examine data he and his co-workers had collected for 1,500 walkers tested at the University of Massachusetts. In a computer analysis of factors that seemed related to the walkers' maximum heart rate, he discovered that three variables seemed most influential: age, body weight, and gender. Using those results, he created a new and reliable formula, the "math-max" formula:

> 210 minus half your age, minus 5 percent of your body weight in pounds, plus 4 for men and zero for women.

Here we have used Sally Reed as an example. She just turned 53 and weighs 120 pounds. Round either up or down if your age divided by two ends in .5. Sally's formula would be

> 210 − 26 − 6 = 178 bpm maximum heart rate

Sally's true and tested maximum heart rate during cycling is 180 bpm. Her math-max and her tested heart rate are different by only 2 bpm, which is very accurate.

Now calculate your maximum heart rate based on this formula by plugging in your numbers:

> 210 minus half your age _____ minus 5 percent of your body weight _____ plus 4 for men and zero for women = _____ bpm

This is your mathematically calculated maximum heart rate, or your math-max heart rate.

## SETTING ZONE 2 (60 PERCENT OF MAXIMUM HEART RATE)

You now have four different ways to determine your first training zone, and it's time to apply this information to a ride. Your zones need to be based on your unique physiology, current fitness level, goals, and other personal factors.

The number of heartbeats in each of your zones is keyed to your maximum heart rate. For the first workout, Crisscross Zone 1 and Zone 2 in Chapter 3, you will use a heart rate that is 60 percent of your maximum heart rate, or RPE 4, a cool and comfortable zone where you can have fun and receive many health benefits.

Since you're not ready to start by red-lining, you're going to determine the average of the four measurements we just recommended and use this to anchor your personal zone 2 of 60–70 percent of your maximum heart rate.

A. Every two minutes bike harder and self-test at an RPE of 4: _____ bpm

B. The highest number you have ever seen or counted x 60 percent: _____ bpm

C. Rate using your favorite workout ride x 60 percent: _____ bpm

D. Rate using a mathematical formula to determine 60 percent of your maximum heart rate: _____ bpm

From these numbers, use your best judgment to determine a heart rate number that best represents the feeling of RPE 4, or about 60 percent of your maximum exertion. Write that number here: _____ bpm.

Here's an example for Sally Reed's individual training zones:

A. Every two minutes bike harder and self-test: 110 bpm

B. The highest number she has ever seen or counted: (175 x 60 percent) 105 bpm

C. Rate using her favorite workout ride: 105 bpm

D. Rate using a mathematical formula to determine 60 percent of her maximum heart rate: 107 bpm

Average of these four measurements: 109 bpm

Her tested maximum heart rate of 180 x 60 percent = 108 bpm

## THE TEN STEPS TO HEART ZONES CYCLING

Systematic training is a way of exercising based on a certain methodology or system. Training systems follow certain rules that are like a set of instructions written into a software program. These rules are based on how the human body responds physiologically to a dosage, also called "training load" or just "load."

The ten steps to Heart Zones Cycling is just that—a systematic and progressive way to approach riding your bike smarter in order that your body responds positively and safely. Training this way leads to realizing benefits and enjoying your rides even more. By measuring and monitoring your riding with this system, you can best manage your cycling program. That's because a heart rate monitor is a management tool for your cycling improvement; it is not a speedometer.

Each of the ten steps proceeds in logical sequence. Think of these steps as forming a ladder. When you reach the top rung of the ladder, you will know more, be fitter, and find more joy in training with methodology. The program is fun, it saves you time, and it helps you get more out of each ride.

| The Ten Steps to Heart Zones Cycling | | |
|---|---|---|
| **Step** | **Task** | **Chapter** |
| 1 | Estimating your maximum heart rate | 1 |
| 2 | Choosing your goals | 2 |
| 3 | Setting your zones | 2 |
| 4 | Creating your 30-day program | 4 |
| 5 | Determining your training spokes | 4 |
| 6 | Assessing your current level of fitness | 5 |
| 7 | Writing your training plan | 7 |
| 8 | Analyzing your training plan | 7 |
| 9 | Logging your workouts and rides | 9 |
| 10 | Reassessing your fitness level | 9 |

## STEP 1: *Estimating Your Maximum Heart Rate*

To estimate your maximum heart rate, simply use your 60 percent estimate and calculate its 100 percent value. The following chart makes this step easy. Circle the 60 percent estimate and then write down the corresponding 100 percent number:

| **100%** | 150 | 155 | 160 | 165 | 170 | 175 | 180 | 185 | 190 | 195 | 200 | 205 | 210 | 215 |
|---|---|---|---|---|---|---|---|---|---|---|---|---|---|---|
| **60%** | 90 | 93 | 96 | 99 | 102 | 105 | 108 | 111 | 114 | 117 | 120 | 123 | 126 | 129 |

My estimated 100 percent maximum heart rate is _____bpm.

You have completed the first step of Heart Zones Cycling by calculating your maximum heart rate. With this number, you can determine each of your five different heart zones because they are anchored to your maximum heart rate. You'll be calculating your heart zones in Chapter 2.

# Heart Zones Cycling

## Maximum Heart Rate

| TRAINING ZONES (% MAXIMUM HEART RATE) | FUEL BURNING | Max HR 150 | Max HR 155 | Max HR 160 | Max HR 165 | Max HR 170 | Max HR 175 | Max HR 180 | Max HR 185 | Max HR 190 | Max HR 195 | Max HR 200 | Max HR 205 | Max HR 210 | Max HR 215 | Max HR 220 |
|---|---|---|---|---|---|---|---|---|---|---|---|---|---|---|---|---|
| **Zone 5** Red-Line Zone 90%–100% Max HR | CARBOHYDRATE BURNING | ◇ | ◇ | ◇ | ◇ | ◇ | ◇ | ◇ | ◇ | ◇ | ◇ | ◇ | ◇ | ◇ | ◇ | ◇ |
| | | 135 | 140 | 144 | 149 | 153 | 158 | 162 | 167 | 171 | 176 | 180 | 185 | 189 | 194 | 198 |
| **Zone 4** Threshold Zone 80%–90% Max HR | | 135 | 140 | 144 | 149 | 153 | 158 | 162 | 167 | 171 | 176 | 180 | 185 | 189 | 194 | 198 |
| | | 120 | 124 | 128 | 132 | 136 | 140 | 144 | 148 | 152 | 156 | 160 | 164 | 168 | 172 | 176 |
| **Zone 3** Aerobic Zone 70%–80% Max HR | | 120 | 124 | 128 | 132 | 136 | 140 | 144 | 148 | 152 | 156 | 160 | 164 | 168 | 172 | 176 |
| | | 105 | 109 | 112 | 116 | 119 | 123 | 126 | 130 | 133 | 137 | 140 | 144 | 147 | 151 | 154 |
| **Zone 2** Temperate Zone 60%–70% Max HR | FAT BURNING | 105 | 109 | 112 | 116 | 119 | 123 | 126 | 130 | 133 | 137 | 140 | 144 | 147 | 151 | 154 |
| | | 90 | 93 | 96 | 99 | 102 | 105 | 108 | 111 | 114 | 117 | 120 | 123 | 126 | 129 | 132 |
| **Zone 1** Healthy Heart Zone 50%–60% Max HR | | 90 | 93 | 96 | 99 | 102 | 105 | 108 | 111 | 114 | 117 | 120 | 123 | 126 | 129 | 132 |
| | | 75 | 78 | 80 | 83 | 85 | 88 | 90 | 93 | 95 | 98 | 100 | 103 | 105 | 108 | 110 |

## Understanding Maximum Heart Rate

To ride smart, you need to know your maximum heart rate. Here are some important characteristics of maximum heart rate:

- Genetically determined; you are born with it
- Altitude-sensitive
- A fixed number, unless you become unfit

- Affected by some medications
- If high, does not predict better athletic performance
- If low, does not predict worse athletic performance
- Varies greatly among people of the same age
- Serves as the anchor for setting an individual's training zones
- Sport-specific

As you move through the next few steps and learn how to ride and get maximum benefit from each pedal stroke, stop for a moment and think about why you want to ride smarter, with more precision, and in less time and miles. The answer is different for everyone. Each person is motivated differently, and learning your source of motivation is important. We suspect that if you are like us, it is because in your heart, you love to ride. This is called "intrinsic" motivation, and it is the deepest kind of force because it is internal, not external. By using a heart monitor and knowing your maximum heart rate, you are better assured that you can ride in your zones to accomplish your goals. Keep reading to discover how to set those internal goals that are the driving force behind riding successfully.

## REFERENCES

Borg, Gunmar. *Borg's Perceived Exertion and Pain Scales*. Champaign, IL: Human Kinetics, 1998.

Edwards, Sally. *The Heart Rate Monitor Book*. Helsinki, Finland: Polar Electro Oy, 1993.

Foster, Carl, et al. A New Approach to Monitoring Exercise Training. *Journal of Strength and Conditioning Research* 15, no. 1 (2001): pp. 109–115.

Wilmore, Jack, and David Costill. *Physiology of Sport and Exercise*. Revised. Champaign, IL: Human Kinetics, 1999.

# 2
# Setting Your Goals and Riding within Your Heart Zones

*Paul Yale is a brilliant software developer, teacher, and author. Success in business came easily for him, but successful fitness had been a challenge for years.*

*When I met Paul through my heart zones training seminar, he was a couch potato who belonged to a prestigious athletic club but never worked out. He gained weight each year and didn't like it. He traveled internationally, so it was hard to stay in shape when the speed of his life was accelerating.*

*He attended his first seminar alone but later brought many relatives and his whole business team. After three years, he completed his first triathlon, ran a marathon in less than five hours, and started to ride to get in better shape. He gained muscle, lost fat, and lost total body weight. I was thrilled by the improvement I saw in his health and his life.*

*We asked Paul why, like so many others, he continued to attend the seminar and bring more people. He answered that business and cycle training share qualities that made it possible for him to integrate both. He applied the way we train and race as competitive athletes to how he conducted his small business.*

*Paul's first discovery was in the "g" word: goals. This chapter will teach you how athletes set attainable goals by training. We rarely "exercise." When we do, we move for the joy or benefit of the movement itself. That's important. When we "train," we move to accomplish a goal. That's critical. For athletes to succeed, we use goals for motivation.*

*Business and most other aspects of life are similar in that if you set goals, the chance to accomplish more increases enormously. But more important than mere goal setting is the feeling of personal accomplishment, self-esteem, and satisfaction when you cross the finish line. The feeling that you did it is one of the best rewards that comes from the process. You set a goal, you write and execute a plan, and you joyfully reach the finish line. That process can empower each of us. Becoming an athlete by practicing the Heart Zones Cycling system gives you access to that feeling and ability. You can apply the same process to every other aspect of your life. In* The Art of Happiness, *the Dalai Lama describes this process: "[In] an approach to bringing about positive changes within oneself, learning is only the first step. There are other factors as well: conviction, determination, action, and effort."*

*I volunteer to finish last in all the Danskin women's triathlon races. I've finished last in more than eighty races in the past thirteen years. I swim with the last swimmer, bike with the last cyclist, and run with the last runner, so that no one else has to finish last. To me it is a privilege to be the sweep athlete.*

*Finishing dead last isn't as much fun as finishing somewhere else in the field, of course. But what counts is that you set goals and accomplish them. Reebok had an advertising campaign with a slogan that I loved: "Life is not a spectator sport." I'd like to rewrite it positively as "life is a participant's sport." You are the athlete. An athlete in my playbook is anyone who trains.*

*You can experience improvement not only in your athletic performance but also in your life. Follow this systematic process and you will realize the outcome by saving time and getting more benefit. In your workout and in your life, you will increase productivity.*

—Sally Edwards

## STEP 2: *Choosing Your Goals*

The second step in your new cycle training program is to choose your athletic goals. As a framework for making those choices, you should set goals that are specific, measurable, action-oriented, realistic, and timely (remember these by the acronym SMART). Setting goals around these factors is smart training. Finally, you also need to decide on short-term and long-term goals.

Next, write down your goals. Determine what it will take to accomplish them. What are your resources? What support systems must you have in place? What tools and skills will you need to be successful? Go get them. Then realistically assess the amount of time you'll need.

Once you've done this, commit your goal requirements to paper or disk in the form of a written plan. We'll call this a training or action plan. Use it to detail your workouts and how you'll complete them. Record your training in a logbook or software program so you can track how well you're doing. In the world of commerce, this kind of planning and recording is called a business plan.

Complete a self-assessment. This is a measurement that gives you a starting point for later comparison. For example, what is your current fitness level? That will be one of your starting points.

It's sometimes wise to get a medical checkup before you begin. Keep a copy of the records; don't just leave them in your physician's files, since they belong to you. Take charge of your health and accept responsibility for its improvement. Athletes and coaches call this your personal "performance evaluation." The term reinforces the business-sports connection, because employers also speak of a personal performance evaluation.

Finally, measure progress at intervals in your training. This procedure helps you see improvement and better manage your training program. You'll be getting healthier, fitter, faster, and stronger. Realizing and enjoying the changes in yourself will also motivate you.

## How Athletes Use Goals in Their Lives

Your athletic goal-setting process leads you to the big moment when you realize you're prepared to face the challenge. Throughout your training, you will have built a structure that puts you on the line—the starting line. You will reach the starting line ready and confident because you have trained like an athlete, and you are an athlete in every mental, physical, and emotional way.

Almost every year, somewhere in the world, Sally Edwards races in an Ironman triathlon. She has completed sixteen Ironman races over the past twenty years. People frequently ask her why she continues to enter that difficult race after doing it so often. Her answer:

> I love challenges and accomplishments. I prefer the hard races—the multiday adventure races like the Eco-Challenge and the bicycle race across the United States called RAAM—because they are as much who I am as what I want to learn and gain from these experiences. Each year, I set my own large and small goals.
>
> To reinforce this lifestyle, I carry with me the memory of how I feel as I head toward the finish banner. The crowds are cheering, and a smile of joy radiates from my face. I look up at the finish clock and recall the number I set in my goal process, the finish time I committed to when I set my goals. And at that moment, I know who I am and the satisfaction in my heart and soul of accomplishing the goals that I set and believed in, which is why I continue to participate in sports and business.

For Sally and so many others, such as former couch potato Paul Yale, that's success. This training can become success for you, too.

## THE FIVE HEART ZONES

All zones have structure, weight, and size. Structurally, the top and bottom of a zone are like a ceiling and floor. The top of zone 3, for example, is structurally the same number as the floor, or bottom, of zone 4. All zones have size. All are in 10 percent increments of your maximum heart rate, with a midpoint in each halfway between bottom and top. Each zone is named in accordance with the benefit derived from riding within its structure.

Each zone is unique. What happens physiologically changes from zone to zone, such as the fuels consumed, your feeling while in the zone, the amount of time you can spend in it, and the training effect that results.

Zones are not cumulative. You can't get the benefit of zone 1 by training in a higher zone such as zone 4. You only get the benefit of the specific zone you are experiencing. Zones have weight or value that corresponds to the number of the zone. The higher the number of the zone, the heavier the weight or multiplier value. All zones are part of a wellness continuum from health to fitness to performance. All zones are relative, which means they are specific to your maximum heart rate and nobody else's.

## Zone 1: The Healthy Heart Zone

| Zone | Zone Name | Percent of Max Heart Rate | Fuels Burned | Calories | Description | RPE |
|---|---|---|---|---|---|---|
| 1 | Healthy Heart Zone | 50%–60% | 10% carbohydrates, 85% fat, 5% protein | 3–5 calories per minute | Easy. Don't sweat. Fun. Relaxing. Recuperative. Sustainable for long periods of time. Breathing is effortless. | 1–2 |

Zone 1 is the kickoff point for those new to training. The reason you start a cycling program with the most time spent in zone 1 is that it builds a healthier heart. Your heart muscle gets stronger and more efficient. You don't burn a lot of calories, but those you do burn come primarily from dietary and body-fat stores.

If you are in shape, the Healthy Heart Zone is a great place for a gentle recovery ride. A health benefit from training is metabolic fitness, including lower blood cholesterol, lower blood pressure, improved self-esteem, and, ideally, a stabilized body weight. You will no longer gain that one pound per year that is so common in even the most conscientious person. Because zone 1 is such low-intensity training, you'll have plenty of time to enjoy the sights and smell the flowers while you ride.

## Zone 2: The Temperate Zone

| Zone | Zone Name | Percent of Max Heart Rate | Fuels Burned | Calories | Description | RPE |
|------|-----------|---------------------------|--------------|----------|-------------|-----|
| 2 | Temperate Zone | 60%–70% | 15% carbohy-drates, 80% fat, 5% protein | 6–8 calories per minute | Cool zone. Breathing is comfortable. Known as the temperate zone. Gain muscle mass. Realize more health benefits. | 3–4 |

Zone 2 has such a strong character that it is known by a variety of names, including the Temperate Zone, the Comfort Zone, the Cruise Zone, and sometimes (though inaccurately) the Fat-Burning Zone. Some of the benefits you'll get from training in the Temperate Zone are increased skeletal muscle mass and decreased body fat. In the Temperate Zone, you train your body to metabolize fat efficiently, which includes fat mobilization, transportation, and utilization. You can read more about this in Chapter 6.

Oxygen is plentiful in this zone, so you will realize improved aerobic function. As you spend more time in the Temperate Zone, you will increase your capacity to burn fat by increasing the number of energy factories, called mitochondria, in each muscle cell. In other words, training in zone 2 allows you to open your fat cells and let the fat out of them while turning on the demand for fat by muscle cells. Simultaneously, because of the body's adaptation to the exercise, your muscles are increasing the number of fat-energy-burning factories.

Zone 2, the Temperate Zone, like its name, is a cool and comfortable zone to ride.

## Zone 3: The Aerobic Zone

Zone 3 gives you one of the biggest fitness benefits in the least time. In the Aerobic Zone, you maximize your efforts because you are burning more calories in the form of carbohydrates and fat. Simultaneously, your body is consuming lots of oxygen, and your cardiopulmonary system dramatically improves. Endorphins, the brain chemicals that blunt pain and are responsible for what's termed the "cyclist's high," are released. These naturally produced opiate-like stress reducers can increase up to fivefold from a resting state.

| Zone | Zone Name | Percent of Max Heart Rate | Fuels Burned | Calories | Description | RPE |
|------|-----------|---------------------------|--------------|----------|-------------|-----|
| 3 | Aerobic Zone | 70%–80% | 55% carbohydrates, 40% fat, 5% protein | 9–11 calories per minute | Cardiovascular zone— improvement in the number and size of blood vessels, in respiratory functions, in cardiac function, endorphins released, shift in fuel utilization toward carbohydrates. You sweat. | 4–5 |

This Aerobic Zone is the key fitness zone because you get fitter and faster when you train within it. During this training time, you dump many of the emotional and physical stored-up toxins. You build resistance to fatigue and increase your endurance. Zone 3 riding builds cardiovascular efficiency while sparing the carbohydrates and burning the fats. The exercise high, or state of euphoria, arising from training here results in mood improvement, reduced anxiety, and improved appetite control. The beauty is that all these benefits last for hours after the workout.

## Zone 4: The Threshold Zone

| Zone | Zone Name | Percent of Max Heart Rate | Fuels Burned | Calories | Description | RPE |
|------|-----------|---------------------------|--------------|----------|-------------|-----|
| 4 | Threshold Zone | 80%–90% | 70% carbohydrates, 25% fat, 5% protein | 12–14 calories per minute | Improved oxygen consumption; increased tolerance to lactic acid production (the burn). Breathing is more difficult. High calorie consumption and more carbohydrates utilized as fuel. | 6–7 |

When you cross into the Threshold Zone, you enter a new territory of high heart rate numbers. Zone 4 leads to improved sports and fitness performance. If you want to get really fit, you need to spend some riding time in this zone. If you only want to stay fit, you never need to cross this threshold.

Somewhere in this zone for most individuals you pass from aerobic to anaerobic exercise. At this point, most athletes are exercising so hard that the muscles become hungry for oxygen. You can continue to exercise without enough oxygen. As a result, you may feel a burning sensation in the working muscle groups because without enough oxygen, there is a build-up of lactic acid.

The Threshold Zone is high-intensity training. It is much too stressful for the beginner, but for anaerobic workout junkies who spend all their riding time hanging out in this zone, producing endorphins and eating up lactic acid as if it were chocolate, it's a delight. This isn't an easy training zone to stay in because it is "hot"; it has high heart rate numbers and high intensity. Even exceedingly fit athletes find it's a challenge to stay in this zone for more than sixty minutes. Your muscular energy factories, the mitochondria, are working at full capacity, burning every calorie that comes their way without distinguishing fat from protein or carbohydrate. Think of the Threshold Zone as one with a high thermostatic climate.

## Zone 5: The Red-Line Zone

| Zone | Zone Name | Percent of Max Heart Rate | Fuels Burned | Calories | Description | RPE |
|---|---|---|---|---|---|---|
| 5 | Red-Line Zone | 90%–100% | 90% carbohydrates, 5% fat, 5% protein | 15–20 calories per minute | Extremely high-intensity zone. Important for maximizing speed and strength but potentially damaging to the physiology. Total amount of calories burned is high. | 9–10 |

The Red-Line Zone is only for competitive athletes. You may have experienced zone 5 by accident if you ever had to sprint to catch the bus, when your heart is beating so hard and your breathing is so labored that you feel your chest will burst. Red-lining is a training zone beyond the anaerobic threshold junkie's favorite. This is the territory where athletes suffer pain as they try to deliver the maximum metabolic demands of the muscles. It's not a sustainable training zone because your heart muscle can't and won't contract at or near its maximum intensity for long. For every second spent in this zone, you are taxing your oxygen capacity, fuels, and heart and skeletal muscles to their limits. Of course, payback comes later during recovery with the possiblility of sore muscles, fatigue, and much more.

This zone is where you work at your maximum heart rate. Stay too long and you will reach complete exhaustion. The Red-Line Zone is tantalizing because if you don't visit it often enough, you can't reach your highest performance levels. But if you overstay your visit (over-train), your body won't readily invite you back.

Each of the five physical heart zones has its own face, name, and character and is as unique as you are. You'll find a reason to spend time in each zone and accomplish different specific goals by doing so. That is what is so attractive about them and about the training system. If the endorphins don't get you in zones 3 to 5, the fat-burning will seduce you in zones 2 to 4.

## Wellness Is a Continuum

Your job, if you want to ride smart, is to cycle within your individual heart zones. You ride in different zones to get different benefits. If, when asked why you ride or what your goals are, you answer that you want to manage your weight, you probably need to ride in the lower heart zones, 1 through 3, because the exercise intensity in those zones enhances fat loss. If you say you want to improve your muscles and endurance, you'll train in zones 2 through 4. To train for high performance like an athlete, you'll train almost entirely in zones 3–5, with an emphasis on the upper two zones, and in zone 2 for recovery.

Training in different zones is designed to accomplish different personal goals at different times. Riding occasionally in order to stay fit, but not to get fitter, is called maintenance, and is accomplished by training in the cool, low-intensity heart zones.

Within the five heart zones, there are no good or bad zones. Plan your cycle training program to include the three Ms—managed, monitored, and measured—and you will realize the cumulative benefits within each heart zone.

The table emphasizes these points:

- Distinctly different benefits are derived from each zone.
- Zones display no hierarchy of superiority. The health zones, 1–3, are merely different from, not better than, the performance zones, 3–5.
- Benefits are not associative. You cannot spend all your time in the performance heart zones and then expect to get the good benefits of the lower zones.
- The fitness zones, 2–4, provide the greatest benefit with the fewest risks.

## STEP 3: *Setting Your Zones*

The next step in creating your training program is to determine your five individual training zones. Remember your estimated maximum heart rate (max HR) from Chapter 1. Here is where it comes into play. Using the table at right, multiply the percent of maximum heart rate times your estimated maximum heart rate.

| My Five Heart Zones | |
|---|---|
| **Heart Zone Percent** | **Beats per Minute** |
| 100 percent of max HR | _____ bpm |
| 90 percent of max HR | _____ bpm |
| 80 percent of max HR | _____ bpm |
| 70 percent of max HR | _____ bpm |
| 60 percent of max HR | _____ bpm |
| 50 percent of max HR | _____ bpm |

## Characteristics of the Five Heart Zones

| Wellness Zone | Zone Number | Zone Name | Improvement Benefits | Negative Aspects |
|---|---|---|---|---|
| Health Zones | 1 2 3 | Healthy Heart Temperate Aerobic | Lower blood pressure, weight loss, stress management. Overall health improvement: smoking cessation, lowers risks such as heart attacks, decreases substance abuse. Improved blood chemistry (cholesterol, triglycerides). Improved muscle mass. | Performance does not improve. Burn rate of total calories is relatively low. |
| Fitness Zones | 2 3 4 | Temperate Aerobic Threshold | Increase the following: delivery of blood, oxygen, and other nutrients to the muscles. Increase in the number and size of mitochondria, the number and size of blood vessels. Increase in the size and strength of the heart. Increase in lung function, oxygen consumption. | Few if any. |
| Performance Zones | 3 4 5 | Aerobic Threshold Red-Line | Improved volume of oxygen consumed, better tolerance to lactate, increased anaerobic threshold, increased muscle speed to contract, improved muscle strength. Optimum athletic performance. Enlargement of fat-burning range. | Overtraining potential: increased red blood cell destruction, increased risk of injuries, diminished ATP energy renewal, potential damage to aerobic capacity and enzymes, potential damage to the immune system. |

| Zone Name | Percent of Max HR | Beats per Minute | Zone |
|-----------|-------------------|------------------|------|
| Red-Line Zone | 90–100% max HR | _____ to _____ | 5 |
| Threshold Zone | 80–90% max HR | _____ to _____ | 4 |
| Aerobic Zone | 70–80% max HR | _____ to _____ | 3 |
| Temperate Zone | 60–70% max HR | _____ to _____ | 2 |
| Healthy Heart Zone | 50–60% max HR | _____ to _____ | 1 |

Setting your zones and choosing your goals is very much like planning a long trip in your car. You plot the various towns or points of interest you are going to stop at and enjoy along the way (short- to mid-range goals) and then the date you plan on arriving at the final destination (race day or the ultimate goal). The gas you choose (heart zones training) provides you with the most effective and highest-octane fuel available. Along with training in the zones, goal setting provides the motivation, conditioning, and confidence needed to complete the journey.

## REFERENCES

Dalai Lama. *The Art of Happiness.* New York City: Riverhead Books, 1998.

# 3

# The Basics of Riding
# with Your Heart

*Salespeople in the cycling business will tell you that fitting people for a new bike for performance and comfort is a challenge because no two bodies are the same. Similarly, there is no single perfect training program for everyone.*

*All exercise, like bikes, should be customized to fit the individual. Several years ago, a popular magazine named the fittest man in the world. The article outlined his training program and left readers with the notion that they should consider following it so they could become as fit as the cover boy. That approach may sell magazines, but it is not good advice for training. You can appreciate and respect other people's training regimens, but follow the one that fits you.*

*Consider maximum heart rate as an example. Maggie Sullivan, vice president of sports marketing for Danskin, is a forty-eight-year-old, hardworking, very slender, tall, high-energy woman. If you saw her, it would be hard to estimate her percent of body fat, cholesterol level, blood pressure, metabolic rate, or maximum heart rate. In a test, she wore a heart rate monitor and measured her maximum heart rate on a treadmill. Surprisingly, her tested maximum heart rate is 215 beats per minute. Maximum heart rate is not related to age.*

*There are two things to note about maximum heart rate. The mathematical formula commonly used (220 minus your age) is extremely inaccurate for much of the population. Maggie's heart rate under this formula would be 220 − 48 years = 172 bpm. Compared with her tested maximum heart rate of 215, there is an error of 43 beats per minute—too large for practical use.*

*Second, Maggie's heart zones are unique to her. She needs to determine her training zones based on her anchor point heart number of 215 bpm, which is entirely different from, for example, Sally Reed's maximum heart rate of 180 bpm. As they say in the shoe business, if the shoe doesn't fit, don't wear it.*

*The same is true for group exercise or cycling programs. We put packs of riders or groups of individuals together, make them follow the same workout programs, and expect them all to do well. The coach or instructor leads the group through the same intensity, duration, and frequency of exercise. Some do well, and others don't. If there are a few stars in the class who lose a lot of weight or win a race, the coach is considered brilliant. We don't consider the participants who fail to accomplish their goals and say that the coach is a failure. We should. The coach has failed the group if he or she hasn't individualized the workout to meet everyone's unique needs.*

*This is common in indoor cycling classes, where the fittest riders hop on the bikes nearest the instructor and the last row can barely hold onto the workout. This tends to happen out of intim- idation or fear. Many of these indoor cycling workouts are called "high, hard, and hot" because participants hold a high heart rate for long periods. Just as in a pack of road riders, the unfit fall off the back and quickly out of the program. We lose them because they're burned out.*

*In contrast, heart zones training, which might be called individualized zone training with heart, is based totally on your individual physiology—your heart zones. This training honors your individual goals, individual physiology, unique sports history, interests, and special needs; it is completely about you. Your heart sets the tempo and the pace. Yours is the smart heart.*

*Your heart rate monitor is the link between your mind and body. It lets your mind see what your heart is saying.*

—SALLY EDWARDS

## UNDERSTANDING WORKOUTS AND TRAINING RIDES

Chapters 3–10 contain both indoor workouts and outdoor rides in which you use your heart rate monitor. *Indoor workouts* are based on your fitness goals. *Healthy heart workouts* will inter- est those whose goals are to build an endurance base and get healthy; these exercises are done at 50–75 percent of maximum heart rate and last 20 to 30 minutes. *Fitness workouts* are for those who want to get fitter. The intensity is higher (50–85 percent), and the ride is longer. *Performance workouts* are for those wanting to get their fittest, with intensities of 50–95 per- cent of maximum heart rate and workouts lasting up to 60 minutes.

Each indoor workout format contains an overview and description of the session. These sessions train your heart, muscles, and energy systems to be more efficient. Whether you are a beginner, intermediate, or competitive cyclist, workouts are driven by heart rate, and how you reach and maintain those heart rates is determined by your specific training goals. As an example, if your goal is to train for strength and power, you will change your training intensity using resistance and gearing. If your goal is to train for improved leg speed and suppleness, your heart rate numbers will be based on cadence or spinning. A person riding at a heart rate of 150 bpm and 60 rpm is training for strength, whereas someone riding at 150 bpm and 150 rpm is training for leg speed. Each rider has the same heart rate number, but two different physiological systems are being stressed.

Outdoor rides also have a brief overview and description. For certain rides, we have highlighted the key interval training sequence, with a ride snapshot.

## Heart Zones Cycling Terms

There are a few basic cycling terms to keep in mind for your workouts and rides because they are referred to throughout the book. Some of these are also included in the table of abbreviations that appears in Appendix F.

### Intensity

The heart rate intensities (percentage of maximum heart rate) during these workouts will range from 50 to 95 percent depending on your current goals and fitness level. Intensity can be measured in other ways, but for our purposes, heart rate is the measure, along with perceived exertion (how you feel).

### Cadence

Cadence, or pedal revolutions per minute (rpm), tends to be underemphasized but is an essential element in training. A comfortable cadence is different for each person. In general, a cadence of 80–110 rpm on flat terrain and 55–70 rpm on hills, depending on the length and grade of the climb, is ideal. Remember that a lower cadence and higher resistance or big gears can strain knees and quickly fatigue the muscles. Maintaining 60 rpm or above when climbing hills allows you to blend strength with cadence. As you get fitter and stronger, you will be able to ride bigger gears or use more resistance at the same rpm and heart rate.

| Pedal Strokes per 6 Seconds | Equivalent in RPM |
|---|---|
| 4 | 40 |
| 5 | 50 |
| 6 | 60 |
| 7 | 70 |
| 8 | 80 |
| 9 | 90 |
| 10 | 100 |
| 11 | 110 |
| 12 | 120 |
| 13 | 130 |
| 14 | 140 |
| 15 | 150 |

Higher cadence during parts of your workout will help recruit slow-twitch muscle fibers designed for hours of use. High-speed cadence, or spinning, is also good for recovery because it promotes circulation and refueling of the working muscle groups.

The best way to determine cadence is with a bike monitor or computer. If you don't have one, you can calculate cadence by counting the downstroke of one leg for six seconds and adding a zero. A heart rate monitor with stopwatch function is handy. Some workouts contain a six-second number in the coaching notes. Use the table on page 25 as a guide for checking cadence.

## Resistance and Gearing

Don't make the mistake of thinking that more resistance or bigger gears is the answer to getting fitter, faster, and stronger. Heavy resistance and big gears in the beginning are a prescription for biomechanical problems such as knee injuries. Many people take up cycling because it is touted as being good for strengthening muscles and tendons surrounding the knees, as well as being a great low-impact activity. Remember, though, that too much, too soon of any type of overload strength training can be detrimental. Honestly evaluate your fitness level and cycling skills, and take it easy on the resistance or gearing in the beginning.

Initially, you should work on your pedal stroke, cadence, and riding position rather than reach for heart rate numbers by excessively overloading your muscles and knees. There are several ways to increase intensity and raise your heart rate; resistance or gearing is just one. The workouts show you how to raise the intensity.

## Form

A smooth pedaling style greatly affects efficiency on the bike. Minimize extraneous movement, keeping your torso steady and letting your legs do the work. Your hips should not rock, bounce, or bob from side to side. Keep your shoulders square and your back elongated and flat. Use your abdominal muscles for support while relaxing your shoulders and neck.

Body position on the bike is specific to the individual. For some, standing is easier than sitting on a long, steep hill or interval, and others prefer to remain seated. Whatever position you choose, try to maintain good form, keeping your body as natural and relaxed as possible. Indoor stationary cycling classes offer myriad positions on the bike. Although fun and entertaining, not all extra space positions apply to outdoor cycling. Simply accept the studio class for what it is: a group exercise setting to improve your fitness level, not necessarily a class to improve your cycling skills.

## Pedal Stroke

Pedal with as smooth a stroke as possible in a circular motion, applying force through the legs to the pedals. You should pedal in circles rather than squares by dropping your heels at the bottom of the stroke and pulling back up using your hamstrings. Imagine that you have a small pencil on the inside of your ankles and the goal is to draw a perfect circle on each revolution. Keeping pedal pressure constant is your objective.

## Intervals

Interval training consists of alternating different speeds and levels of effort in one session. Intervals add variety to training and result in the training effect. They are used to get the cyclist faster and fitter in a shorter period of time. Interval training has been supported by a tremendous amount of research to validate the theory that raising and lowering your heart rate or intensity during a single workout produces multiple benefits, including these:

- Improved endurance or aerobic capacity, measured by the amount of oxygen you can use ($VO_2$ max)
- More total calories burned as you increase your intensity
- More fun, by adding variety
- Helps individuals stay on their training program

The primary reason for intervals is to train the energy systems to use specific fuels and deliver nutrients to your muscles more efficiently. You train your fuel systems as much as you strengthen specific muscle groups.

Steady-state riding is training at a fixed heart rate number. The reason to ride at a constant speed, cadence, or heart rate is to train yourself to become more efficient at this specific intensity level. Review the following sidebar on interval training and techniques to familiarize yourself with the types of intervals you'll be doing in the workouts.

## Choice

When the word "choice" is included in the workout, you must decide what to work on—strength, power, speed—and whether to cycle standing or seated. For building leg strength and practicing climbing out of the saddle (your bike seat), you will use more resistance or harder gears at a specific heart rate. When focusing on spin or leg speed, you will use less resistance or easier gears and a higher cadence. You may also choose to sprint to a certain heart rate within a given time to simulate a jump or fast start.

# Interval Training Skills and Techniques for Indoor Cycling

| Technique/Definition | Cycling Benefits |
| --- | --- |
| **Isolated Leg Training (ILT)** Pedaling with only one leg; resting the other on a box or stool or just dangling it at the side. | Improved strength, speed, and pedaling techique. |
| **Spin Ups** Increase cadence progressively by 5 to 10 rpm at regular intervals. | Improved neuromuscular adaptation, leg speed. |
| **Power Starts** From a slow spin or stopped position, seated or standing, expend 10 seconds all-out effort with heavy resistance or hard gear. 20-second recovery, alternate lead foot. | Improved power, acceleration, balance. |
| **Surges** Moderate to heavy resistance with 15- to 30-second cadence increases, then back to original cadence. | Improved muscle recruitment, strength, and power. |
| **Hill Climbing** Put front wheel on a 4-inch block of wood to simulate climbing. | Improved specific strengthening of hill-climbing muscle groups and body position. |
| **Pedaling Circles** Concentrate on a round pedal stroke, minimizing the "dead spot" at the top of the stroke by pulling up and across the top. | Improved suppleness, pedaling efficiency, and muscular endurance. |
| **Ups and Downs** Number of times up to a certain heart rate and recover back down to a given heart rate in a period of time. | Improved muscular power, speed, and endurance. Test for recovery heart rate. |
| **Tempo** Steady cadence with increases in resistance/gearing. | Improved muscular strength and endurance. |
| **Lactate Threshold** Maintain the highest sustainable heart rate for a period of time. | Improved oxygen and fuel utilization and lactate clearance systems. Getting fitter, faster, and stronger. |
| **Jumps** 1. Alternate standing and seated to a count; 2. Seated or standing, short, fast accelerations. | 1. Improved strength, balance, muscle recruitment. 2. Improved power, acceleration, and balance. |
| **Hovers** Hover just above the seat with the body weight over the seat post. | Improved strength, balance, muscle recruitment. |
| **Slides** From a hover position, slide weight forward over handlebars, drop toes, then slide weight back over saddle dropping weight over the heels. Usually done to a count. | Improved strength, balance, muscle recruitment. |
| **Ladders** Incremental increases in heart rate during certain periods of time. | Improved physiological adaptation to an increasing workload at different periods of time. |
| **Pyramids** Incremental increases and decreases in heart rate during certain periods of time. | Improved adaptation to increasing workload at different periods of time. |
| **Repeats** Repeat effort and recovery intervals a number of times. | Improved muscular strength and endurance. |

## Stretching

Stretching is a vital part of every workout and ride. Incorporate stretching before your warm-up and after you warm down on the bike. If you avoid stretching, you will pay the price down the road in the form of injuries, inefficiency, and restriction in your range of motion.

## Music

Music should be motivating and enjoyable. It is more important to choose music that sets a feeling or mood rather than to pick music just because it has a certain number of beats per minute. Indoor cycling music may be purchased at several popular websites, including www.exercise.about.com.

# Indoor Workouts

Beginning with this chapter, we present four indoor workouts and four outdoor rides in each chapter. We describe the goal and concept of each indoor workout and include a chart profiling the intensity followed by a step-by-step workout sequence.

## Workout Profiles

The profile illustrates the heart rate changes during the indoor workout. It is a workout-at-a-glance picture of the entire session. If you were to train with a downloadable heart rate monitor and transfer the resulting heart rate data into a software program, the profile of your heart rate numbers would resemble our workout profile. Try it!

There are different parts to a workout profile. In the sample that follows, named Five-by-Five, you can see that every 5 minutes, you change the intensity of the ride so that your heart rate changes by 5 beats every 5 minutes. The profile of this workout looks like a hill. The first half of the workout is like riding the uphill part. As the profile ascends, your heart rate increases, and as it rises, you progressively ride in more difficult heart zones, from zone 1 through zone 4. Likewise, as you descend the hill, your heart rate slows, and your intensity declines. On the down side of the hill, the workout is lighter and easier. Finally, you descend the hill to the bottom in the warmdown phase during the last few minutes.

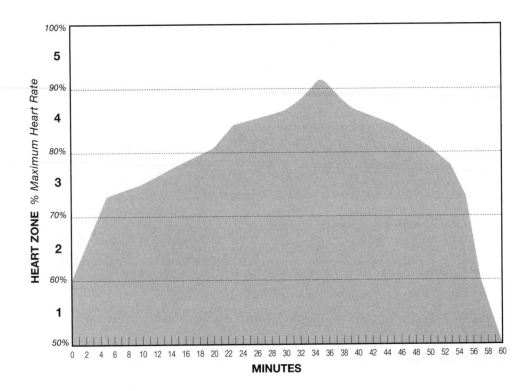

## Workout Sequences

A workout sequence describes how to do a given workout minute-by-minute, step-by-step (see, for example, the sequence chart for the Five-by-Five workout). As the minutes elapse, you will be asked to make riding adjustments to either increase or decrease your heart rate. You will also be instructed to change body position on the bike. As you do this, you will ride through different heart zones. Take the time before you ride to complete the column labeled "Your Heart Rate," because these are the heart rate values you will train at during the ride.

The "Interval Time" column represents the total amount of time that you sustain a given heart rate or stay in a certain range. In the Five-by-Five workout, you sustain each heart rate for 5 minutes and then change it up or down, according to the instructions.

How you make changes in your training intensity can be by your "choice," or we may suggest ways to change intensity that suit the goal of the particular workout. For example, if you are working on building strength, you will be directed to change your exercise intensity primarily by resistance and body position on the bike. By changing riding resistance these ways, you build muscle strength and ultimately riding power. The following workout outline has been completed to show you how to fill in your own form before you start to ride.

| Elapsed Time (min.) | Workout Plan | Heart Zone | Your Heart Rate (bpm) | Interval Time (min.) |
|---|---|---|---|---|
| \| **Sequence for Five-by-Five Workout for a Rider Whose Maximum Heart Rate Is 200 bpm** | | | | |
| 0–5 | Warm up to bottom of Z2 | 2 | 120 | 5 |
| 5–10 | Increase HR to maximum HR minus 50 bpm (bottom of mountain) | 3 | 150 | 5 |
| 10–15 | Increase HR 5 bpm, choice | 3 | 155 | 5 |
| 15–20 | Increase HR 5 bpm, choice | 3 | 160 | 5 |
| 20–25 | Increase HR 5 bpm, choice | 4 | 165 | 5 |
| 25–30 | Increase HR 5 bpm, choice | 4 | 170 | 5 |
| 30–35 | Increase HR 5 bpm, choice | 4 | 175 | 5 |
| 35–40 | Increase HR 5 bpm, choice (top of hill) | 5 | 180 | 5 |
| 40–45 | Decrease HR 5 bpm, choice (be careful to only drop 5 bpm in a controlled recovery) | 4 | 175 | 5 |
| 45–50 | Decrease HR 5 bpm, choice | 4 | 170 | 5 |
| 50–53 | Decrease HR 5 bpm, choice | 4 | 165 | 3 |
| 53–55 | Decrease HR 5 bpm, choice | 3 | 160 | 2 |
| 55–57 | Decrease HR 10 bpm, choice | 3 | 150 | 2 |
| 57–59 | Decrease to bottom of Z2 | 2 | 120 | 2 |
| 59–60 | Warm down to bottom of Z1 | 1 | 100 | 1 |

## Heart Zones Training Points

Each workout also contains a "Stats and Tips" section that has a column indicating the total heart zones training (HZT) points earned in the workout. HZT points are an easy way to compare the difficulty of different workouts and, ultimately, to track your training and set training goals. (For more information on developing an HZT point–based training program, see *Heart Zone Training* by Sally Edwards [Adams Publishing, 1996].)

All you need to know here is how HZT points are calculated. It's simple: You earn one point per minute of your workout, so first determine how many

| Heart Rate Ranges for a Rider Whose Maximum Heart Rate Is 200 bpm | |
|---|---|
| **Zone Number and Zone Name** | **% of Max Heart Rate (bpm)** |
| 5. Red-Line Zone | 180–200 |
| 4. Threshold Zone | 160–180 |
| 3. Aerobic Zone | 140–160 |
| 2. Temperate Zone | 120–140 |
| 1. Healthy Heart Zone | 100–120 |

minutes, or "points," you have, then multiply the number of points by the level of the zone you are training in. For example, on a 40-minute zone 1 ride, you would earn 40 points (40 minutes x 1 = 40); for a 30-minute zone 3 ride, you would earn 90 points (30 minutes x 3 = 90); and for a 25-minute zone 2 ride, you would earn 50 points (25 minutes x 2 = 50).

Essentially, the more HZT points a workout provides, the more training you're getting. It's a new way of measuring total training effort, also known as "training load," and it's blissfully simple to use. Have fun with it!

## READY TO RIDE

You are about to have some of the best rides of your life. In this and each subsequent chapter, you will have your choice of four indoor workouts and four outdoor rides based upon your goals and fitness level. Remember, healthy heart workouts are shorter in duration, typically 30 minutes, and heart rate ranges between 50 and 75 percent of your maximum. Fitness workouts are longer in duration, typically 45 to 50 minutes, and heart rate ranges are between 50 and 85 percent. Performance workouts are the longest and the most difficult. They are for the very fit individual and those wanting to reach their peak level of performance. Heart rate ranges from 50 to 95 percent.

The reading on your monitor is accurate 99 percent of the time and tells you exactly the relative intensity of effort your heart is experiencing. So if you think the workout or ride is too easy and you should sweat and go harder, no matter how strong the urge, follow your heart, not your head. If you listen to the voice of your heart, you will learn to hear it tell you more about who you are. When you listen to your inner heart speak, your outer world also undergoes beneficial changes.

Finally, remember to stretch before and after you get on the bike to maintain and increase your flexibility. Warming up and warming down are important parts of a workout, so don't sacrifice them, even if you have time constraints. These are all important parts of your workout that allow you to *keep* working out, year after year.

## WORKOUTS: Indoor Training

### HEALTHY HEART  Workout 1: Crisscross Zone 1 and Zone 2

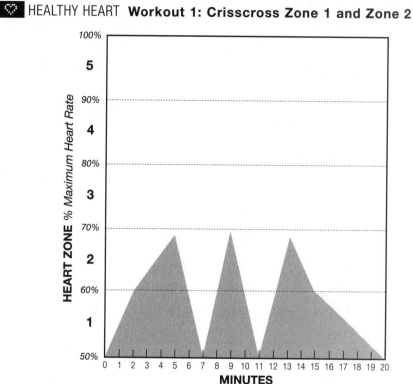

## Overview

If you are just getting started on a fitness program, this 20-minute workout will help build an endurance and aerobic base. Zones 1 and 2 are the Healthy Heart and Temperate Zones and lead to the development of a stronger heart muscle. In addition, by riding in low heart zones, you are investing in such healthy changes as lower blood pressure, lower serum cholesterol levels, stabilization of body weight changes, and improvement in your self-esteem.

The workout profiles are a graphic way of representing the workouts. Crisscrossing any one or two heart zones is a training ride of peaks, valleys, and rebounds. Each time you hit the heart rate number that corresponds with the top of the zone, decrease the intensity and allow your heart to recover until it reaches the bottom of the heart zone. When you reach the bottom of the zone, pick up the pace and increase intensity again, bouncing from the bottom to the top and then back to the bottom again.

| Stats and Tips for Workout 1: Crisscross Zone 1 and Zone 2 | | | |
|---|---|---|---|
| Zone Number and Name | Minutes in Zone | Heart Zones Training Points | Estimated Calories |
| 5. Red-Line | | | |
| 4. Threshold | | | |
| 3. Aerobic | | | |
| 2. Temperate | 10 | 20 | 60–80 |
| 1. Healthy Heart | 10 | 10 | 30–50 |
| Totals | 20 | 30 | 90–130 |

**Tip 1:** Use easy gearing or light resistance.

**Tip 2:** Focus on a round, smooth pedal stroke.

## Description

This workout will give you a feel for the two lowest-intensity zones, the Healthy Heart Zone (50–60 percent of your maximum heart rate) and the Temperate Zone (60–70 percent of your maximum heart rate). The low heart zones are known as the comfort zones because they are friendly and pleasant. Additionally, low heart zones training offers a much needed sanctuary of rest and recovery (rec) from higher-intensity training.

| Sequence for Workout 1: Crisscross Zone 1 and Zone 2 | | | | |
|---|---|---|---|---|
| Elapsed Time (min.) | Workout Plan | Heart Zone | Your Heart Rate (bpm) | Interval Time (min.) |
| 0–2 | Warm up to bottom of Z1, easy pedal | 1 | _____ | 2 |
| 2–5 | Increase HR to bottom of Z2 (60% of max. HR) with (R) or cadence/rpm | 2 | _____ | 3 |
| 5–7 | Increase HR to top of Z2 (70% of max. HR), choice | 2 | _____ | 2 |
| 7–9 | (Rec) to bottom of Z1 | 1 | _____ | 2 |
| 9–11 | Increase HR to top of Z2 (70% of max. HR), choice | 2 | _____ | 2 |
| 11–13 | (Rec) to bottom of Z1 | 1 | _____ | 2 |
| 13–15 | Crisscross[a] from bottom of Z1 to top of Z2, choice | 2 | _____ | 2 |
| 15–17 | (Rec) to bottom of Z2 | 2 | _____ | 2 |
| 17–20 | Warm down to bottom of Z1 | 1 | _____ | 3 |

[a] Crisscross: Increasing heart rate from the bottom of a zone to the top of a zone and back to the bottom.

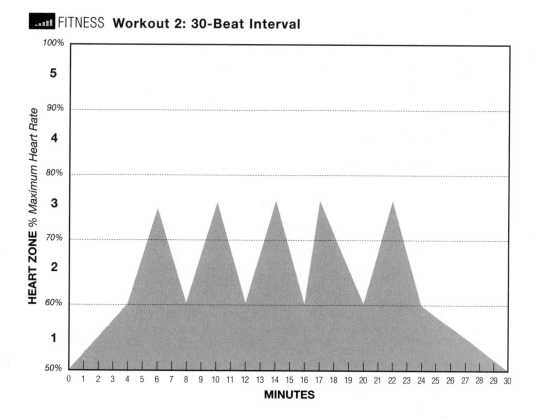

**FITNESS Workout 2: 30-Beat Interval**

## Overview

If your cardiovascular goal is to get fitter and you have been working out three or more times per week, choose this 30-minute, 30-beat interval workout. If you have never tried interval workouts before, you'll find they are fun and challenging. An interval is defined as alternating periods of higher intensity with periods of lower intensity. The interval in this workout is 2 minutes, and the intensity is a 30-beat increase in heart rate (HR). The recovery is a 30-beat decrease in heart rate in 2 minutes. The intensity will range from 50 percent to 75 percent of your maximum heart rate.

Completing this 30-beat interval ride will challenge your heart muscle to respond to both time and intensity intervals. Here is your chance to put the pedal to the metal and blow out the carbon! You will reap the benefits of lowering your cholesterol and blood pressure and increasing your capacity to burn fat. As you transition into zone 3, the benefits include an increase in the size and strength of your heart and an increase in your fat-burning metabolism.

## Description

This 30-minute workout includes a 4-minute warm-up, a 22-minute main set, and a 4-minute cooldown. It covers three zones with intensity ranging from 50 percent to 75 percent.

Begin in the Healthy Heart Zone and cross the Temperate Zone on your way to the midpoint of the Aerobic Zone. The 30-beat, 2-minute interval begins at the bottom of zone 2 (60 percent) and goes to the midpoint of zone 3 (75 percent). The rest or recovery interval drops 30 beats in 2 minutes to the bottom of zone 2. The main set has five 30-beat intervals.

Be aware of the following: (1) As you increase your heart rate to the midpoint of zone 3 (75 percent), you may exceed the heart rate goal. That's fine; just remember that on the next work interval you may have to "ease up" a few beats before you reach the 75 percent heart rate goal. (2) The recovery interval is what we call an "active" recovery versus an absolute recovery. In other words, you are pedaling with very little effort as your heart rate drops. Be careful not to let your heart rate fall below the recovery heart rate goal.

| Stats and Tips for Workout 2: 30-Beat Interval | | | |
|---|---|---|---|
| Zone Number and Name | Minutes in Zone | Heart Zones Training Points | Estimated Calories |
| 5. Red-Line | | | |
| 4. Threshold | | | |
| 3. Aerobic | 10 | 30 | 90–110 |
| 2. Temperate | 12 | 24 | 72–96 |
| 1. Healthy Heart | 8 | 8 | 24–40 |
| Totals | 30 | 62 | 186–246 |

**Tip:** An "active" 30 bpm in 1 minute is an excellent recovery heart rate (12 bpm or less is poor; 20 bpm is good; 40 bpm or more is the recovery rate of elite athletes). The more bpm the better!

| Sequence for Workout 2: 30-Beat Interval | | | | |
|---|---|---|---|---|
| Elapsed Time (min.) | Workout Plan | Heart Zone | Your Heart Rate (bpm) | Interval Time (min.) |
| 0–4 | Warm up in Z1, easy pedal | 1 | _____ | 4 |
| 4–6 | Increase resistance (R) or cadence (rpm) bottom of Z2 | 2 | _____ | 2 |
| 6–8 | Increase HR 30 beats to the midpoint of Z3 (75%). Your choice of (R), (rpm), or a combination of both; stay seated | 3 | _____ | 2 |
| 8–10 | "Active" (rec) to the bottom of Z2, easy pedal, no (R) | 2 | _____ | 2 |
| 10–12 | Increase HR 30 beats to midpoint of Z3 (75%), your choice | 3 | _____ | 2 |
| 12–14 | Recover (rec) to the bottom of Z2 | 2 | _____ | 2 |
| 14–16 | Increase HR 30 beats to 75%, standing | 2 | _____ | 2 |
| 16–18 | (Rec) to the bottom of Z2 | 3 | _____ | 2 |
| 18–20 | Increase HR 30 beats to 75%, high (rpm) | 2 | _____ | 2 |
| 20–22 | (Rec) to the bottom of Z2 | 3 | _____ | 2 |
| 22–24 | Increase HR 30 beats to 75%, heavy (R) | 2 | _____ | 2 |
| 24–26 | (Rec) to bottom of Z2 | 1 | _____ | 2 |
| 26–30 | Warm down with easy pedal | | _____ | 4 |

## PERFORMANCE  **Workout 3: Allez! Allez!**

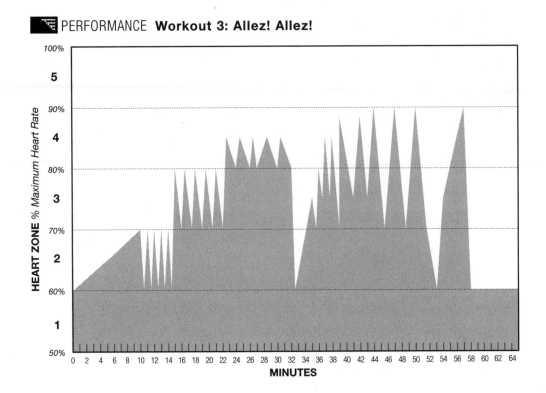

## Overview

Two ways to get faster on your bike!

1. The strongest muscle in the body is the cardiac pump. By developing a riding technique using a faster cadence, Tour de France winner Lance Armstrong puts greater demands on his heart and lungs versus drawing on strength in his leg muscles, which would be required for lower cadences in higher gears. Carried along by a huge aerobic capacity, Armstrong can then save his legs for that final climb and sprint to the finish.

2. It is always important to improve your pedaling technique. Being able to pedal efficiently is an essential element of good riding technique, and one that is necessary in order to be comfortable riding at higher cadences. Efficient pedaling involves applying equal force throughout the entire revolution of a pedal stroke, not just on the downstroke.

## Description

This workout will help you improve your pedaling technique and your overall aerobic fitness as you adopt a faster cadence and eventually develop more power. The first half of the workout is done with moderate resistance and fast cadence, the second half with heavy resistance and the same fast cadence. When riding outside, you want to increase your speed; try increasing your cadence first rather than shifting to harder gears. You may notice a rise in your heart rate, but the power requirement on your legs will not be as great as if you had shifted gears. Over time your heart muscle will adapt, your aerobic capacity will increase, your legs won't tire as fast, and you will recover more quickly. Train your heart as much as, if not more than, your legs.

To determine how good your pedaling technique is, ride your bike up a wet incline. If your wheels tend to skid with every downstroke of your legs, you may not be applying an even force. Try again in an easier gear, this time concentrating on applying even force throughout the pedal stroke. To do this, imagine scraping mud off the bottom of your shoes on the bottom of your stroke. Then from about the 10 o'clock position, pedal as though you are standing on a barrel and pushing it with your feet. You will soon realize a huge improvement in your traction on the uphills as you power up them evenly. Incorporate this feeling into your technique and muscle memory, and pedal better and with greater efficiency.

| Stats and Tips for Workout 3: Allez! Allez! | | | |
|---|---|---|---|
| Zone Number and Name | Minutes in Zone | Heart Zones Training Points | Estimated Calories |
| 5. Red-Line | 3 | 15 | 45–60 |
| 4. Threshold | 30 | 120 | 360–420 |
| 3. Aerobic | 16 | 48 | 144–176 |
| 2. Temperate | 16 | 32 | 96–128 |
| 1. Healthy Heart | | | |
| Totals | 65 | 215 | 645–784 |

**Tip:** Think of moderate (R) as riding in your small front chainring and heavy (R) as riding in your large chainring.

| | Sequence for Workout 3: Allez! Allez! | | | |
|---|---|---|---|---|
| Elapsed Time (min.) | Workout Plan | Heart Zone | Your Heart Rate (bpm) | Interval Time (min.) |
| 0–5 | Easy pedal warm-up | 2 | _____ | 5 |
| 5–10 | Increase HR to bottom of Z3 | 3 | _____ | 5 |
| 10–15 | Moderate (R), 95 rpm, 30 sec. followed by 30 sec. easy pedal (rec). Repeat interval a total of 5 times | 3 2 | _____ _____ | 5 |
| 15–22.5 | Slightly increase (R), 95 rpm, 60 sec. followed by 30 sec. easy pedal (rec). Repeat interval a total of 5 times | 4 3 | _____ _____ | 7.5 |
| 22.5–32.5 | Slightly increase (R), 95 rpm, 90 sec. followed by 30 sec. easy pedal (rec). Repeat interval a total of 5 times | 4 3 | _____ _____ | 10 |
| 32.5–35 | (Rec) | 2 | _____ | 2.5 |
| 35–38 | Heavy (R), 95 rpm, 30 sec. followed by 30 sec. easy pedal (rec). Repeat interval a total of 3 times | 3 4 | _____ _____ | 3 |
| 38–44 | Heavy (R), 95 rpm, 60 sec. followed by 60 sec. easy pedal (rec). Repeat interval a total of 3 times | 4 | _____ | 6 |
| 44–53 | Heavy (R), 95 rpm, 90 sec. followed by 90 sec. easy pedal (rec). Repeat interval a total of 3 times | 4 5 | _____ _____ | 9 |
| 53–55 | Easy pedal (rec) | 2 | _____ | 2 |
| 55–56 | Moderate to heavy (R), 75%, choice | 3 | _____ | 1 |
| 56–57 | Increase (R), 80%, choice | 4 | _____ | 1 |
| 57–58 | Increase (R), 85%, choice | 4 | _____ | 1 |
| 58–59 | Increase (R), 90%, choice | 5 | _____ | 1 |
| 59–65 | Easy-pedal warm down | 2 | _____ | 6 |

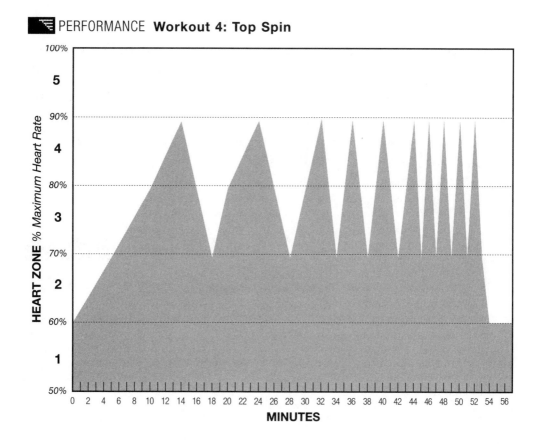

PERFORMANCE **Workout 4: Top Spin**

## Overview

This is one of our favorite workouts and a play on words if you are a tennis player. You will spin yourself to the top of four zones in 60 minutes. You can also change this workout to meet your goals by dropping down a zone on each 4-minute interval, which makes it a great workout for those wanting to get fitter. The last 10 minutes will challenge your sprint and recovery capabilities and give you a taste of how fit you really are.

Top Spin is designed to improve your ability to respond to approximately 20-beat and 40-beat intervals. It will also help you measure your fitness level by timing recovery rates. You may choose to do the 20-beat intervals by increasing cadence or adding resistance. If you choose resistance, keep a steady tempo or cadence. Do an "active" recovery by soft pedaling or easy pedaling. The 40-beat intervals are your choice in terms of using cadence, resistance, body position, or combinations that increase heart rate; do whatever it takes to get to the top of the zone quickly and back down. This is a good workout to do monthly to see if your recovery times are improving.

## Description

The Top Spin workout is a series of approximately 20- and 40-heartbeat repeats. The work-to-recovery ratio is 2:1, meaning that for every 2 minutes of effort, there is a 1-minute recovery. The last 10 minutes of the main set is very challenging and designed to see how many times you can do the 40-beat recovery interval. We can give you this gauge—and perhaps something to shoot for: In heart cycling classes, eight times up and down is the most we have seen.

This workout is fun to do with a group of people, especially during the first 10 minutes when everyone is sprinting and recovering at different times. Bring your towel and water bottle for this workout.

| Stats and Tips for Workout 4: Top Spin | | | |
|---|---|---|---|
| Zone Number and Name | Minutes in Zone | Heart Zones Training Points | Estimated Calories |
| 5. Red-Line | | | |
| 4. Threshold | 28 | 112 | 336–392 |
| 3. Aerobic | 20 | 60 | 180–220 |
| 2. Temperate | 10 | 20 | 120–160 |
| 1. Healthy Heart | 2 | 2 | 6–10 |
| **Totals** | **60** | **194** | **642–782** |

**Tip:** Relax, breathe long and deep rather than short and quick.

| Sequence for Workout 4: Top Spin | | | | |
|---|---|---|---|---|
| Elapsed Time (min.) | Workout Plan | Heart Zone | Your Heart Rate (bpm) | Interval Time (min.) |
| 0–5 | Warm up to the bottom of Z2 | 2 | _____ | 5 |
| 5–10 | Increase HR to the top of Z2 with cadence (rpm) | 2 | _____ | 5 |
| 10–14 | Increase HR to the top of Z3 with (R) | 3 | _____ | 4 |
| 14–18 | Increase HR to the top of Z4, your choice of sprint, (R), or combination, seated | 4 | _____ | 4 |
| 18–20 | Recover (rec) to the top of Z2 | 2 | _____ | 2 |
| 20–24 | Increase HR to the top of Z3 with (R), standing | 3 | _____ | 4 |
| 24–28 | Increase HR to the top of Z4, your choice of sprint, (R), or combination, first 2 min. seated, second 2 min. standing | 4 | _____ | 4 |
| 28–30 | (Rec) to the top of Z2 | 2 | _____ | 2 |
| 30–32 | Seated sprint to the top of Z3 | 3 | _____ | 2 |
| 32–34 | Standing sprint to the top of Z4 | 4 | _____ | 2 |
| 34–36 | (Rec) to the top of Z2 | 2 | _____ | 2 |
| 36–38 | All-out sprint to the top of Z4 | 4 | _____ | 2 |
| 38–40 | (Rec) to the top of Z2 | 2 | _____ | 2 |
| 40–42 | All-out sprint to the top of Z4 | 4 | _____ | 2 |
| 42–44 | (Rec) to the top of Z2 | 2 | _____ | 2 |
| 44–54 | Count the number of times to top of Z3 and (rec) to the bottom of Z3 in 10 min., your choice | 4 | _____ | 10 |
| 54–60 | Warm down to the bottom of Z2 | 2 | _____ | 6 |

## Outdoor Training and Rides
### Three Maximum Heart Rate Tests

The safest way to take a true maximum heart rate test is in an exercise or human-performance lab. This test is available in most major cities in the world, and the price for it varies. If you don't have access to or don't want to visit an exercise lab, you can determine your tested maximum heart rate at your own risk. Do these three rides only if you are fit, have no history or symptoms of cardiac, respiratory, or vascular conditions, and are under age fifty for women and forty for men. In addition, be sure you are fully rested before you test yourself in order to get your most accurate measurement.

### Workout 5: The Largest Number

This is an easy and quick assessment that takes you near your maximum heart rate. Turn on your bike monitor or bike computer and warm up completely. Start your stopwatch, and every 15 seconds, increase your heart rate 5 bpm until your heart rate no longer rises. When you reach a point of near exhaustion, slow down and recover. If your heart rate monitor does not store peak heart rate, mentally record the highest number you see. Always have a friend with you for both safety and motivation. Ride on roads with little vehicular traffic or interruptions.

### Workout 6: The All-Out Trip

This is another test that takes you to a point near your maximum heart rate. Find a 1,000-meter or half-mile measured distance that is flat and has no obstructions. Warm up adequately. Sprint the distance as hard as you can at full speed with a friend riding nearby to encourage you. Motivation is an essential factor in trying to get close to your true maximum HR. Do this twice. The second time should be more difficult than the first and probably will be the lower of the two numbers. Use the higher of the two numbers as your maximum heart rate for cycling.

### Workout 7: Hill Sprints

Select a hill that you can sprint to the top of in approximately one minute. Do three all-out sprints to the top with very little rest in between. Use the highest number you see on your heart rate monitor as your maximum heart rate.

## Workout 8: Crisscross Zone 3

This 70-minute ride takes you on a tour through three zones, leaving you feeling energized and smiling from all those endorphins. The goal is not to go into zone 4, even on the hills. Pick a riding route through relatively flat to moderately rolling terrain. The idea is to spin your way up any hills using easy gearing and staying in the saddle. Select gears that keep your cadence between 70 and 90 rpm. This is a great opportunity to work on your pedal stroke and body position. Relax, enjoy the scenery, and spin your way along. You may choose not to use the large chainring. If that is the case, your cadence may be slightly higher than 90 rpm. Stay away from big gears on the hills, and pedal on the downhills to maintain your heart rate.

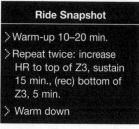

**Ride Snapshot**
- Warm-up 10–20 min.
- Repeat twice: increase HR to top of Z3, sustain 15 min., (rec) bottom of Z3, 5 min.
- Warm down

Warm up for 10 to 20 minutes, gradually working your way up to the bottom of zone 3. Slowly increase your heart rate to the top of zone 3 and hold it there for 15 minutes, then recover to the bottom of zone 3 for 5 minutes. Repeat; 15 minutes to the top of zone 3, and 5-minute recovery to the bottom of zone 3. Warm down for 10 minutes with easy pedaling in zones 2 and 1.

The winner is the one who has the most fun!

# 4

# Your First 30 Days of Riding and Training

*I'll never forget my first studio bike class in the mid-1990s. Instructor Maureen Rusty had just finished Johnny G's (originator and trademark owner of Spinning) Mad Dogg Athletics training. Twenty black-metallic Schwinn spin bikes sparkled in the mirrors of the athletic club's former aerobics room, which amplified every enthusiastic shout.*

*The real power of that experience came not from the instructor's enthusiasm, the fancy new bikes, or knowing a club had made an early commitment to invest in this valuable form of exercise. Instead, what wholly consumed me was the information from my heart rate monitor during the workout.*

*A monitor, spin bike, great instructor, and rocking music are 95 percent of the formula needed to create an exceptional workout; the other 5 percent is the personal attitude it takes to be willing to suffer a little to enjoy the physical sensations of a high, hard, and hot session. Without a monitor, I would not have known that for almost 60 minutes, I was red-lining at above 90 percent of my maximum heart rate.*

*The pool of sweat under the bike should have shown me I was nearing exhaustion. I was competing mentally with the cyclist next to me, who was also red-lining and couldn't speak. In fact, everyone in the room seemed to feel the same way: Ride until you drop.*

*I could see how hard I was working because of the constant display on the monitor of my current heart rate. My maximum heart rate on a bike is 185 bpm. Throughout the workout, my hamstrings and quadriceps were spewing lactic acid as I experienced total muscle depletion. Rather than ease back if it seemed too hard as the instructor had suggested, I decided just to ride and watch my monitor.*

*Sure enough, I fried. So did all the other riders. I could barely walk after dismounting, but it was such an exercise "high," I promised myself that day to write, lecture, and teach others how to enjoy indoor group cycling without frying. Training smart allows you to realize all the benefits without the penalties.*

—SALLY EDWARDS

It seems easier for highly competitive athletes to fry when they train. We know our competition is training hard, so we train harder. But to train that hard and that high for so long leads to an increased potential for muscle and immune-system impairment and possible damage from overtraining.

## TRAINING ACTIVITY

Training is highly sport-specific. To be a great cyclist, you need to ride your bike and train your specific bike muscle systems and their complementary energy systems. Similarly, to improve as a triathlete, you must train your specific triathlon muscle systems, teaching them how to metabolize fuel efficiently. Sport-specific training is important. However, complementing that training with rest days for the sport-specific muscles and activity days for your auxiliary systems can take you to even higher levels of fitness. This type of training program is called sport-specific cross-training.

## WORKOUT TYPES

Your training may encompass three basic workout types: a continuous, steady-state workout session, an interval workout session, or a combination of the two.

Both continuous and interval workouts can be divided into subcategories based on the length and heart zone of that workout. A steady-state workout is confined mainly within a narrowly described heart zone, or "at, about, or around" a certain heart rate number. A good example would be cycling a 10-mile time trial at the midpoint of zone 3, or 75 percent of maximum heart rate. Such an aerobic ride would be designated a steady-state zone 3 workout.

Training in intervals is a technique alternating between short, intense efforts of exercise followed by periods of rest. They are designated short intervals, middle-distance intervals, and long intervals and are measured by either time or distance. As the interval time lengthens, the sustainable heart rate typically decreases.

A combination workout or ride includes multiple heart zones and both types of training rides—interval and steady-state. Examples of combination workouts include ladders, pyramids, zig-zags, and other workouts with mixed intensity levels.

## STEP 4: *Creating Your 30-Day Program*

Since no one knows your physiology and psychology as well as you, it's essential that you learn to write your own 30-day program. You know your schedule and can best assess your strengths and weaknesses, goals and ambitions, dietary needs, and support system. If a coach or personal trainer with cycling expertise is available, get feedback on your plan. Incorporate all or some of these elements:

*Balance.* Your training fits your life; it doesn't consume it. For example, it must realistically reflect the amount of time you have available.

*Appropriate.* Your training must match your current level of fitness.

*Relevant.* Plan a program that is consistent with your goals and values.

*Reward-based.* Your training should compensate you for your investment.

*Obstacle recognition.* You need to recognize hurdles you'll encounter and design your training so that you can overcome them.

*Individualized.* Training must fit your unique and special qualities, including the emotional and physical. This element comes from the heart as much as the head.

*Joyful.* Your program should offer pleasure and some celebration.

*Milestones.* Training should offer feedback and test events because you can best manage what you can monitor and measure.

*Step-by-step process.* Training should have clearly defined steps to master to save you time and enhance your life.

Now use those parameters to design your personalized 30-day training program. You will love the process of planning, making decisions, and committing to a schedule. You'll even enjoy the design phase after you finish the 30 days and realize you need to fine-tune your plan. To start, your first venture into building a viable long-term training plan is to use a calendar.

For many busy people, a 30-day calendar works well because it gives you a look at your other commitments such as family, travel, and meetings. Remember that a training program needs to fit into your life, not the reverse.

Using a calendar or the sample 30-day template that follows, write in your favorite training rides. For example, some people ride Tuesdays and Thursdays when organized rides are offered. Since you're just getting started, your ride frequency should be three to five times per week, for 30–120 minutes, in heart zones 1 to 3. Decide how you will train on your non–riding days— stretching classes, weights, complementary training such as swimming, skiing/snowshoeing, running, or skating—and add those to the weekly activities on appropriate days along with a day of complete recovery or rest.

Your challenge is to set up a program that works. Don't fret over details or spend too much time creating the program at this point. Just commit to writing this action plan and to doing the program for 30 days. Keep the heart rate intensities variable so you can gain the maximum benefit. Finally, try to commit to a time of day. If you know you're going to indoor cycle on Wednesday with a group, write down the time and show up, which is half of being successful; the rest is to have a goal and a plan.

## 30-Day Training Plan

Total Weekly Training Time:

|        | 1  | 2  | 3  | 4  | 5  | 6  | 7  |    |
|--------|----|----|----|----|----|----|----|----|
| WEEK 1 | 1  | 2  | 3  | 4  | 5  | 6  | 7  |    |
| WEEK 2 | 8  | 9  | 10 | 11 | 12 | 13 | 14 |    |
| WEEK 3 | 15 | 16 | 17 | 18 | 19 | 20 | 21 |    |
| WEEK 4 | 22 | 23 | 24 | 25 | 26 | 27 | 28 |    |
| WEEK 5 | 29 | 30 |    |    |    |    |    |    |

Total Monthly Training Time:

## Sample 30-Day Training Program for a Fit Intermediate Cyclist

| Week: | Monday | Tuesday | Wednesday | Thursday | Friday | Saturday | Sunday |
|---|---|---|---|---|---|---|---|
| 1 | Ride Z3, continuous, with Mike at 10 a.m. for 30 minutes. Take a 1-hour stretching class at 6 p.m. | Take a 1-hour stretching class at 6 p.m. | Ride Z2–4, indoor cycle class at the club 6–7 a.m., 45 minutes. | Rest day. | Out-of-town meetings all day–no training time available, going out with the family in evening. | Ride Z2–3, continuous pacing for one hour, at 7 a.m. with Judy. | Ride Z3–4 hills. Leave the house at 8 a.m. with Tom for 2-hour ride. |
| 2 | Rest day. | Ride mountain bike for 60 minutes, Z3 on trails near the house. | Ride, Heart Zones Cycling class at the club 12–1 p.m., Z3–4, 50 minutes, all intervals. | Cross-train: swim laps after a Z2 warm-up for 30 minutes. | Ride, Z2–3 after work with Liz, continuous, mid-point Z3, 90 minutes. | Ride indoor trainer, do Ladder to Success workout (#42). | Rest day. |
| 3 | Ride Z3, continuous, with Mike at 10 a.m. for 1 hour. | Take a 1-hour stretching class at 6 p.m. | Ride, Z2–4, indoor cycling class at the club 6–7 a.m., 50 minutes. | Rest day. | Rest day. | Ride indoor trainer, Heartbeat workout (#18). | Ride Z3–4 hills. Leave the house at 8 a.m. with Tom for 3-hour ride. |
| 4 | Rest day. | Ride mountain bike for 1 hour, Z3 on trails near the house. | Ride, Heart Zones Cycling class at the club 12–1 p.m., Z3–4, 50 minutes, all intervals. | Cross-train: swim 20 laps with Zoomers after a Z2 warm-up for 15 minutes. | Ride Z2–3 after work with Liz, continuous, mid-point Z3 for 90 minutes. | Ride indoor trainer, Fast Lane workout (#50). | Crisscross Z2–3 workout (# 10), for 60 minutes. |

**Note:** This schedule is designed for an intermediate cyclist who has ridden for more than one year, is currently fit and healthy, and has no injuries or other complications.

As you design your 30-day riding plan, keep in mind frequency, workout type (interval, continuous, or combination), intensity, time of day, and mode (indoor or outdoor).

Some training partners or students will ask their partners or coaches to write their workouts. Asking them to review, analyze, and question you on your workout is okay. Your role here, however, is to learn how to train based upon your individual physiology and how to use these principles to write a training plan.

## Multiple Zones Give Multiple Benefits— The Wellness Continuum

Who said you can't have your cake and eat it too? The Heart Zones Training program provides just that—all the benefits of health, fitness, and performance if you apply it in your daily life, packaged and prepared in the "wellness continuum."

As you know by now, each of the heart zones is part of a "wellness continuum" from health (zones 1–3) to fitness (zones 2–4) to performance (zones 3–5). If you want health benefits, you train in the health zones. If you want fitness benefits, you train in the fitness zones. Performance resides in the high-hard zones of 3–5. If you want all of these benefits, you must train in all the zones.

Wouldn't it be wonderful if training benefits were associative, allowing you to train in zone 3 while reaping the benefits of zones 1 and 2? This isn't possible, because each zone features its unique specific metabolic and exercise stress characteristics. If you wondered whether training only in zone 5 would enable you to lower your blood pressure and triglycerides, the answer is no. The fact is you would increase your blood pressure by riding all of your time in zone 5, because you would be adding huge amounts of exercise stress to your other daily stresses.

However, you certainly can train each day in a different zone and derive all the wellness benefits that way. One day, cycle in zone 1 and use this as a recovery day—a fun, nonintense, calorie-burning workout. The next day, ride in and out of zone 5 (intervals) and use this as your supercompensation day, when you train your physiology to its highest ability so that it can recover to a higher fitness level. The following day, train in zone 2 for the benefits of improved self-esteem, effortlessly burning a lot of fat with little to no pain. Then train in zone 3, the Aerobic Zone, multiplying your mitochondria. Take off the next day for a full rest and recovery. Resume with training in zone 4 in different sports, and cross-train so you'll get fitter in your cycling.

Variety is the spice that allows us to maximize benefit and time. You can have and eat that cake; but first, write a 30-day training plan to make it happen.

☞ **TIP:** ADVANCED TRAINING CONCEPT—EXERTION FACTOR

Different types of activities have different weights or values based on the nature of the activity. For example, does running for 20 minutes at 150 beats per minute equal a 20-minute bike ride at 150 beats per minute? Are the two workouts equal in their training value, workload, calories burned, and effects on the muscles and cardiovascular system?

The answer is "no." Running is harder on the body's skeletal system because of the impact forces of the activity. Running also consumes more oxygen and thus burns more calories per minute than cycling. You may know from running that it's a jarring sport and stresses your legs and feet tremendously. You also don't have the rest phases of downhills or backing off the cadence as you do with cycling.

As a result of these impact forces, the recovery time from running is longer than from cycling. This impact factor, along with the stress of using different muscle groups in different activities, provides for a way to establish an "exertion factor." This factor differs by sport activity as well as the intensity level of the workout. Using an exertion factor allows you to compare workouts in different sports.

Impact impairment from running, for example, increases as the speed increases. The faster you run, the greater the impact. Similarly, the faster you cycle, the more joint stress. So if you are running or cycling at high heart rates, the impact-stress or exertion factor of the activity is higher. The slower you move and the lower your heart rate, the lower the exertion or impact factor.

☞ **TIP:** ADVANCED TRAINING CONCEPT—TRAINING VOLUME AND TRAINING LOAD

Training volume is how long you exercise or how far you ride, usually measured in minutes/hours or by distance in yards/meters. Think of volume as the size of something: a mass, in this case duration or distance traveled. Your weekly training volume is the workout frequency times the distance or total amount of training time for the week.

If you ride 4 days a week for 60 minutes each and each ride is 18 miles, your weekly training volume is calculated as follows:

Weekly training volume (by duration) = 4 days x 60 minutes = 240 training minutes per week
Weekly training volume (by distance) = 4 days x 18 miles = 72 miles per week

Training load is the amount, or dosage, of exercise activity. Training load is more important to monitor because it includes how hard you exercised during that 72-mile or

240-minute week. While the load can be calculated different ways, in the Heart Zones Cycling program we simply multiply by the time spent in each of the zones to determine the training load, expressed in heart zones training (HZT) points.

In the preceding example, imagine all the workouts were performed in zone 3. Following is the individual workload for the week:

Weekly training volume (by duration) = 4 days x 60 minutes x 3 (zone 3) = 720 HZT points

You now have an easy way to analyze your training dosage.

## TRAINING BALANCE

By now, you may have realized that training involves more than glancing at a flashing heart icon and pushing your heart rate to maximum. A common mistake is to use a heart rate monitor as if it were a speedometer to see how hard and fast we can go. In reality, a monitor is more like a tachometer, showing us what's really happening under the hood and how our body is responding to stress. The more feedback we have, the better our chances of making good decisions in training and riding. You can use a heart rate monitor to balance your training.

Do you know people who think they haven't had a good workout unless they've pushed themselves so hard they can barely finish? They spend their training time in a big black anaerobic hole, never glimpsing the daylight of rest and recovery. High-intensity training has a purpose, but at some point the body will rebel against abuse. You simply can't cycle in zones 4 and 5 all the time without adequate rest and recovery.

If you don't allow your body recovery time to rebuild itself, you'll develop the classic symptoms of overtraining: persistent fatigue; leaden legs; irritability; insomnia; an increase in resting heart rate; and decreasing performance. You may be on the fast track to becoming less fit and possibly seriously damaging your body by training too long in the high, hot, and hard zones.

Spend time in each zone based on your fitness goals and training program and you will reap the benefits each zone has to offer. Your training program will change as your goals change; your goals change because your life changes.

Training balance is important to your success. Brian was one of those people who pushed themselves to the limit. He showed up in Sally Reed's Heart Zones Cycling class, heart rate monitor in hand and ready to ride. What he failed to tell anyone was his motivation for being there. Brian had recently undergone an angiogram, then an angioplasty, followed by triple-bypass surgery. His heart muscle was strong from previous years of training as a triathlete, so the doctor's orders were to continue to exercise and change his diet. Over two years, Brian rarely missed a class. His motivation to be stronger and fitter came from his awareness of friends who didn't survive their first heart attack. Brian wanted to strengthen not only his heart but his whole body as well. He didn't wait to get serious about being fit and healthy. He wisely said, "Today is a gift. I'll never have a better opportunity, and I can't let it go by."

## FIT

How do you fit your goals into a training schedule that will work for you? How do you quantify your training sessions to ensure you're growing progressively fitter and not under- or over-training? One way to answer these questions is by using the formula FIT. This acronym stands for frequency, intensity, and time, the three key factors in designing and measuring your training. FIT is a way of evaluating how often, how hard, and how many minutes you train.

In the past, there were four ways to measure exercise intensity: blood lactate, $VO_2$ (gas exchange), rate of perceived exertion (RPE), and pulse. The first two methods are fairly accurate but require special equipment and are usually expensive and applied primarily in a clinical setting. RPE is commonly used for many activities but is highly subjective and unreliable. Pulse rate taken manually is not accurate enough and is awkward to assess. Today, with the development of the heart rate monitor, it is easy to quantify exercise intensity.

Because intensity is now readily measurable, workouts can be quantified. Here is the formula to measure the total quantity of exercise dosage:

F x I x T = Training load, where

F = Frequency or "how often" or number of workouts per week (one per day is a frequency of seven workouts)

I = Intensity or "how hard" or the number of the zone in which you are training

T = Time or "how many minutes" in each zone (in heart zones training it is called TIZ, or time in zone [in minutes]).

This formula measures the total exercise dosage applied to the individual and quantifies the workload in heart zones training (HZT) points, currently one of the only ways to measure applied workload. Here is an example:

5 days/week x (zone) 3 (70 percent of maximum heart rate) x 30 minutes = 450 HZT points

The American College of Sports Medicine recommends exercising most days of the week at an intensity range of 60 percent to 90 percent of your maximum heart rate for a minimum of 30 minutes to get fit. These guidelines cover a wide range of activities. The ACSM also recognizes that lower intensity levels are beneficial in reducing degenerative diseases. Healthy adults must work at higher frequencies and intensity levels for additional benefits.

It's important to remember that you'll be working out in multiple zones and for varying times, and that each person will have a different exercise capacity. Competitive athletes may have more than 3,000 HZT points per week, whereas someone who just wants to get healthier and fit may register 100 to 1,000 points per week. As you saw in Chapter 3, each indoor workout in this book gives you a percentage of time in each zone followed by the total points for the workout. You will decide your magic number of HZT points each week based on your goals.

## THE TRAINING WHEEL

Training is a cyclical process. For most athletes, there's a start of the training season, different phases within a training season, and an end. This cycle of training is called the "training wheel" because it resembles the wheel of your bike, with spokes dividing the training into distinct parts.

In the center of the training wheel is the hub—the focus, a connection piece through which each spoke threads. Symbolically, the hub might represent your training goals. There are five spokes to the training wheel:

- Base training
- Endurance training
- Strength training
- Interval speed training
- Peak power training (racing)

The rim of the training wheel represents time, that all too precious commodity that is both free and an equalizer. We all have exactly the same amount of time in every day; managing it best means using a training system for guidance.

Unlike on a bike wheel, the spokes on the training wheel are not spaced equally apart. You spend different lengths of time within spokes, depending on your individual needs and goals. If you are new to cycle training, spend more time in the first two spokes: base and endurance. Experienced and fit cyclists will have a well-established base and can cycle through them in a short time to the other three spokes: strength (hills), intervals (speed), peak power (a combination of all the spokes).

You'll find it easy to build your own training wheel if you consider what specific short-term or long-term goal you have set. To determine the time to spend in each spoke, count back from the goal to establish the number of weeks you have to prepare (14 weeks in the training wheel example). Next, divide these weeks and assign them to each of the spokes of the training wheel. This sets the number of weeks you'll be riding in each spoke.

## The Training Wheel Model

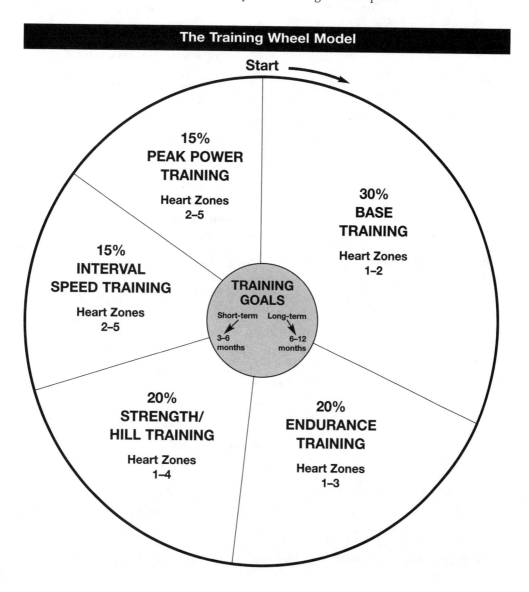

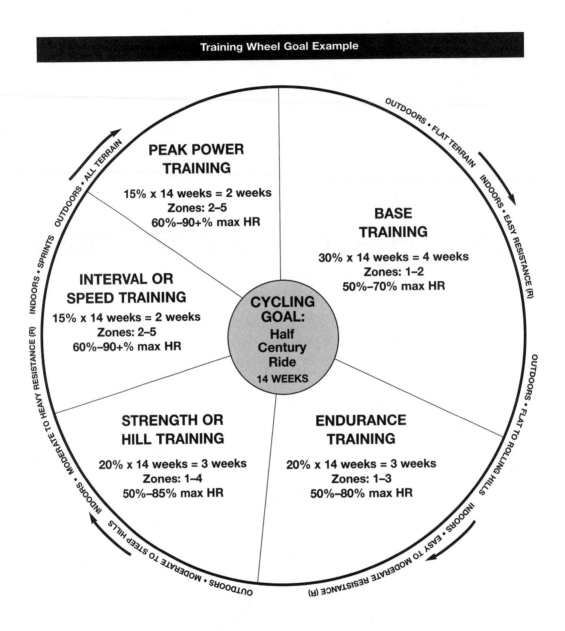

**Training Wheel Goal Example**

PEAK POWER TRAINING
15% x 14 weeks = 2 weeks
Zones: 2–5
60%–90+% max HR

BASE TRAINING
30% x 14 weeks = 4 weeks
Zones: 1–2
50%–70% max HR

INTERVAL OR SPEED TRAINING
15% x 14 weeks = 2 weeks
Zones: 2–5
60%–90+% max HR

CYCLING GOAL:
Half Century Ride
14 WEEKS

STRENGTH OR HILL TRAINING
20% x 14 weeks = 3 weeks
Zones: 1–4
50%–85% max HR

ENDURANCE TRAINING
20% x 14 weeks = 3 weeks
Zones: 1–3
50%–80% max HR

OUTDOORS • FLAT TERRAIN
INDOORS • EASY RESISTANCE (R)
OUTDOORS • FLAT TO ROLLING HILLS
INDOORS • EASY TO MODERATE RESISTANCE (R)
OUTDOORS • MODERATE TO STEEP HILLS
INDOORS • MODERATE TO HEAVY RESISTANCE (R)
INDOORS • SPRINTS
OUTDOORS • ALL TERRAIN

The wheel is an individual cycle training program, so make it fit your schedule. Training is a blend of art and science, and research shows that you should progressively vary exercise load by training in different spokes during different phases for improvement.

The key point to improve your fitness is to change your training. By moving from one spoke on the training wheel to the next, you'll get fitter. As you become fitter, you will get faster, and you will have lower training heart rates at the same bike speeds.

| Calculating Time to Spend in Each Spoke | | | | |
|---|---|---|---|---|
| Spoke | Percentage of Total Training (14 weeks) | Time in Spoke Based on Example of 14-Week Training Season | Weeks and Months for My Training Wheel | Primary Training Heart Zone |
| Base | 30% | 4 weeks | | Zone 1–2 |
| Endurance | 20% | 3 weeks | | Zone 3 |
| Strength | 20% | 3 weeks | | Zone 2–4 |
| Interval/Speed | 15% | 2 weeks | | Zone 3–5 |
| Peak Power | 15% | 2 weeks | | Zone 2–5 |
| TOTAL | 100% | 14 weeks | | |

## STEP 5: Determining Your Training Spokes

Before you select which one of the five training spokes best matches your current fitness level, you must determine how fit you are. This is best accomplished by taking self-tests and subjectively making a determination. As you get fitter and faster, you will be moving from one spoke to the next. This is systematic training because you are periodizing your training program. You'll be adding different types of rides emphasizing different heart zones and different training regimens. The following brief descriptions of the five different spokes will help you to determine which spoke to start with.

## Base Rides

Early-season training rides, short to medium in length or time. All base rides are in the low heart zones (1 and 2), and they are fun, easy, and aerobic. You'll be in your base period from two to eight weeks; each week, you'll be building your cardiovascular aerobic system. When outdoors, ride flat to gentle hills. Ride at a higher rpm and use easier gearing.

## Endurance Rides

You've developed your base aerobic capacity and are ready for longer, slightly harder rides that push the heart rate intensity higher (50–80 percent of max HR, or zones 1, 2, and 3). Building a bigger and more powerful base is instrumental to the rest of your training season, because this base is the aerobic foundation supporting the other training spokes. Your goal in this two-to six-week training spoke is to develop cardiovascular and muscular endurance.

When outdoors, ride flat to rolling hills. Ride at a higher rpm using easy to moderate gearing. Increase your time in the saddle.

## Strength/Hill Rides

In this training spoke (50–85 percent of max HR, or zones 1, 2, 3, and 4), you'll work on developing muscle strength—your muscles' ability to generate force against resistance—to give your sport-specific riding muscles more power.

When outdoors, ride moderate to steep hills, ride into the wind, or climb hills both standing out of the saddle and seated. Ride this training spoke for two to six weeks.

## Intervals/Speed

One of the best ways to get faster on your bike is to ride repeatedly faster for short periods of time followed with recovery time. That's interval training. This is one of the most important times to use your monitor, because you'll be riding into the highest of heart zones, red-lining into zone 5. Intensity ranges from 60–90-plus percent of max HR, or zones 2, 3, 4, and 5. Doses of high-intensity training improve your recovery and your ability to sustain high heart rates and thus your ability to train at or above your anaerobic threshold.

When outdoors, ride all types of terrain faster and at varying time and distance intervals.

## Peak Power Rides

During this training (at 60–90-plus percent of max HR), you'll combine all three spokes into your weekly program—endurance, strength, and speed. You'll train for acceleration, top speed,

| Recommended Indoor Workouts | | | | |
|---|---|---|---|---|
| **Base Spoke:** 50%–70% of Max HR | **Endurance Spoke:** 50%–80% of Max HR | **Strength Spoke:** 50%–85% of Max HR | **Speed Spoke:** 60%–90+% of Max HR | **Power Spoke :** 60%–90+% of Max HR |
| Change of Heart | Heartbeat | The Zipper | Top Spin | Knock Your Socks Off |
| Crisscross Z1 & Z2 | Ladder to Success | Tailwind | Pumped | Happy Feet |
| Recovery Intervals | 30-Beat Interval | Afterburner | Sitting Bull | Escalator |
| Peekaboo | A Positive Spin | Seattle Ridge | La Bicicletta | Spentervals |
| Talk Is Cheap | Fast Lane | Winner's Circle | Salty Dog | Red Light, Green Light |
| Five-by-Two | Crisscross Z2 & Z3 | | | Seattle Ridge |
| Lancelot | | | | |
| Out of Rock Bottom | | | | |

| Recommended Outdoor Rides | | | | |
|---|---|---|---|---|
| **Base Spoke:** 50%–70% of **Max HR** | **Endurance Spoke:** 50%–80% of **Max HR** | **Strength Spoke:** 50%–85% of **Max HR** | **Speed Spoke:** 60%–90+% of **Max HR** | **Power Spoke :** 60%–90+% of **Max HR** |
| The Observation Trip | Crisscross Z3 | The Heat Is On | Biggest Number | Saturday Night Fever |
| Steady-State Pace Ride | Recovery Interval Ride | The Spoke 'n' Word | All-Out Time Trial | Rock 'n' Roll |
| Noodling | Cruisin' | Pyramid Scheme | Anaerobic Threshold Ride | Sign Here, Press Hard |
| Doublemint | Paceline Ride | Aerobic Time Trial | Need for Speed | S-Squared |
| Steady Eddie | | Head for the Hills | Hill Sprints | Snookie |
| | | Hill-Billy | All-Out Trip | |
| | | Over the Hill | Spitfire | |
| | | | Five-by-Five | |
| | | | SOS | |

and top endurance. This combination of high intensities, speed, hill intervals, and endurance can lead to overtraining, so be careful and check your resting heart rate often. (Chapter 5 describes how to do this.)

When outdoors, ride hills and do time trials. Use the large chainring to develop strength and power, but be careful not to overstress your knees.

## WORKOUTS: Indoor Training

### HEALTHY HEART **Workout 9: Five-by-Two**

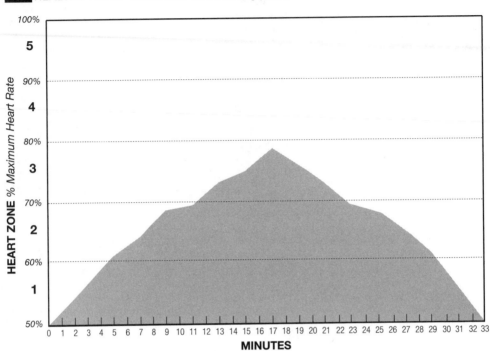

## Overview

Many of the newer pieces of cardiovascular equipment, such as treadmills, elliptical machines, and rowers, have on the console a workout profile chart like the one shown here. Some pieces of equipment even give you the opportunity to select a setting for a workout profile that resembles the workout you want to experience. When you select a profile, the exercise machine is electronically programmed into a mode that varies the resistance in a way that changes your required effort to match the profile. The high-end machines have an additional feature called "heart rate control" that uses the data from your heart rate monitor to set the resistance. Most exercisers prefer these machines because they get an individualized workout programmed to match their heart rate response rather than a certain fixed amount of resistance.

Indoor studio or spin bikes have none of these features. Few have any electronics whatsoever. Rather, you must program the bike with your mind by making all of the adjustments for resistance, speed, and heart rate response. There is joy in simplicity of this sort. But even more, there's the challenge of paying attention to the protocol to experience the workout. In this Five-by-Two workout, every 2 minutes you must be the programmer and increase your heart rate by 5 beats.

| Stats and Tips for Workout 9: Five-by-Two | | | |
|---|---|---|---|
| Zone Number and Name | Minutes in Zone | Heart Zones Training Points | Estimated Calories |
| 5. Red-Line | | | |
| 4. Threshold | | | |
| 3. Aerobic | 10 | 30 | 90–110 |
| 2. Temperate | 16 | 32 | 96–128 |
| 1. Healthy Heart | 7 | 7 | 21–35 |
| Totals | 33 | 69 | 207–273 |

**Tip 1:** "By monitoring your heart rate, you can be sure you are safely and effectively exercising" (Kirkpatrick and Birnbaum 1997, 49).

**Tip 2:** Riding in the lower three heart zones results in improvement of health parameters or metabolic fitness, including lower blood pressure and improved blood chemistry.

## Description

The workout profile of Five-by-Two resembles a ladder. On the uphill side of the ladder your exercise intensity increases, and on the downhill side you decrease the resistance and your heart rate should drop to match it. Reaching the top of this workout ladder is only half of the evenly balanced profile; some people may find that coming down the ladder in a controlled manner may be hard until they gain more experience with their individual response to changes in intensity. Then, just as you achieve the desired heart rate, it is time either to boost or reduce your heart rate, depending on the direction of your travel and the elapsed time in the workout. Watch your monitor and focus on precision heart zones training.

| Sequence for Workout 9: Five-by-Two | | | | |
|---|---|---|---|---|
| Elapsed Time (min.) | Workout Plan | Heart Zone | Your Heart Rate (bpm) | Interval Time (min.) |
| 0–5 | Warm up in Z1 | 1 | _____ | 5 |
| 5–9 | Increase intensity to max HR minus 70 bpm | 2 | _____ | 4 |
| 9–11 | Increase HR 5 bpm | 2 | _____ | 2 |
| 11–13 | Increase HR 5 bpm | 2 | _____ | 2 |
| 13–15 | Increase HR 5 bpm | 2 | _____ | 2 |
| 15–17 | Increase HR 5 bpm | 3 | _____ | 2 |
| 17–19 | Increase HR 5 bpm | 3 | _____ | 2 |
| 19–21 | Increase HR 5 bpm | 3 | _____ | 2 |
| 21–23 | Decrease HR 5 bpm | 3 | _____ | 2 |
| 23–25 | Decrease HR 5 bpm | 3 | _____ | 2 |
| 25–27 | Decrease HR 5 bpm | 2 | _____ | 2 |
| 27–29 | Decrease HR 5 bpm | 2 | _____ | 2 |
| 29–31 | Decrease HR 5 bpm | 2 | _____ | 2 |
| 31–33 | Warm down to bottom of Z1 | 1 | _____ | 2 |

## ▚▁▍▍ FITNESS **Workout 10: Crisscross Zone 2 and Zone 3**

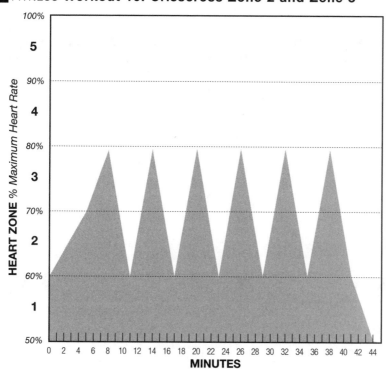

## Overview

This is one of our favorite 45-minute workouts because you cross two zones and experience some significant physiological changes or training effects in your body. You are cycling between 60 percent and 80 percent of your maximum heart rate, which is similar to an easy-to-moderate outdoor ride. You go from being very comfortable to slightly uncomfortable, and from no sweat to dripping wet. The body's choice of fuel is shifting to more carbohydrates, and respiration is more rapid and deeper to meet the additional need for oxygen. Endorphins, the brain chemicals that blunt pain and are responsible for what is termed "runner's high" (or what we call "spin grins"), are one of the benefits of zone 3 riding.

## Description

This workout is a tour of the two most enjoyable heart zones and should leave you feeling better than when you started. You are burning more calories and consuming lots of oxygen, and your cardiopulmonary system responds by dramatically improving. By training in the fitness zones, you will get fitter and faster. The exercise high that often develops as you travel through zone 3 results in mood improvement, reduction in anxiety, and improved appetite control. The benefits last for hours after the workout, and people may think you have been on vacation because of the grin on your face.

| Stats and Tips for Workout 10: Crisscross Zone 2 and Zone 3 | | | |
|---|---|---|---|
| Zone Number and Name | Minutes in Zone | Heart Zones Training Points | Estimated Calories |
| 5. Red-Line | | | |
| 4. Threshold | | | |
| 3. Aerobic | 21 | 63 | 189–231 |
| 2. Temperate | 23 | 46 | 138–184 |
| 1. Healthy Heart | 1 | 1 | 3–5 |
| Totals | 45 | 110 | 330–420 |

**Tip:** You should feel great after this workout, thanks to your natural endorphins!

| Sequence for Workout 10: Crisscross Zone 2 and Zone 3 | | | | |
|---|---|---|---|---|
| Elapsed Time (min.) | Workout Plan | Heart Zone | Your Heart Rate (bpm) | Interval Time (min.) |
| 0–5 | Warm up to the bottom of Z2 | 2 | _____ | 5 |
| 5–8 | Increase HR with resistance (R) or cadence (rpm) bottom of Z3 | 3 | _____ | 3 |
| 8–11 | Increase HR with resistance (R) or cadence (rpm) to the top of Z3 | 3 | _____ | 3 |
| 11–14 | (Rec) to the bottom of Z2 | 2 | _____ | 3 |
| 14–17 | Increase HR to the top of Z3; your choice of (R) or rpm, seated | 3 | _____ | 3 |
| 17–20 | (Rec) to the bottom of Z2 | 2 | _____ | 3 |
| 20–23 | Increase HR to the top of Z3; your choice of (R) or rpm, seated | 3 | _____ | 3 |
| 23–26 | (Rec) to the bottom of Z2 | 2 | _____ | 3 |
| 26–29 | Increase HR to the top of Z3;alternate (R) and rpm, seated | 3 | _____ | 3 |
| 29–32 | (Rec) to the bottom of Z2 | 2 | _____ | 3 |
| 32–35 | Increase HR to the top of Z3; alternate (R) and rpm, standing | 3 | _____ | 3 |
| 35–38 | 3 minute (rec), bottom of Z2 | 2 | _____ | 3 |
| 38–41 | Increase HR to the top of Z3, all-out sprint fast rpm, seated | 3 | _____ | 3 |
| 41–45 | Warm down to the bottom of Z2 then Z1 | 2 1 | _____ _____ | 4 |

## PERFORMANCE **Workout 11: Tailwind**

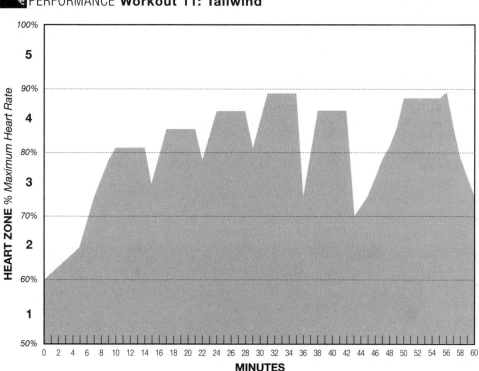

## Overview

"Tailwind" is one of those words you love as a cyclist. Wind pushing you from your back—a tailwind—is a cyclist's dream. When air is pushing you from behind, it's as if an unseen hand is patting you and saying, "Good job."

## Description

Tailwind is an interval workout, a combination of moderate- to high-intensity work followed by brief periods of recovery. More than half of your riding time is in zone 4. Always be aware that when you spend a large part of your training time at or above your aerobic threshold metabolism, you're taxing your physiology. This session is loaded with challenges. Vary the work intervals by changing cadence, changing position on the bike, adding resistance, or changing gears. For example, you may want to "spin" your way up the first two-thirds of the work interval using high cadence and low resistance or easy gearing and then add resistance or harder gearing to power your way up the last third. As you crest the hill or approach the end of the work interval, feel the relief as the tailwind again pushes at your back.

| Stats and Tips for Workout 11: Tailwind | | | |
|---|---|---|---|
| Zone Number and Name | Minutes in Zone | Heart Zones Training Points | Estimated Calories |
| 5. Red-Line | | | |
| 4. Threshold | 36 | 144 | 432–504 |
| 3. Aerobic | 17 | 51 | 153–187 |
| 2. Temperate | 7 | 14 | 42–56 |
| 1. Healthy Heart | | | |
| Totals | 60 | 209 | 627–747 |

**Tip:** To develop a smooth, round pedal stroke, envision your knee reaching up as if to touch the handlebar at the top of the stroke.

| Sequence for Workout 11: Tailwind | | | | |
|---|---|---|---|---|
| Elapsed Time (min.) | Workout Plan | Heart Zone | Your Heart Rate (bpm) | Interval Time (min.) |
| 0–5 | Warm up to bottom of Z2 (60%), easy pedal | 2 | _____ | 5 |
| 5–7 | Add 10 bpm with cadence/rpm | 2 | _____ | 2 |
| 7–11 | Add 5 bpm each min. for 4 min. with cadence/rpm | 3 | _____ | 4 |
| 11–15 | Sustain HR at bottom of Z4 (80%), choice | 4 | _____ | 4 |
| 15–17 | 2 min. (rec) to midpoint of Z3 (75%) | 3 | _____ | 2 |
| 17–22 | Increase HR to max HR minus 30 bpm, sustain for 5 min., choice | 4 | _____ | 5 |
| 22–24 | (Rec) to midpoint of Z3 (75%) | 3 | _____ | 2 |
| 24–29 | Increase HR to midpoint Z4 (85%), sprint | 4 | _____ | 5 |
| 29–31 | Decrease HR to bottom of Z4, 90 rpm (9) | 4 | _____ | 2 |
| 31–36 | Increase HR to top of Z4 and sprint first 3 min. then heavy (R) last 2 min., 60 rpm (6), standing | 4 | _____ | 5 |
| 36–38 | Decrease HR to max HR minus 50 bpm | 3 | _____ | 2 |
| 38–43 | Increase HR 25 bpm, choice | 4 | _____ | 5 |
| 43–45 | (Rec) to bottom of Z3 | 3 | _____ | 2 |
| 45–50 | From bottom of Z3, increase HR 5 bpm each min. for 5 min. | 3/4 | _____ | 5 |
| 50–55 | Increase HR 10 bpm and sustain, choice | 4 | _____ | 5 |
| 55–56 | Increase HR to top of Z4, choice | 4 | _____ | 1 |
| 56–57 | Decrease HR to bottom of Z4 | 4 | _____ | 1 |
| 57–58 | Decrease HR to bottom of Z3 | 3 | _____ | 1 |
| 58–60 | Warm down to bottom of Z2 | 2 | _____ | 2 |

## PERFORMANCE **Workout 12: La Bicicletta**

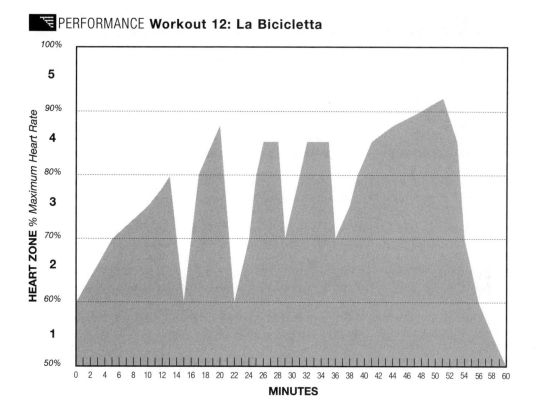

Consider a man riding a bicycle. Whoever he is, we can say three things about him. We know he got on the bicycle and started to move. We know that at some point he will stop and get off. Most important of all, we know that if at any point he stops moving and does not get off the bicycle he will fall off it. That is a metaphor for the journey through life of any living thing, and I think of any society of living things.

—WILLIAM GOLDING, *A MOVING TARGET*

## Overview

There are about 1.1 billion bicycles in use around the world. That's about one bike for every three people.

The bicycle was invented sometime between 1816 and 1863 and sketched as early as the 1500s by Leonardo da Vinci on a notebook page. The first pedal-driven bicycle patent came in 1866 by a French emigrant who later sold his patent for $1,000 and worked the rest of his life as a machinist building the velocipede he had introduced to the world.

| Stats and Tips for Workout 12: La Bicicletta | | | |
|---|---|---|---|
| Zone Number and Name | Minutes in Zone | Heart Zone Training Points | Estimated Calories |
| 5. Red-Line | 3 | 15 | 45–60 |
| 4. Threshold | 28 | 112 | 336–392 |
| 3. Aerobic | 16 | 48 | 144–176 |
| 2. Temperate | 11 | 22 | 66–88 |
| 1. Healthy Heart | 2 | 2 | 6–10 |
| Totals | 60 | 199 | 597–726 |

**Tip:** Like the leaning tower of Pisa, this is a "lean" and mean workout.

## Description

This workout begins with two moderate to difficult hill climbs followed by two intervals of sprint work called Rock 'n' Roll. These sprints are done at high intensity and are designed to improve your leg speed and power. The last interval is a gradual increase in heart rate up to 90 percent of max and then a gradual decrease back down to finish off the set.

| Sequence for Workout 12: La Bicicletta | | | | |
|---|---|---|---|---|
| Elapsed Time (min.) | Workout Plan | Heart Zone | Your Heart Rate (bpm) | Interval Time (min.) |
| 0–5 | Easy-pedal warm-up | 2 | _____ | 5 |
| 5–10 | Increase HR (R) moderate hill | 3 | _____ | 5 |
| 10–12 | Increase HR to midpoint of Z3, high rpm | 3 | _____ | 2 |
| 12–13 | Increase HR 5 bpm, rpm | 3 | _____ | 1 |
| 13–15 | Increase HR to bottom of Z4, rpm | 4 | _____ | 2 |
| 15–17 | Timed (rec) to bottom of Z2 | 2 | _____ | 2 |
| 17–19 | Increase HR to bottom of Z4, heavy (R), rpm (6) | 4 | _____ | 2 |
| 19–20 | Increase HR 10 bpm, choice | 4 | _____ | 1 |
| 20–22 | Increase HR 5 bpm, heavy (R) | 4 | _____ | 2 |
| 22–24 | Timed (rec) to bottom of Z2 | 2 | _____ | 2 |
| 24–29 | Rock 'n' Roll, 15 sec. hard effort followed by 15 sec. easy pedal, choice | 3 4 | _____ _____ | 5 |
| 29–31 | (Rec), drink water! | 3 | _____ | 2 |
| 31–36 | Rock 'n' Roll, repeat | 3 4 | _____ _____ | 5 |
| 36–38 | Timed (rec) 1 min. and 2 min. | 3 2 | _____ _____ | 2 |
| 38–39 | Increase HR to 75% of max, choice | 3 | _____ | 1 |
| 39–41 | Increase HR to 80% of max, choice | 4 | _____ | 2 |
| 41–44 | Increase HR to 85% of max, choice | 4 | _____ | 3 |
| 44–48 | Increase HR to 88% of max, choice | 4 | _____ | 4 |
| 48–51 | Increase HR to 90% of max, choice | 5 | _____ | 3 |
| 51–53 | Decrease HR to 88% of max | 4 | _____ | 2 |
| 53–54 | Decrease HR to 85% of max | 4 | _____ | 1 |
| 54–60 | Easy-pedal warmdown | 2 | _____ | 6 |

## Outdoor Training and Rides

### Workout 13: The Observation Trip

All of us have a favorite ride. Most of these rides have names. It might be the lunchtime ride or the river ride or the Tuesday night ride. On your first ride with a heart rate monitor, simply ride and observe your heart rate. Ride as you always do and ride comfortably. Don't change anything. You'll have a tendency to disagree with your heart rate monitor on your first ride and think it isn't working. In most cases, the monitor is right and the cyclist is wrong. As humans, we tend to want something different: a higher number here (as in bike speed); a lower number there (as in heart rate); more of this (such as altitude changes); less of that (such as the time it takes to finish the ride); and so on. Most of us react this way.

On your observation trip, just ride and watch and be detached from the numbers. They don't mean much until they are put into relationship with each other. Don't form an opinion; this is called riding with detachment. Be in the present and just look, feel, wonder, and think. Don't fight with what you are observing or argue with yourself about it. For now, just accept the information.

When you finish this observation trip, note the following information by entering them in your training logbook or software program.

Today's date

Elapsed time—(chrono on watch, heart rate monitor, or bike monitor)

Distance

Average speed—(bike monitor)

Maximum speed—(bike monitor)

Peak heart rate—(highest number you saw on your HRM)

Average heart rate—(if your heart rate monitor has this function)

That's it. That's all you have to do. Just note this information and get ready for the steady-state ride.

### Workout 14: Steady-State Pace Ride

For this ride you will need a monitor that gives your average heart rate for the total exercise time. You simply will ride according to how you feel, holding a constant speed that is comfortable. If we were to say ride in your "comfort zone," which might be a heart zone that you can maintain while still talking continuously, that is the intensity level to ride. Try not to vary your pace or speed. The goal is to hold the speed constant throughout the trip. Ride at a steady state for a fixed distance. Five miles is recommended if you are a beginner, 10 miles if you are an intermediate rider, and if you are more experienced, such as a century rider, then do a 25-mile ride. The key is not the distance you cover but that you keep your pace the same throughout.

At the end of the ride, you have only one key number to record: your average heart rate. Note that number in your logbook or software program.

## Workout 15: The Recovery Interval Ride

How quickly you recover is a measurement of how fit you are. The faster your heart rate can recover, the fitter your cardiovascular system. This is an assessment you'll periodically do to see if the promise of getting fitter is a reality, and if your training system is working for you, not against you (called overtraining).

This ride is a series of intervals. An interval is alternating hard to easy bouts within a workout set or session. For this trip (it has a lot of variations once you understand the importance of both interval training and the power of recovery), you will do 3 intervals of hard effort and 3 intervals of recovery. Warm up for a period of 15 to 20 minutes or until you feel ready to ride hard. Ride hard for 5 minutes at a fixed speed. Beginners should use 12 mph, intermediate riders 18 mph, and advanced riders 20-plus mph. Then drop the speed by 5 mph for 5 minutes. This is the recovery time. Repeat this hard effort and recovery interval 2 more times. Finish by riding easy and cooling down. Record the following information in your logbook:

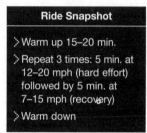

**Ride Snapshot**

> Warm up 15–20 min.
> Repeat 3 times: 5 min. at 12–20 mph (hard effort) followed by 5 min. at 7–15 mph (recovery)
> Warm down

Average heart rate

Chrono time (elapsed time)

Average speed (mph or km)

The purpose of workouts 13 through 15 are to set some benchmarks and become more familiar with your heart rate monitor. Using your heart rate monitor allows you to measure your improvement and individualize your training. That's what we call "smart training."

## Workout 16: The Heat Is On

Power and speed are related like identical twins in a family. To the outsider they may mean the same thing, but they are distinctly different. The "speed twin" is able to sprint at high rpm in any gear and can hold that red-line effort for short periods of time; "quick" would be his middle name. On the other hand, the "power twin" is all about strength, pace, and perseverance. Headwinds and hills are nothing more than appetizers to this cyclist.

So why as a cyclist do you care about power or speed? You may not unless you want to go faster, cover more ground, and not be dropped by your friends on the hills. The following ride will help you develop more power and make you a better all-around cyclist.

Warm up for at least 15 to 30 minutes. Choose a course that is flat to rolling terrain. You will be using a lower cadence and bigger gears during this ride, so beware if you have knee problems; this may not be the ride for you. Listen to your body and increase the cadence and use easier gearing if needed.

> **Ride Snapshot**
>
> ⟩ Warm up 15–30 min.
> ⟩ Repeat 5–8 times: 10 sec. accelerations, hard gearing, seated, (rec) bottom of Z2 (40 rpm)
> ⟩ Warm down or continue ride

Ride along at 40 rpm in your large chainring in front and in the middle of your rear sprocket. In other words, use some hard gearing. Stay seated and accelerate as hard as you can for 10 seconds, then recover by spinning in a lower gear until you have reached the bottom of zone 2. Repeat five to eight times.

Developing power can also be accomplished by riding in rolling terrain and charging up short hills in the saddle without shifting down or letting your cadence drop. You can even try to increase your cadence. Watch your heart rate increase, especially if you try to increase your cadence. As you develop more power, you will notice your heart rate is lower for the same effort. That is exactly what you want—a lower heart rate for the same power output.

On longer hills, shift to a harder gear halfway up, then stand and power over the top. As you get increasingly stronger, don't forget to wait for your friends.

## REFERENCES

American College of Sports Medicine. *ACSM's Guidelines for Exercise Testing and Prescription.* 5th ed. Baltimore: Williams & Wilkins, 2000.

Francis, P., M. J. Guono, and A. Stavig. Physiological Response to a Typical Spinning Session. *Health and Fitness Journal* 3, no. 1(1999): pp. 28–34.

Kirkpatrick, Beth, and Burton Birnbaum. *Lessons from the Heart.* Champaign, IL: Human Kinetics, 1997.

Rippe, J. (M.D.). Counting Pulse Rate Compared to Heart Rate Monitor. Unpublished manuscript. University of Massachusetts, 1991.

# 5

# Using Your Monitor to Measure Your Fitness Level

*Heart monitors are formidable management tools, yet too frequently, we merely strap them on and casually use them to judge our performance. We look at the number and hastily decide it's too low or too high, but our judgment isn't based on facts about our personal fitness.*

*Paul Camerer is an example of how numbers can be wrong. On our way to celebrate his eightieth birthday, he proudly exhibited his new monitor, displaying his average heart rate for his indoor cycling workout that day: 152 bpm for 60 minutes.*

*Paul had happily debunked the old "220 minus your age" formula. He had been using a monitor that automatically calculated his maximum heart rate based on that formula (220 minus 80 = 140 bpm), which predicted that his maximum heart rate should sink as he aged. Yet for an hour, Paul had maintained an average heart rate 12 bpm higher than the formula said he could maintain for even a minute.*

*When I first tested Paul's maximum heart rate when he was 72 years old, it measured 188 bpm. Twelve years later, at age 84, his maximum heart rate was still 188 bpm. Maximum heart rate, at least in some people, doesn't decline with age; instead, our fitness level drops with age as we lapse into a more sedentary lifestyle. Paul continued to train, and although his maximum oxygen uptake probably changed and his muscle strength perhaps declined, his maximum heart rate remained unchanged.*

—SALLY EDWARDS

The American College of Sports Medicine regularly issues position papers recommending how people should exercise. In one report that cited 262 scientific references, the ACSM specified how much exercise is enough and what type of exercise is best for developing and maintaining fitness (ACSM 1998).

Although the report is long, it's worth reading. One of its key points is the need for standardization of testing and measurement procedures. Each researcher uses different ways of testing; as the article points out in one long sentence: "Despite an abundance of information available concerning the training of the human organism, there is a lack of standardization of testing protocols and procedures, of methodology in relation to training procedures and experimental design, and of a preciseness in the documentation and reporting of the quantity and quality of training prescribed, making interpretation difficult" (ACSM 1998, Appendix D).

In other words, there is no single universally agreed-upon way to measure fitness, including using heart rate measurements for showing changes in fitness. Fitness is measurable in many ways.

### STEP 6: *Assessing Your Current Level of Fitness*

Despite the confusion, a few simple tests and measurements can be reliably used to determine some baseline thresholds of fitness. Remember that the definition of physical fitness is the individual's ability to perform moderate-to-vigorous levels of physical activity without excessive fatigue. A heart rate monitor is an ideal tool to help you measure your current level of fitness.

The heart rate monitor might well be one of the best tools we have for measuring fitness outside the laboratory. Today you can buy a heart rate monitor to test your fitness for less than $50.

## Resting Heart Rate

Resting heart rate is taken in the morning, usually before you rise from bed. After wakening, simply count your heart rate before you get up, stretch, or perform other activities. The rate should vary within a range of 5 bpm in day-to-day readings. Measure your resting heart rate for five consecutive days, and average those measurements for your baseline resting heart rate value. If you notice your heart rate exceeding this number at times, you may be experiencing some change in your physiology. Likely causes for the increase or decrease in heart rate may be response to stress, overtraining, a poor night's rest, or a startled response to awakening too quickly.

## Ambient Heart Rate

A key heart rate indicator for stress measurement, your ambient heart rate is measured with your body in a sedentary position but biologically awake. You're in ambient heart rate mode when you are reading or watching television or in a quiet conversation with friends. The lower your ambient heart rate, the better for your health and fitness. Ambient heart rate can decrease quickly with improvements in your physical fitness, and it improves dramatically when you remove the stressors in your life, which can be anything from food allergies to lack of sleep or time.

You can measure ambient heart rate several ways. The easiest is to wear your monitor all day and periodically observe it when you are sitting and inactive. Note the number. Take a half dozen or more measurements and average them. Compare the daily changes using your monitor as a type of window into your heart. Like a window, it affords you a view of what's happening to your internal physiology.

To assess your ambient heart rate more accurately, measure the total number of beats over an extended period. One athlete has described wearing his monitor for a 24-hour workday that included 8 hours of sleep and a 30-minute run. He reported his average heart rate for the 24 hours was "61 bpm (30 percent maximum) with a maximum heart rate during my 'up-tempo' run of 175–180 bpm. My heart beat 87,840 times in the day" (Ackland 1998, p. 129). To complete your recording of ambient heart rate, you'll need a heart rate monitor that can either sample heart rate or count each individual heartbeat for several hours. Several models provide this feature.

Perform this measurement on yourself several times throughout the month. If your ambient heart rate is dropping because you are reducing the stress in your life, you'll notice that the total number of heartbeats in a 24-hour period will decrease. This happens because your stroke volume is higher and you are more efficient, so your heart doesn't need to beat as often to supply the nutrients required.

## Delta Heart Rate

The Greek word for change is "delta." This measurement shows the change in heart rate as a result of a change in body position. Also known as the orthostatic test, delta heart rate is simple and takes little time in return for the information it generates. Lie down and remain still for about 2 minutes, noting the lowest heart rate number in this position. As you slowly stand, note the spike in the heart rate, which gradually drops to a standing heart rate number. Remain

## Listening to Your Emotional Heart

Heart rate monitors give you continuous biofeed-back information as to the relative level of your exercise intensity. There's no guesswork involved. It provides information immediately and without the complications of manual measurement.

A monitor is the link between the heart and mind. That may be its most powerful use. When you have information about what's going on inside your body, you can mentally respond to it.

Using a monitor is a way of opening your heart muscle by giving it a voice. The language it speaks is numbers—how many heartbeats per minute. When you listen to your heart, you will find more joy and be more successful in your training. That is because a heart rate monitor is a bridge between the mental and the emotional states.

standing and note your heart rate every 15 seconds until it levels off. Subtract the prone heart rate number (P in the formula that follows) from the standing rate (S) to determine your delta heart rate. The higher the number, the more stressed the body. The chart shows a general range of scores for you to compare with your delta heart rate for assessing your training:

| Delta Heart Rate | Recommendation |
| --- | --- |
| Over 30 bpm | Take the day off from training. This is not a good number. |
| 20–30 bpm | This is a cautionary range. It's high and you should note this. Train at least one zone lower than you had planned and make it a recovery day. |
| 10–20 bpm | Normal; everything is fine. |
| 0–10 bpm | Excellent. Be happy that you are in a healthy state with regard to your heart's ability to respond to a change in body position. |

Use the delta heart rate assessment to help you recognize the amount of training and other stress you might be experiencing. The graph shows a sample heart rate profile from the following delta heart rate assessment:

Delta heart rate =

S (70 bpm) − P (60 bpm) = 10 bpm

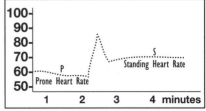

There are days when I don't want to train even though it's in my ride plan. I struggle like everyone else to get to the club or get on my mountain bike, and I find every excuse not to do it. This reluctance is stressful. My ambient heart rate numbers for the day show that stress by increasing. My athletic heart says go ride, but my emotional heart wants the freedom to skip training.

My monitor records the stress that occurs during this debate between these two hearts—the athletic heart talking to the emotional heart. Usually on these days, I follow my emotional, intuitive heart and ditch the ride. It's usually the right decision. The next day, I usually realize that I needed a day of rest. Be careful not to further stress your heart muscle by worrying or feeling guilty about missing a ride or workout. Turn it to your advantage and thank your heart for communicating with you that it, too, needs a complete recovery day.

—*Sally Reed*

## R-to-R Variability

This is a highly sophisticated measurement that is available only on very high-end heart rate monitors and Holter monitors. It measures the variability in the time between heartbeats known as the beat-to-beat variation. The greater the variability, the better the cardiac muscle responsiveness to small changes. A person who is highly stressed has very little beat-to-beat variability because the heart muscle doesn't respond to minor changes.

| Using a Heart Rate Monitor for Diagnosis | |
|---|---|
| Resting heart rate | Lower the better. Indicates that you are in low stress and physically fit. |
| Ambient heart rate | An indicator for the current amount of stress in your life. |
| Delta heart rate | Same as ambient HR. |
| R-to-R variability | The greater the variability, the healthier the total physiological system. |

Heart rate changes can be used as a diagnostic measurement. Changes in the heart rate values can indicate certain health changes.

Heart rate monitor information is also valuable for measuring improvement on your bike. The following several rides show you how to measure fitness gains using your monitor.

## Speed Test/Time Trial Test

This simple test uses three variables for determining improved fitness: speed, heart rate, and time. Hold any two variables constant and measure the changes in the third. For example, you can use a fixed-distance test. A good distance for cycling is a 1-mile loop, completing from 3 to 10 loops. Warm up and hold a constant heart rate, such as 80 percent of your maximum heart rate, for a fixed distance, such as 3 miles or 3 loops. Note the average speed. The higher the speed you can ride with distance and heart rate constant, the fitter you are.

Similarly, hold your speed and heart rate constant and notice the change in distance traveled. Finally, maintain a constant speed and distance over a measured time and note the changes in heart rate. This is one of the best ways to test true cardiovascular improvement without the need for lactate or gas analyzers, which measure the concentration of lactic acid in your blood or the volume of oxygen you consume.

## Average Heart Rate Test

Average heart rate is an important feature for your monitor to display because average exercise intensity seems to be one of the best measurements to determine training benefits. Knowing your average heart rate, regardless of whether you're doing an interval session or a steady-state continuous workout, helps you to quantify your training load.

## *Recovery Heart Rate— Intrarecovery and Interrecovery*

There are two types of recovery heart rate. Intrarecovery heart rate occurs between sets of interval sessions. Interrecovery heart rate changes between workout days and daily recovery episodes.

Training is a series of physiological stresses followed by recovery, which results in improvement of your riding energy systems. For training to lead to improved fitness, an appropriate cycle of physical stress and recovery must be applied to obtain the training effect.

Recovery is the ability of your physiological system to return to a normal (pre-exercise) state, or homeostasis. Depending on the type of physical stress applied and the dosage, recovery can be immediate or take as long as several days or weeks to occur.

Both interrecovery and intrarecovery times can be used to fine-tune your training because they help measure your improvement. Here are a few simple rules to follow when using recovery times and recovery heart rate to improve or diagnose your training:

*Rule 1. The harder the workout, the longer the recovery time needed.*

This is the principle of high, hot, and hard training rides. If you spend long periods of time in zones 4 and 5, you must allow a longer recovery. High heart zones are physiologically stressful, but it's appro-

You can also use average heart rate to determine if you are getting fitter. That improvement test is simple: Hold a constant time, speed, and course and compare the average heart rate. If it's lower, you may be getting fitter; if it's higher, you may be less fit or, worse, overtraining.

Average heart rate data are especially useful for the indoor cyclist who has the ability to measure distance. Hold your heart rate at a constant number—say, 140 bpm—for a fixed period of time from 5 to 30 minutes. As your training progresses, note whether your distance traveled for this identical workout increases—a clear indication that the training effect is working for you.

More advanced heart rate monitors feature average heart rate per lap or split. This measurement can be useful if you are doing interval training or want to know your average heart rate per mile or kilometer during an event.

Neil Craig, one of Australia's best sports physiologists, explains the usefulness of average heart rate this way:

priate to train there as long as you complement them with recovery rides in the lower heart zones. A good way to measure if you have achieved sufficient interrecovery is to measure your resting heart rate. If it approaches 5 beats per minute of normal, you have probably recovered adequately.

### Rule 2. Inability to recover indicates insufficient recovery time.

If your heart rate doesn't recover between workouts, you may be overtrained, or you may not have recovered from the previous ride. You could be experiencing some effects from medication or environmental conditions, or you may have compromised your immune system. Another possibility is that you may be feeling physiological effects from other life stresses.

### Rule 3. Shortened intrarecovery time means greater fitness.

Measure with your monitor and your watch the time required between intervals for your heart rate to recover to a designated percentage of maximum heart rate. If this period decreases from week to week, you are probably getting fitter—your body can recover more quickly from a period of physical stress.

Why is average heart rate an important reading? Well, look at the following exercise and training principle: the average relative intensity of training dictates the extent of adaptation regardless of whether the training is done continuously or intermittently. This principle was formulated back in the mid-1970s and revisited by Canadian researchers in 1992 who looked at the value of either training continuously at anaerobic threshold or continuously but with alternating intensities above and below the anaerobic threshold. Their results confirmed that neither method was superior and that it is the average relative intensity of exercise that is the key to getting a good aerobic training effect. (Craig 1999)

In other words, for aerobic training at least, it doesn't matter whether your training is continuous or intermittent or interval in nature; provided the average heart rate is similar, you will get similar aerobic exercise benefits.

You can collect other good average heart rate examples by riding on a hilly course, resting on the downhills, and working hard on the uphills. A key number to know would be the average of those hard and then easy periods, so that you can determine whether you accomplished your training goal for that session.

If you are multizone training, average heart rate is valuable information. For example, if you like to warm up at 65 percent of your maximum heart rate for 5 minutes, then your workout design calls for 10 minutes in zone 3, 5 minutes in zone 4, and 2.5 minutes in zone 5, plus a cooldown of 10 minutes at 55 percent of your maximum heart rate. You can use your monitor's lap-split feature to give you your average for every zone and time period as well as for the entire workout.

## Hill Climb Test for Maximum Heart Rate

We all receive genetically specified distinguishing biomarkers within our DNA code. One of those markers is our individual maximum heart rate. As you now know, there are a number of different protocols to determine maximum heart rate. Connie Carpenter and Davis Phinney recommend using a hill climb:

Select a hill and do several hill sprints with little rest on a day when you are feeling good (don't try this when you are fatigued). Make each effort harder than the last, and use a heart-rate monitor or take your heart rate after each sprint. After several sprints, your pulse will peak at or near your maximal heart-rate value. (Carpenter and Phinney 1992, 140)

## Indoor Graded Maximum Heart Rate Test

For indoor cycling, the following graded maximum heart rate test seems to be the most accurate: Warm up adequately. Comfortably cycle at 120–130 bpm until you are ready to begin the test. Hold cadence steady and slowly increase resistance every 15 seconds. Carefully control the resistance so that heart rate increases 5 beats every 15 seconds. A typical test will last 2 to 4 minutes. Toward the end of the test, you may require support from others to encourage you to continue to reach true maximum effort. You'll be able to hold your maximum for 5–30 seconds before you reach exhaustion. Warm down completely before you dismount.

Assessing your fitness with your heart rate monitor is one of the most valuable reasons to use one. Paul Camerer learned that as he got older, he could ride harder than the mathematical formulas that predicted, inaccurately, his maximum heart rate. Get the most out of your monitor by using it for measuring your current fitness and your fitness improvement.

## The Submax Test for Cycling

This test uses your "feeling" of intensity level—the "rating of perceived exertion" (RPE)—combined with your fitness level and your heart rate as registered on your heart rate monitor. This 10-level test is designed for an indoor stationary bicycle. An increase in cadence or resistance may be used to increase exercise intensity.

### Administering the Test

Warm up for a minimum of 5 minutes at about 100 bpm. Begin the test at level 1 by increasing your heart rate to 110 bpm and maintaining that for 2 minutes. At the end of 2 minutes, record your RPE number and begin level 2 by increasing your heart rate to 120 bpm and holding that for 2 minutes. At the end of the 2 minutes, record your RPE number and begin level 3 by increasing your heart rate to 130 bpm and holding that for 2 minutes. (You may stop the test after this level if your RPE number is 7 or higher.) At the end of 2 minutes, record your RPE number. Begin level 4 by increasing your heart rate to 140 bpm and maintain that number for 2 minutes. At the end of the 2 minutes, record your RPE number. (You may stop the test after this level if the RPE number is 7 or higher.) Begin level 5 by increasing your heart rate to 150 bpm and maintain that number for 2 minutes. At the end of the 2 minutes, record the RPE number. Continue up the levels until you reach an RPE number of 7.

Warm down for a minimum of 5 minutes until your heart rate is below 100 bpm.

To determine your estimated maximum heart rate, complete the calculations by adding bpm to the various levels of heart rate as indicated by the Testing Chart. Maximum heart rate estimates are then averaged to determine maximum heart rate.

## Submax Cycling Test

Name_____

Date_____

Begin by warming up 5–10 minutes.

| Levels (A) | Heart Rate (bpm) (B) | RPE from Testing Chart Column (2) (C) | BPM from Testing Chart Column (3) (D) | Estimated Max HR: Column B + D (E) |
|---|---|---|---|---|
| 1 | 100 | 1 | 90 | 190 |
| 2 | 110 | 2 | 80 | 190 |
| 3 | 120 | 3 | 70 | 190 |
| 4 | 130 | 4.5 | 55 | 185 |
| 5 | 140 | 6 | 40 | 180 |
| 6 | 150 | 7 | 30 | 180 |
| 7 | 160 | | | |
| 8 | 170 | | | |
| 9 | 180 | | | |
| 10 | 190 | | | |
| | | | Estimated Max HR: Average of Column (E) | 185 |

| Testing Chart | | | | |
|---|---|---|---|---|
| Descriptive Words | RPE (2) | BPM (3) | Feeling (4) | % Max HR (5) |
| Very little effort | 1 | 90 | Very light to easy | |
| | 1.5 | 85 | | |
| Very comfortable | 2 | 80 | Easy | <35% |
| | 2.5 | 75 | | |
| Easy to talk, no problem to continue | 3 | 70 | Moderate | 35%–50% |
| | 3.5 | 65 | | |
| Could continue for a long time | 4 | 60 | Somewhat hard | 50%–60% |
| | 4.5 | 55 | | |
| Still somewhat Comfortable | 5 | 50 | Strong | 60%–70% |
| | 5.5 | 45 | | |
| More challenging, not as comfortable | 6 | 40 | Hard! | 70%–80% |
| | 6.5 | 35 | | |
| Tough, very heavy, must push self | 7 | 30 | Very hard | 80%–85% |
| | 7.5 | 25 | | |
| Challenging, breathing deep and rapid | 8 | 20 | #x*! hard | 85%–90% |
| | 8.5 | 15 | | |
| Uncomfortable, rapid breathing | 9 | 10 | #x*!, #x*! hard | 90%–95% |
| | 9.5 | 5 | | |
| Cannot talk, ready to stop | 10 | 0 | Maximal | 95%–100% |

## WORKOUTS: Indoor Training

### HEALTHY HEART **Workout 17: Recovery Intervals**

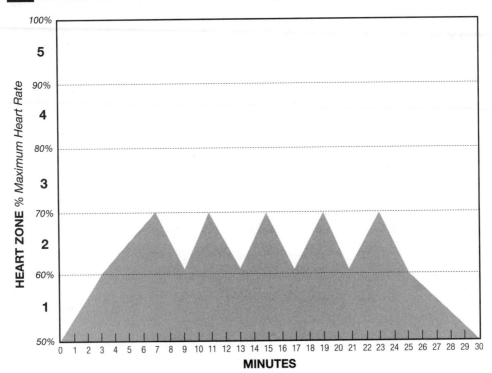

## Overview

There are days when your legs need a break—a recovery day. Here's a way to use your recovery day as a way to maintain your fitness, burn a few extra calories, and just ride for joy without crossing into the Threshold or Red-Line Zones (4 and 5, respectively). This workout is also a great way to measure your "active" recovery (easy-pedal) heart rate. The recovery interval is 15–20 bpm, depending on your maximum heart rate numbers. This recovery interval is perfect for testing and for giving yourself a break, as you will see. If you have more than 30 minutes to ride, then add several more intervals.

## Description

A main set is that period of time in a workout when most of the training takes place. During the main set of this recovery workout, you will be riding in heart zone 2, or between 60 and 70 percent of your maximum heart rate. Training in the low heart zones, zones 1 and 2, helps you develop a healthier heart. Keep the resistance low and "noodle" or "easy pedal" your way up and down each interval. Measure the elapsed time of each of your recoveries. Count how many seconds it takes for you to drop from the top of zone 2 at 70 percent of your maximum heart rate to the bottom of zone 2 at 60 percent. As you get fitter, it takes fewer seconds to recover because your heart is healthier. Retest your recovery time each month in a standardized way such as this one.

Another way you can do the recovery test is to measure how many heartbeats you drop in 2 minutes of easy pedaling (active recovery).

| Stats and Tips for Workout 17: Recovery Intervals | | | |
|---|---|---|---|
| Zone Number and Name | Minutes in Zone | Heart Zones Training Points | Estimated Calories |
| 5. Red-Line | | | |
| 4. Threshold | | | |
| 3. Aerobic | 10 | 30 | 90–110 |
| 2. Temperate | 14 | 28 | 84–112 |
| 1. Healthy Heart | 6 | 6 | 18–30 |
| Totals | 30 | 64 | 192–252 |

**Tip:** Make sure your recovery cadence is the same on each recovery and use easy gearing or very little resistance.

| Sequence for Workout 17: Recovery Intervals | | | | |
|---|---|---|---|---|
| Elapsed Time (min.) | Workout Plan | Heart Zone | Your Heart Rate (bpm) | Interval Time (min.) |
| 0–3 | Warm up, easy pedal | 1 | _____ | 3 |
| 3–5 | Warm up, easy pedal to bottom of Z2 | 2 | _____ | 2 |
| 5–7 | Increase HR to midpoint of Z2 (65%) | 2 | _____ | 2 |
| 7–27 | Increase HR steadily to bottom of Z3 (70%) for 2 min., then active recovery for 2 min. to the bottom of Z2 and sustain.[a] Record the number of seconds to recover. Repeat a total of 5 times | 3 2 | _____ | 20 |
| 27–30 | Warm down to bottom of Z1 | 1 | _____ | 3 |

[a] Recovery may be timed and a new interval started once the bottom of Z2 is reached. Count the number of completed work/recovery intervals in 20 min.

## ▦ FITNESS **Workout 18: Heartbeat**

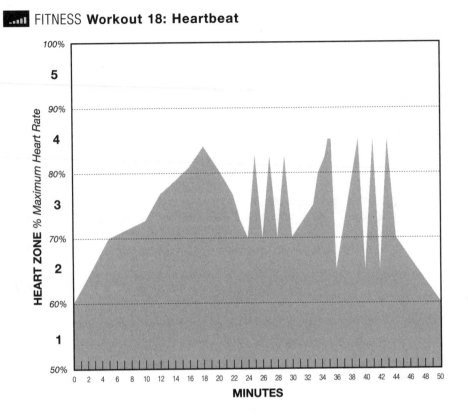

## Overview

This workout gives you four different workout challenges. It starts with a Five-by-Two ladder. Next, you're challenged to finish a crisscross from the bottom to the top of zone 3. Third, you ride yourself through a set of power and sprint intervals. Finally, you finish with a crisscross from the midpoint of zone 2 to the midpoint of zone 4.

## Description

Each of these four challenges produces its own outcome. The Five-by-Two ladder simulates a long uphill pull that continuously gets steeper. It also includes a controlled recovery down the ladder that simulates a long downhill to give you some breathing time. A 2-minute, crisscross interval follows to train your aerobic system in zone 3. The next interval pushes the heart rate higher as the heart and muscles are trained to respond quickly in 10-second sprints followed by 20-second recoveries. The last interval is a final push through two zones as you race against the clock. Finish with a series of 5 standing power sprints (10 seconds all-out with a 20-second recovery) followed by 3 minutes of recovery.

| Stats and Tips for Workout 18: Heartbeat | | | |
|---|---|---|---|
| Zone Number and Name | Minutes in Zone | Heart Zones Training Points | Estimated Calories |
| 5. Red-Line | | | |
| 4. Threshold | 14 | 56 | 168–196 |
| 3. Aerobic | 21 | 63 | 189–231 |
| 2. Temperate | 15 | 30 | 90–120 |
| 1. Healthy Heart | | | |
| Totals | 50 | 149 | 447–547 |

**Tip:** Use your monitor to test for improvements in your recovery heart rate.

| Sequence for Workout 18: Heartbeat | | | | |
|---|---|---|---|---|
| Elapsed Time (min.) | Workout Plan | Heart Zone | Your Heart Rate (bpm) | Interval Time (min.) |
| 0–5 | Warm up to bottom of Z2 | 2 | _____ | 5 |
| 5–10 | Increase HR to bottom of Z3 with cadence/rpm | 3 | _____ | 5 |
| 10–20 | From the bottom of Z3 add 5 bpm every 2 min., choice of (R) or (rpm), seated | 3 4 | _____ _____ | 10 |
| 20–25 | Decrease HR 5 bpm every min. for 5 min. to bottom of Z3 | 4 3 | _____ _____ | 5 |
| 25–33 | Increase HR from bottom of Z3 to bottom of Z4 in 1 min., your choice, followed by a 1 min. (rec) to bottom of Z3, count recovery beats (RHR). Repeat 3 times with a final 2 min. (rec) at the bottom of Z3 | 3 4 3 4 3 4 3 | _____ _____ _____ _____ _____ _____ _____ | 8 |
| 33–36 | [Power starts[a] with heavy (R), standing for 10 sec. followed by 20 sec. seated (rec).] Repeat a total of 6 times | 3 4 4 4 4 | _____ _____ _____ _____ _____ | 3 |
| 36–39 | Easy pedal (rec) to bottom of Z2 | 2 | _____ | 3 |
| 39–45 | Increase HR from midpoint of Z2 (65%) to midpoint of Z4 (85%) and (rec) to midpoint of Z2 (65%). Count number of times you complete this interval in 6 min. | 2 4 2 | _____ _____ _____ | 6 |
| 45–50 | Warm down to bottom of Z2 | 2 | _____ | 5 |

[a] From a slow spin or stopped position, seated or standing, expend in 10 seconds all-out effort with heavy resistance followed by a 20-second recovery. Alternate your lead foot.

## PERFORMANCE **Workout 19: Escalator**

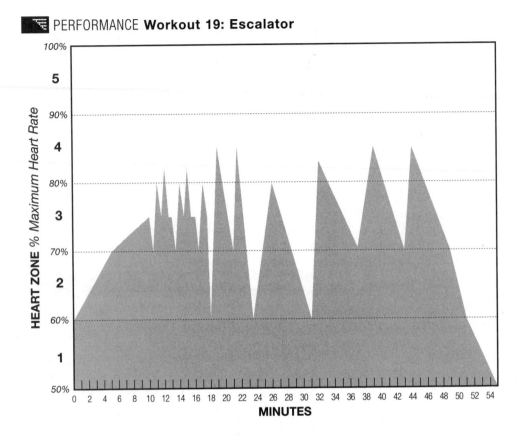

## Overview

This workout may remind you of being a kid again and riding the escalators at the local department store. Remember how fun it was to climb the moving steps and speed up the trek to the next floor? This workout has plenty of ups and downs, and you don't have to worry about getting off on the next floor and looking like a klutz if you misjudge the final step.

## Description

A series of 30-second efforts and recoveries will help you develop more power in your pedal stroke. Then you do four longer steady-state intervals to build your aerobic power.

| Stats and Tips for Workout 19: Escalator | | | |
|---|---|---|---|
| Zone Number and Name | Minutes in Zone | Heart Zones Training Points | Estimated Calories |
| 5. Red-Line | | | |
| 4. Threshold | 29 | 116 | 348–406 |
| 3. Aerobic | 13 | 39 | 117–143 |
| 2. Temperate | 13 | 26 | 78–104 |
| 1. Healthy Heart | | | |
| Totals | 55 | 181 | 543–653 |

**Tip:** Recruit your hamstrings by pulling your heels up toward the bottom of your seat on the upstroke.

| Sequence for Workout 19: Escalator | | | | |
|---|---|---|---|---|
| Elapsed Time (min.) | Workout Plan | Heart Zone | Your Heart Rate (bpm) | Interval Time (min.) |
| 0–5 | Easy-pedal warm-up | 2 | _____ | 5 |
| 5–10 | Increase HR to bottom of Z3 | 3 | _____ | 5 |
| 10–18 | 30 sec. hard effort followed by 30 sec. easy pedal (rec), adjust (R) as needed for Z3 or Z4 | 3 4 | _____ _____ | 8 |
| 18–19 | Easy pedal (rec) | 2 | _____ | 1 |
| 19–24 | Moderate to heavy (R), 30 sec. hard effort, midpoint of Z4 (85%), followed by 30 sec. easy pedal (rec) for a total of 5 min. | 4 | _____ | 5 |
| 24–29 | Steady-state HR, bottom of Z4, (R), 80 rpm (8), seated | 4 | _____ | 5 |
| 29–31 | Easy pedal (rec) | 2 | _____ | 2 |
| 31–36 | Steady-state HR, bottom of Z4 plus 5 bpm, (R), 80 rpm (8), seated | 4 | _____ | 5 |
| 36–38 | Easy pedal (rec) | 3 | _____ | 2 |
| 38–43 | Steady-state HR, midpoint of Z4 (85%), (R), 80 rpm (8), choice | 4 | _____ | 5 |
| 43–45 | Easy pedal (rec) | 3 | _____ | 2 |
| 45–50 | Steady-state HR, midpoint of Z4 (85%), (R) as needed, 95 rpm (9.5), seated or standing | 4 | _____ | 5 |
| 50–55 | Easy pedal (rec) | 2 | _____ | 5 |

**Workout 20: Two-by-Twenty Anaerobic Threshold Test**

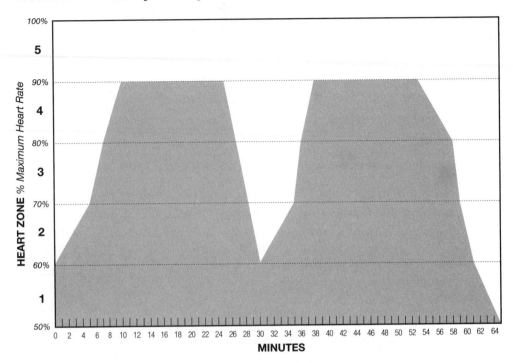

## Overview

This is an anaerobic heart rate test designed by David Martin, Ph.D., at Georgia State University. The goal of this workout is to sustain the highest heart rate number you can for 20 minutes followed by a 5-minute recovery and then sustain the same high number again for 20 minutes. After completing both 20-minute intervals, answer this question: Was that the hardest I could work for the time allotted (40 minutes)? If the answer is yes, then that heart rate number is an excellent estimate of your anaerobic threshold heart rate. The following chart shows sample threshold rates for individuals considered sedentary, fit, and superfit.

Anaerobic threshold testing is one way of measuring fitness. The higher the percentage of maximum heart rate you can sustain for the duration of the test, the fitter you are. This translates into being able to cycle faster for a longer duration. If you have never done this test before, you may want to be conservative the first time until you get the feel for what is happening and what is expected. Retest in a month or six weeks to see if you are getting fitter. It is important that you are fully rested before doing this test and that you give yourself a minimum of 48 hours of rest from riding above heart zone 3.

| RPE | Feeling | Sedentary | Fit | Superfit | Descriptive Words | Zone | % of Max HR |
|-----|---------|-----------|-----|----------|-------------------|------|-------------|
| | | | | **Anaerobic Threshold Chart** | | | |
| 1 | Rest | | | | Very little effort | | <35% |
| 2 | Easy | | | | Very comfortable | | <35% |
| 3 | Moderate | | | | Easy to talk | | 35–50% |
| 4 | Somewhat strong | | | | Could continue for a long time | 1 | 50–60% |
| 5 | Strong | X | | | Feels hard | 2 | 60–70% |
| 6 | Heavy | X | X | | More challenging | 3 | 70–80% |
| 7 | Very strong | | X | | Tough | 4 | 80–85% |
| 8 | Hard | | | X | Very challenging | 4 | 85–90% |
| 9 | Very, very hard | | | X | Uncomfortable | 5 | 90–95% |
| 10 | Extremely strenuous | | | | Can't talk, ready to stop | 5 | 95–100% |

Note: "X" indicates the anaerobic threshold RPE and percentage of maximum heart rate for a sedentary, fit, or superfit individual.

## Description

Warm up for 5 minutes to the bottom of zone 2, then gradually increase heart rate for the next 5 minutes until you reach the heart rate number that you think you can sustain for 20 minutes. Sustain that number for 20 minutes. You may choose to use cadence, resistance/gearing, or any combination you wish to sustain your heart rate. After 20 minutes, recover to the bottom of zone 2 for 5 minutes. Make sure you drink plenty of water and allow your legs and body to relax.

After 5 minutes of recovery, begin to increase your heart rate again over the next 3 minutes until you have reached the same heart rate number that you sustained for the first 20 minutes. Sustain that heart rate for a second 20 minutes, then warm down over the next 7 minutes to zone 1.

| Sequence for Workout 20: Two-by-Twenty | | | | |
|---|---|---|---|---|
| Elapsed Time (min.) | Workout Plan | Heart Zone | Your Heart Rate (bpm) | Interval Time (min.) |
| 0–5 | Warm up to bottom of Z2 | | _____ | 5 |
| 5–7 | Increase HR, bottom of Z3 | 2 | _____ | 2 |
| 7–10 | Gradually increase HR to highest sustainable HR number | 3 | _____ | 2 |
| 10–30 | Sustain HR goal, choice of rpm or resistance (R) | | _____ | 20 |
| 30–35 | Recover (rec) to the bottom of Z2, easy pedal | | _____ | 5 |
| 35–36 | Increase HR, bottom of Z3 | 2 | _____ | 1 |
| 36–38 | Gradually increase HR to same sustainable HR number | 3 | _____ | 2 |
| 38–58 | Sustain HR goal, choice of rpm or resistance (R) | | _____ | 20 |
| 58–65 | Warm down gradually to Z1 | | _____ | 7 |

## Outdoor Training and Rides

### Workout 21: The Distance Improvement Ride

Do you want to cycle farther and at a lower heart rate in less time? That is the purpose of this ride. After an adequate warm-up, you will start at 70 percent of your maximum heart rate if you are a healthy beginner, 75 percent of your maximum heart rate for a fit intermediate rider, and 80 percent if you are very fit. Record your distance traveled in 15 minutes at your chosen heart rate percentage using your bike computer. As you get stronger and fitter, the distance you travel should become greater. When you retest to check your improvement, make sure you are cycling under similar conditions such as wind, heat, and humidity and on the same course. Record your results in your log and compare them once a month or however often you want to measure your improvement.

### Workout 22: The Anaerobic Threshold Ride

First, you need a clear idea of what anaerobic threshold means, because there is much confusion about the concept of anaerobic training. In short, during any training you are riding at an intensity level that requires your body to consume fuels—a combination of carbohydrates, fats, and proteins. For most cyclists, when you are in the aerobic intensity levels (zones 1, 2, and 3) as measured with your heart rate monitor, you have sufficient oxygen and are producing lactic acid but not in sufficient quantity to limit your exercise time. There is a heart rate point that can be measured when you shift your fuels and the metabolic process from aerobic to anaerobic. This is called the "crossover point," where oxygen is insufficient to sustain the exercise intensity and you produce too much lactic acid, so it builds up in the working muscles and causes them to fatigue. The rate of lactate accumulation will depend on how high above this threshold the intensity is and how effective the body is at clearing blood lactate.

To measure blood lactate precisely, you need access to a gas exchange analyzer or a lactate analyzer. Such equipment isn't readily available, but there is a way to estimate your anaerobic threshold heart rate by doing a ride we affectionately call the Two-by-Twenty. (This ride can also be done indoors as the Two-by-Twenty Anaerobic Test in Chapter 5.) This is a strenuous ride and not for the faint of heart.

After you are warmed up adequately, set your heart rate monitor so you can get an accurate reading of average heart rate. Then, time trial a steady-state heart rate for 20 minutes. This heart rate needs to be the highest rate you think you sustain for the 20-minute period. Choose your route carefully, making sure you have no stop signs or other interrupting factors. Focus on your heart rate monitor as much as possible. Mount it on your handlebars so you have a clear view of it throughout the ride.

This workout is only for the very fit cyclist. It isn't easy, because for most people it's a zone 4 threshold ride. This is an ideal training ride once a month to see if your average heart rate improves—that is, if it slowly increases. The closer your anaerobic threshold heart rate is to your maximum heart rate, the fitter you are. Make sure you are fully rested before doing this ride, and take an easy recovery ride or a day off the next day.

## Workout 23: Aerobic Time Trial

Choose a flat 5-mile section of road that has no stop signs, roaming dogs, or other distractions. After an adequate warm-up, ride 5 miles at 75 percent of your maximum heart rate, or the midpoint of zone 3. Stay in the same gear for the entire time trial. Record your time. Retest yourself periodically (once a month). The conditions must be the same from one time trial test to the next. This includes the amount of rest since your last high-intensity workout, the length and intensity of your warm-up, the weather and road conditions, and the gear you used in the previous test. As you become fitter, your time should decrease. This is a good test to do on the endurance spoke of the training wheel and to use as a retest as you progress to the other training spokes.

## Workout 24: The All-Out Time Trial

Find a 5- or 10-mile course that has no stop signs and only limited traffic. Pick a day when there is no wind and the roads are dry. Make sure you have the same weather conditions when you retest.

This time trial means "all out," as fast as you can go for the entire course. Make sure you have a good warm-up. It's helpful to use a downloadable heart rate monitor for this trial because you can save the printout and compare your results with those you achieve the next time you do this time trial. If you don't have a downloadable monitor, the next best thing is to use a monitor that will calculate average heart rate. Elapsed time or chronograph functions are also handy.

Record your results, elapsed time, and average heart rate in your logbook and also note the weather, time of day/year, and how you felt. As you get fitter, you will notice that the time to complete the course decreases and your heart rate declines. That's good, because you can generate more power at a lower heart rate. If you are faster and your average heart rate goes slightly higher, this means that your anaerobic threshold is higher. Good. You are getting fitter. If that is your goal, there is no better way to measure fitness than to put the pedal to the metal and see the results. The process is extremely motivating, and you will soon forget the pain when you see that your training is working.

## REFERENCES

Ackland, Jon. *Precision Training: Training Programmes for 27 Sports Using Heart Rate Monitors.* Auckland, New Zealand: Reed Books, 1998.

American College of Sports Medicine. Position Paper. The Recommended Quantity and Quality of Exercise for Developing and Maintaining Cardiorespiratory and Muscular Fitness and Flexibility in Healthy Adults. *Medicine and Science in Sports and Exercise* 30 (June 1998): pp. 975–991.

Carpenter, Connie, and Davis Phinney. *Training for Cycling: The Ultimate Guide to Improved Performance.* New York: Perigee Books, 1992.

Craig, Neil. *Performance Matters.* Newsletter. June 1999.

*Susan Smalls, Don Cox, and Sue Dills riding a Heart Zones Cycling class on two different types of indoor cycles.*

# 6

# The Fat-Burning Range

*Marie was like so many of us, trying to lose that elusive ten pounds after gaining twenty in five years due to trauma and health challenges. She went through menopause, had a bilateral mastectomy, and experienced a severe ankle fracture. After twenty sedentary years, cancer compelled her to begin working out with other cancer survivors. She lost ten pounds but had reached a plateau.*

*A quietly intense and competitive person, Marie was using a heart rate monitor and confessed to spending a lot of her training time in the higher zones. As you will see, she was more successful when she changed that approach.*

—SALLY EDWARDS

Burning nutrient- and calorie-packed fuels is important to the successful cyclist. This isn't a simple task. It requires effort to combine a healthy diet with a physical and psychological training program to become a better cyclist. Eating optimally combined with training soundly can result in an entire lifestyle shift toward a healthier and longer life.

Eating optimally always leads to the question of the role of dietary and body fat as well as fat burning. One of the questions Sally Edwards is most frequently asked is what heart zone(s) burns the most fat. She prefers to broaden the question to how fuels are used in each of the different heart zones.

Countless magazine articles and reports give conflicting explanations and information about the fat-burning zones. In fact, there's only one best answer to this complex question about fat. Because it's a major issue for those interested in weight management, the process of burning fuels, including fat, is important to understand clearly.

Different types of fuels are burned in different percentages depending on the zone. The three principal types of calories used for cycling are protein, carbohydrates (also known as sugar, muscle glycogen, and blood glucose), and fat (also known as free fatty acids and triglycerides). When you ride in different heart zones, you burn a different ratio of carbohydrates (carbs) and fat. In practical terms, the percentage of protein used for energy remains relatively constant at approximately 5 percent in each heart zone. The higher the heart zone, the higher the percentage of carbohydrates burned and the lower the percentage of fat burned. In fact, you burn the highest percentage of fat compared to total calories when you're asleep! In zone 5 most individuals burn no additional fat; all additional calories consumed are from carbohydrates. This means that most people are burning as many fat calories in zone 4 as in zone 5. You do, however, burn more total calories in zone 5.

The preceding sentence raises another important point: the difference between total calories burned and the percentage of calories burned. The higher the exercise intensity, the more total calories burned in one minute. For example, as a rough estimate, in one minute of exercise, a 150-pound rider would burn the following number of calories from combined protein, fat, and carbohydrates:

| Calories Burned by a 150-Pound Rider | |
| --- | --- |
| Heart Zone | Calories Burned (per min.) |
| 1 | >5 |
| 2 | >8 |
| 3 | >11 |
| 4 | >14 |
| 5 | >20 |

That same person burns a different ratio of calories in each of the heart zones. The higher the exercise intensity, the more glycogen or muscle sugar (carbohydrates as glycogen) is burned, and the lower the percentage of fat calories burned.

## FREQUENTLY ASKED QUESTIONS: FUELING THE ZONES

Following are Sally Edwards's answers to ten frequently asked questions about the fat-burning heart zones. As you read the answers, remember that each person is unique, and thus we display highly individual differences in our response to foods as fuels. As a result, we burn fat, carbohydrates, and protein in an individual way and each according to a number of different factors.

## 1. In What Heart Zone Do I Burn the Most Fat?

The fitter you are, the more total fat you burn in each of the heart zones. The less fit you are, the less fat you burn in each zone. For example, if you are unfit, you will burn the most fat in the lower range, from zones 2 to 3. If you are tremendously fit, you'll burn the most fat in zone 4 or zone 5. For long-term weight-management goals, the total number of calories you burn matters most, not the percentage of fat.

Oxygen must be present for fat to burn. When you exercise aerobically, with plenty of oxygen and without shortness of breath, you burn a high amount of fat. As soon as you cross over to the anaerobic exercise intensity, the point where there is not enough oxygen to sustain the exercise, you don't burn any additional fat as the source of calories fueling your muscles. The following chart shows an example of the percentage of calories used and the calorie consumption in each heart zone during a 30-minute bike ride:

| | | | | | | |
|---|---|---|---|---|---|---|
| **Calorie Consumption for a 30-Minute Ride** | | | | | | |
| Zone | Percent of Max HR | Wellness Zones | Fuels Burned | Calories Burned for 30 Minutes | RPE | Description of Feeling |
| 5 | 90–100% | Performance | 85% carb 10–15% fat appx 5% protein | 450–600 | 9–10 | #x*!, #x*! hard to maximal |
| 4 | 80–90% | Fitness/ Performance | 80–90% carb 10–20% fat appx 5% protein | >450 | 7–8 | Very to #x*! hard |
| 3 | 70–80% | Fitness | 50–85% carb 40–60% fat appx 5% protein | >330 | 5–6 | Strong to hard |
| 2 | 60–70% | Health | 25–50% carb 50–70% fat appx 5% protein | >240 | 3–4 | Moderate to somewhat hard |
| 1 | 50–60% | Health | 10–25% carb 70–85% fat appx 5% protein | >180 | 1–2 | Very light, easy |

**Note:** These are estimates of calories used for a 150-pound fit rider.

**Source:** The descriptions of feelings are adapted from Foster's Perceived Exertion chart (Foster 2001).

## 2. Which Fuels Are Burning in Each Heart Zone?

As mentioned earlier, a different ratio of fuels is burned in each of the five heart zones. The higher the heart zone or the level of exercise intensity, the higher the percentage of carbohydrates oxidized. The lower the zone, the higher the percentage of fat calories used. If you are training for weight-management goals, are you interested in burning a high percentage of fat calories or a high number of total calories? Research still has not provided the complete answer to that question, but what there is suggests that burning a high number of total calories promotes a more successful weight-management program. To help clarify the issue, the following chart shows the percentage of calories burned in each of the five different heart zones during a 30-minute ride:

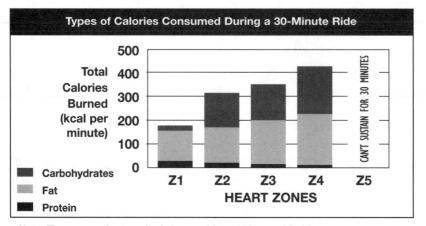

**Note:** These are estimates of calories used for a 150-pound fit rider.

The overall conclusion is that it's best for weight loss or maintenance to exercise longer periods of time in heart zones that you can sustain.

## 3. Do We All Burn Calories the Same Way?

No. There are enormous individual differences. If you've ever read or thought that a calorie is always just a calorie, think again. The issue is not simply the way we metabolize or burn energy. Energy balance is highly individualistic. Recent research shows that burning fuels is more complex than previously thought (Blair et al. 1985).

If you want to achieve an "energy shift" that results in successful weight changes, you can change many factors that influence your individual energy balance:

1. The *ratio of fuels* in your current diet. If you eat a high-fat diet, you'll burn a higher percentage of fat calories when you train.

2. Your current *fitness level*. The fitter you are, the more fat you'll burn at the same exercise intensity.

3. What you have *just eaten*. If you just ate food and are training or racing with that fuel simultaneously being digested, it will affect the ratio of fuels burned.

4. Your current *body composition*. Your percentage of body fat to lean body weight affects fat-burning capacity. People with a higher percentage of body fat burn more fat as a percentage than those who have lower body fat.

5. The amount of *alcohol* in your diet. Alcohol is a diuretic. Acute alcohol ingestion results in adverse performance, impairing both psychological and physiological ability.

6. The length of *time* you exercise. How long you ride affects your requirements for fuel. Before, during, and after a workout, fueling depends on frequency, intensity, type, and duration of exercise.

7. *Gender* plays a role in weight management. For the female, different hormonal levels result in different ways fat is utilized and deposited. Further, water retention varies at different times during the female menstrual cycle. Female athletes have lower energy requirements than men do. According to Butterfield and Gates (1994), "Provision of a high carbohydrate diet as recommended for the male endurance athlete may not be realistic for the female athlete, given her requirements for other micro- and macro-nutrients."

8. Food palate, or *taste preference*. You need to respect the joy of eating food as well as the need for a varied and balanced diet, one that provides adequate nutrient intake.

9. Total *daily number of calories* consumed. An adequate energy intake is required to prevent fatigue and low individual energy levels. Excessive fuel intake results in a shift in energy balance and eventual body fat accumulation.

10. *Genetic makeup* is significant. Though complicated, genetics greatly affects your body composition.

11. *Environment.* Factors such as rural versus city dwelling, pollution, and a sedentary job that doesn't foster human-powered transportation can affect your energy balance and overall health.

12. *Past sports experience.* If you've been fit before, it's sometimes easier to get fit again not only because of the familiarity but also due to the emotional impact of fitness improvements.

13. *Stress.* A high-stress lifestyle can lead to an energy shift toward holding back on fat release (hoarding), because the body responds to stress by automatic preservation of body fat.

You have a degree of control over many of these factors. Understanding and adjusting them can have an impact on how you refuel and manage weight. That is the basic tenet of energy shifting for body-weight changes.

## 4. How Does Fat Burn in Each of the Heart Zones?

Fat comes in two basic forms: the kind we burn in the form of fat calories for basic metabolic and movement requirements, and the kind that's stored in different parts of our bodies, such as in adipose tissue, our blood, and the fat that protects our organs. For most people, liberating the stored fat in the adipose tissues is a major goal. To burn adipose tissue, your metabolic pathways must allow fat cells to release fat in the form of triglycerides, transport the fat to the working muscles, and then burn it off preferentially. We want to burn fat before we burn any of the other sources of fuel.

During low-intensity riding in zones 1 through 3, fat is effectively chosen as the preferred fuel source. Though this burns fewer total calories per minute, it results in the improvement of metabolic fat-burning pathways, which depend on the presence of aerobic enzymes. Low heart zone training high in oxygen availability effectively frees fat from the fat cell (called fat release) and then allows it to be transported to the muscle (fat transportation). When these molecules of fat reach the working muscles, low-intensity exercise permits the cell membrane to open and allows the fat, each gram packed with nine calories of energy, to be burned by the body's energy factories (the mitochondria).

Burning body fat is a complex process that takes time to occur. Short, brief zone 5 bursts of energy can't match longer, slower, less energetic heart zones 1 to 3 workout sessions for burning fat. If you want to burn fat preferentially and in sizable amounts from your stored body fat, then train in low heart zones for longer periods of time and, simultaneously, have more fun.

## 5. Is Cycling the Best Activity for Fat Burning?

If you are a cyclist, probably yes. If you are a swimmer, the best fat-burning activity is probably swimming. This isn't because one activity burns fat better than the other. Each burns different amounts of fat based on several factors. However, what's known—and fairly easy to guess—is that those who stick with an exercise program tend to burn more fat long term than those who quit. This is called "exercise compliance," or the ability of the exerciser to stay on a training program. Compliance strongly relates to the enjoyment of the experience. If you love to ride your bike, your compliance to bicycle riding will be high. If you train in the fitness heart zones, you'll burn lots of fat and lots of calories, stay on the training program, and achieve results. If you're a cyclist who turns to running and doesn't find joy in it, your unwillingness to stay on the running program may derail your success.

Ultimately, it comes down to whether you are training at all, not which zones you occupy. Review of the scientific literature shows that those who are overweight usually get too little exercise; they don't overeat.

You'll probably experience a direct and absolute relationship between exercise and weight loss. Training on your bike can result in steady, slow but long-term, effective weight loss and weight maintenance. That's the best way to reach your weight-management goal.

## 6. What About Bike Weight Versus Body Weight?

One of the nice things about riding a bicycle is that your body weight is supported by your bike frame and tires rather than by your skeletal frame. Cycling may be easier on your joints, but sooner or later that extra weight must go up a hill. That's where you might say the rubber meets the road. Extra weight (either as body fat and muscle or bicycle weight) can slow down the cyclist on hills. Since climbing a hill is work against gravity, a lighter climber is pushing fewer pounds and thereby gaining an advantage over a heavier cyclist.

According to Arnie Baker, M.D., "a 5 percent loss in either body weight or bicycle weight or a combination of both could result in as much as three minutes in an hour's climb" (Baker 1997). That may not sound like much, but it could mean the difference between winning the race or coming in last. Or it could mean the difference between keeping up with the gang or dropping behind to grind your way to the top alone.

Three tactics will get you to the top of the hill faster. You can buy your way to the top with expensive equipment (which doesn't work very well if you're not fit), or you can train your way to the top by losing extra fat pounds and gaining muscle strength. A third option is to combine technology with training.

## 7. What Are the Best Foods to Eat Before, During, and After Cycling?

It's up to you to decide what fuels are best suited to your body and its metabolism, whether you're off or on the bike. First, consider a couple of your nutritional choices. Carbohydrates are one of the most important energy sources to enhance athletic performance. They are essential for cycling and prolonged endurance activities. Exercise scientists have long known that a diet rich in carbohydrates and a body trained to utilize blood glucose are factors that improve performance and endurance. The more glycogen you can pack into your muscle cells and the more stored, readily accessible fuel you possess, the less you will fatigue during long rides.

Your daily energy needs for cycling will depend both on the duration and the intensity of your training. The harder and longer you cycle, the more calories you'll need to consume to maintain the same pace for longer periods. Beware though: Cycle training is not an invitation to eat anything and everything. Training smart means eating the right mix of food from the three major fuel sources to ensure proper energy. Current research supports a nutrient-rich diet of 60–65 percent carbohydrates, 25–30 percent fat, and 10–15 percent protein, with a calorie intake adequately geared to intensity and duration on a daily basis.

As already noted, only carbohydrates and fats are used extensively during cycling. Your working muscles prefer burning carbohydrates because their energy contents are easily and quickly released and used by the body.

In general, your pre-ride meal should be high in carbohydrates and low in fats and proteins. It should contain adequate amounts of fluid to ensure that you are well hydrated. Pancakes, waffles, cereals, pasta, bagels, toast, fruit, fruit juices, and liquid carbohydrate and food supplements are all good food choices. For those with no time to feast, an energy bar can suffice but isn't a replacement for real foods. It is important to eat before cycling, so forget about skipping breakfast—it's too important.

For rides lasting more than one hour, consume about 100 to 150 calories of carbohydrates every half-hour throughout the ride. Most 8- to 12-ounce servings of sport drinks provide about 300 to 400 calories of carbohydrates and fat, so drinking 8–12 ounces every 30 minutes should help fight off fatigue.

Fluid supplementation such as energy drinks during long rides provides electrolytes, water, and carbohydrates. Water is the most critical because dehydration that exceeds 2 percent of body weight greatly reduces performance. Energy drinks also provide sodium, an electrolyte, which enhances water absorption from the intestine into the bloodstream. Most energy drinks are 5–10 percent carbohydrates, the range for optimizing fluid absorption and providing carbohydrates to power your muscles. If you can grab a cool energy drink, do it. Cool fluids empty faster from your stomach than warm fluids.

If you are riding over several hours, you might consider some solid food such as energy or sport bars. Drink several ounces of fluid with the energy bar. Choose high-carbohydrate energy bars low in fat and protein. Select bars that are more than 80 percent carbohydrate and less than 10 percent fat. Another energy source is high-energy concentrated carbohydrate gel, which offers quick energy for sustained performance. Each package is premeasured carbohydrates and relatively easy to consume on the bike. It can also be used immediately after exercise to help with recovery. The gel is not designed to replace food, energy drinks, or bars, however. A better choice might be to eat real food—bananas, fruit, cookies, bagels, peanut butter sandwiches, and nuts.

Carbohydrate-rich foods like fresh fruits, breads, cereals, and energy bars, along with energy drinks, are important tools. The secret is to try different forms to determine which works best for you.

What and when you eat after a long ride can be as important as what you eat before and during it. You may require up to 24 hours to resynthesize muscle glycogen, provided ample carbohydrates are consumed. Try to eat carbohydrates as soon as possible after a ride. If you aren't hungry, drink an energy drink or high-carbohydrate beverage to replace needed fluids. By ingesting them at the end of a ride, you stimulate glycogen replacement, thereby shortening recovery time and leaving more available energy for the next day.

## 8. How Much Water Should I Drink?

Don't leave home without water. How much to drink invites another "it depends": on the ride's intensity, duration, and environmental factors, such as heat, humidity, and wind. It also depends on how your body dissipates heat produced by fuel metabolism. It depends on how many workouts per week you do and their intensity.

Hydration is the key to prolonged activity and performance. If you fail to drink enough during a long ride, you'll suffer dehydration and an inability to sweat, which means a rise in body temperature and premature fatigue. Excessive dehydration can also increase the risk of heat exhaustion and even heat stroke.

Your cycling speed declines often because dehydration reduces the water portion of the blood (plasma), decreasing blood volume. Less blood is sent to the muscles for fuel and oxygen and to the skin to help with cooling, and heart rate and body temperature climb. Your heart rate monitor indicates dehydration when your heart rate drifts upward with no increase in effort. This phenomenon is called "cardiac drift."

The key to avoiding dehydration is to drink often, before you are thirsty. Drink at least 10–20 ounces every 30 minutes, or about a standard water bottle's worth every 30–45 minutes. You should carry two water bottles on your bike for long rides and plan a stop to refill. A water pack on your back can carry considerably more water; try it out first on short rides. For rides longer than an hour, you'll need extra carbohydrates and electrolytes to help maintain your blood glucose levels and your electrolyte balance.

## 9. How Do I Lose Weight Cycling by Using My Heart Rate Monitor?

If it were possible to distill the basics of what research and experience have shown to be the world's best weight plan, it would read something like this: Lower the amount of fat you eat, and increase the amount of fat you burn when exercising.

Most people who cycle for the purpose of weight loss want either to lose fat or to keep it off. Cycling allows you to expend large amounts of calories either by riding for long periods of time or riding at high intensities. Consider both sides of this formula: what you eat and how much you exercise.

If you are interested in fat loss, you can reduce your fat intake to 20 to 30 percent of your total calories; reduce your body fat by exercising, especially at 60 to 80 percent maximum heart rate; reduce your total ingested calories; and increase your muscle mass.

Using your heart rate monitor along with smart eating and exercising is one of the keys to your success. The following chart shows the ratio of fuels burned at various intensities. A good suggestion for achieving smart weight management is to count fat grams, not just calories. Read labels and keep track of the number of fat grams you eat. Eat to feed your lean mass.

You lose weight during cycling by using your heart monitor in your aerobic zones. To begin, stay in these moderate zones for at least 20 to 30 minutes a day. As your body adapts to this time period, you'll notice how quickly the time passes and that you're eager to stay longer in the fat-burning zones. For weight-loss purposes, the key is to extend the length of time you are in these zones, not to move into the higher ones.

To help release fat from fat cells, ride in low-intensity zones for progressively longer and longer periods of time. When 30 minutes seems easy, move on to the next phase of your training. If you can extend your workout to 45 minutes a day, you'll be burning more fat calories. You'll also be giving your fat cells more time to release fat molecules and your bloodstream more time to carry them to your muscles where they will be readily metabolized. Your goal is to extend your workout to 50 or 60 minutes a day, 3 to 6 days a week. You'll find that by

| Fat and Calorie Chart | | |
|---|---|---|
| Calories per Day | 20% Fat (grams) | 30% Fat (grams) |
| 1,200 | 27 | 40 |
| 1,300 | 29 | 43 |
| 1,400 | 31 | 46 |
| 1,500 | 33 | 50 |
| 1,600 | 36 | 53 |
| 1,700 | 38 | 56 |
| 1,800 | 40 | 60 |
| 1,900 | 42 | 63 |
| 2,000 | 44 | 66 |
| 2,100 | 47 | 70 |
| 2,200 | 49 | 73 |
| 2,300 | 51 | 76 |
| 2,400 | 53 | 80 |
| 2,500 | 56 | 83 |
| 2,600 | 58 | 86 |
| 2,700 | 60 | 90 |
| 2,800 | 62 | 93 |
| 2,900 | 64 | 96 |
| 3,000 | 67 | 100 |

cycling in the lower and middle zones, you'll also be rewarded with more than burning more fat: You also will realize lower blood pressure, lower resting heart rate, reduced percentage of body fat, stabilized weight, and lower LDL, or "bad" cholesterol.

Marie applied these lessons. She stopped using her heart rate monitor as a speedometer. She decided to shift her energy equation. For a month, she kept a food diary and found that she was snacking too much and on the wrong things. She added more fruit, subtracted some fat from her diet, and spent more time in the lower and middle zones, burning more calories and building endurance. Today, she's happy, her doctor is pleased with her lowered cholesterol, and her self-image has changed from middle-aged couch potato to emerging athlete.

## 10. Can You Give Me a Sample Program to Lose Weight?

The time factor is a major key to losing weight and keeping it off. Short-term thinking doesn't work the way commitment to your plan and goals will. Your goal is to start by spending more time in the lower zones and gradually increase your frequency and intensity. Decide how many total workout minutes a week you want to do, and divide those into the number of workouts per week (frequency) and the number of minutes in each zone (intensity). The sample chart shown here is a preview of a 12-month program that includes use of a heart rate monitor to manage your riding in the different heart zones.

| Sample Cycle Training Program | | | | | | |
|---|---|---|---|---|---|---|
| Month | | Zone 1 | Zone 2 | Zone 3 | Zone 4 | Zone 5 | Total Time Riding and Other Training |
| 1 | WEEKLY TIME IN ZONE | 60 | 60 | 0 | 0 | 0 | 120 |
| 2 | | 100 | 100 | 20 | 0 | 0 | 220 |
| 3 | | 100 | 150 | 50 | 0 | 0 | 300 |
| 4 | | 100 | 140 | 100 | 0 | 0 | 340 |
| 5 | | 100 | 160 | 160 | 10 | 0 | 430 |
| 6 | | 100 | 175 | 200 | 20 | 0 | 495 |
| 7 | | 100 | 190 | 210 | 30 | 0 | 530 |
| 8 | | 100 | 200 | 250 | 30 | 0 | 580 |
| 9 | | 100 | 200 | 260 | 40 | 0 | 600 |
| 10 | | 100 | 200 | 300 | 40 | 0 | 640 |
| 11 | | 100 | 200 | 350 | 50 | 0 | 700 |
| 12 | | 100 | 200 | 400 | 60 | 0 | 760 |

☞ **TIP:** BURN RATE ON THE BICYCLE

The quest for the ideal heart zone in which to burn maximal amounts of fat requires a basic review of fat-burning facts:

1. Fat burns in every heart zone.

2. In every zone, a different ratio of fat to carbohydrates is burned.

3. The burn rate of the ride is key to weight loss.

4. Power output on the bike is proportional to the energy burn rate.

5. No additional fat is burned in riding intensities above the anaerobic threshold.

6. Oxygen and carbohydrates must be present for additional fat to burn.

When you start a ride, your muscles first start to contract and burn fuel. During this warm-up phase in the lower heart zones, the burn rate, as measured in calories per minute per power output, remains low. In the highest heart zones, you reach the highest burn rate, highest power output, highest total number of calories consumed, and the highest absolute amount of fat and carbohydrates utilized.

The burn rate of caloric expenditure is a key calculation, yet it is currently impossible to measure without sophisticated equipment. The burn rate is the sum of burning three fuel sources: glycogen, or muscle carbohydrates; a small amount of protien; and fat. To maximize the amount of fat burned, you should ride at a heart rate intensity just below your anaerobic threshold. However, to maximize the burning of both carbohydrates and fat in total calories, the higher the intensity, the more total calories burned. For example, the graph shows a rider's ratio of nutrients used and total calories consumed when riding at a steady-state power output. Because burn rates are affected by so many variables, rates are best given only in percentage ranges.

Energy burn rate and nutrient proportion depend primarily on five events:

| Burn Rates | | | | |
|---|---|---|---|---|
| Heart Zone | Name | Carbohydrates Burned (glycogen) | Fat Burned | Protein Burned |
| 5 | Red-Line Zone | 85–90% | 10–15% | approximately 5% |
| 4 | Threshold Zone | 80–90% | 10–20% | approximately 5% |
| 3 | Aerobic Zone | 50–85% | 40–60% | approximately 5% |
| 2 | Temperate Zone | 25–50% | 50–70% | approximately 5% |
| 1 | Healthy Heart Zone | 10–25% | 70–85% | approximately 5% |

1. Ratio of foods in your current diet

2. Time of your last meal

3. Workout intensity

4. Whether you eat during the ride

5. Your bicycle fitness level

## WORKOUTS: Indoor Training

### 💟 HEALTHY HEART **Workout 25: Change of Heart**

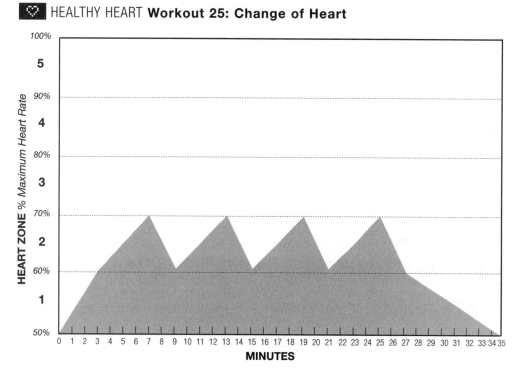

## Overview

In March 2000, people who traded in the equity stock market for Internet stocks experienced a change of heart. The high-flying balloon of Internet stock values deflated. This adjustment occurred in part because these companies' burn rate—or the amount and the utilization of their money resources needed for them to survive—was extremely high. They were metabolizing cash faster than what was reasonable. Stocks were considered overvalued and underperforming.

In contrast, a cyclist's burn rate on a bike is related in large part to the amount and the utilization of oxygen and nutrients. To keep your burn rate efficient so you do not burst your energy bubble, training in the lower zones is ideal. Whenever you exercise, your body burns a blend of the three fuels to create energy: protein, carbohydrates, and fats. Because Change of Heart takes place in the lower three heart zones, you burn a high rate of fat as the source of your energy. Remember, the higher the heart rate numbers, the higher the percentage of carbohydrates and the higher the amount of total calories burned.

## Description

Riding a Change of Heart workout can be powerful because it is in the lower three heart zones. Most of the riding time is in zone 2, the Temperate Zone. It's named that because it is cool and comfortable, a zone you can ride in for long periods of time.

By riding in the lower three heart zones, you earn heart zone training points that lead to lower blood pressure, lower resting heart rate, lower percentage of body fat, stabilized body weight, and lower LDL cholesterol (the kind you do not want).

During the Change of Heart ride, you increase your riding intensity four times to the lower limit of zone 3, that is, its bottom. After just kissing the zone 3 entry heart rate, back off and ride gently. Change of Heart is a moderate-intensity ride that is ideal for performance riders as a recovery day and challenging for new riders to learn their heart rate response to different dosages of riding resistances.

| Stats and Tips for Workout 25: Change of Heart | | | |
|---|---|---|---|
| Zone Number and Name | Minutes in Zone | Heart Zones Training Points | Estimated Calories |
| 5. Red-Line | | | |
| 4. Threshold | | | |
| 3. Aerobic | 8 | 24 | 72–88 |
| 2. Temperate | 19 | 38 | 114–125 |
| 1. Healthy Heart | 8 | 8 | 24–40 |
| Totals | 35 | 70 | 210–253 |

**Tip 1:** To burn the highest number of total calories, train in the highest heart zones.

**Tip 2:** To burn the highest percentage of fat, train in the lowest heart zones.

| Sequence for Workout 25: Change of Heart | | | | |
|---|---|---|---|---|
| Elapsed Time (min.) | Workout Plan | Heart Zone | Your Heart Rate (bpm) | Interval Time (min.) |
| 0–3 | Warm up in Z1 | 1 | _____ | 3 |
| 3–5 | Warm up to bottom of Z2 | 2 | _____ | 2 |
| 5–29 | Increase HR 10 bpm and sustain for 2 min., then increase intensity (HR) to bottom of Z3 and sustain for 2 min., followed by an easy pedal (rec) to bottom of Z2 in 2 min. Repeat a total of 4 times. Your choice of cadence or resistance (R), standing or seated | 2 3 2 | _____ _____ _____ | 24 |
| 29–32 | Recover (rec) to bottom of Z2 | 2 | _____ | 3 |
| 32–35 | Warm down to Z1, easy pedal | 1 | _____ | 3 |

## FITNESS **Workout 26: Afterburner**

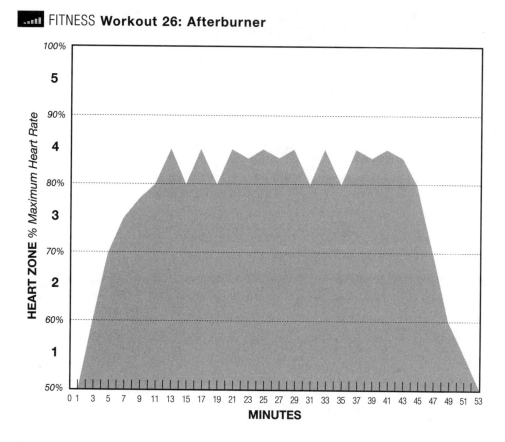

## Overview

This workout is a major fat burner. The goal is to spend as much time at or just below your estimated anaerobic threshold heart rate in order to burn the most fat. Pick a heart rate number that you can train at (or just below) for an extended period of time.

## Description

One of the best ways to maximize your fat-burning potential is to train near your "crossover point" and work to raise it. The crossover point, also known as your anaerobic threshold heart rate, is the point where if you cross it to a higher heart rate, your body's cells will switch from aerobic to anaerobic metabolism, and you will not be burning any additional fat, just additional carbohydrates. However, the higher your anaerobic threshold number, the higher your burn rate for fat.

This workout assumes your anaerobic threshold to be about 85 percent of your maximum heart rate. Your individual crossover heart rate may be higher or lower than this percentage, depending on your fitness level.

| Stats and Tips for Workout 26: Afterburner | | | |
|---|---|---|---|
| Zone Number and Name | Minutes in Zone | Heart Zones Training Points | Estimated Calories |
| 5. Red-Line | | | |
| 4. Threshold | 36 | 144 | 432–504 |
| 3. Aerobic | 8 | 24 | 72–88 |
| 2. Temperate | 4 | 8 | 24–32 |
| 1. Healthy Heart | 5 | 5 | 15–25 |
| Totals | 53 | 181 | 543–649 |

**Tip:** To lose 1 pound of body fat, you must burn approximately 3,500 more calories than you eat.

| Sequence for Workout 26: Afterburner | | | | |
|---|---|---|---|---|
| Elapsed Time (min.) | Workout Plan | Heart Zone | Your Heart Rate (bpm) | Interval Time (min.) |
| 0–5 | Warm up to bottom of Z2 (60%) | 2 | _____ | 5 |
| 5–7 | Increase HR to bottom of Z3 (70%) | 3 | _____ | 2 |
| 7–9 | Increase HR 10 bpm, choice | 3 | _____ | 2 |
| 9–11 | Increase HR 5 bpm, choice | 3 | _____ | 2 |
| 11–13 | Increase HR bottom of Z4 (80%), choice | 4 | _____ | 2 |
| 13–21 | Increase HR 10 bpm or to AT for 2 min., choice, then decrease HR to bottom of Z4 for 2 min. Repeat | 4<br>4 | _____<br>_____ | 8 |
| 21–29 | From bottom of Z4 increase HR 10 bpm for 2 min., choice, then decrease HR 5 bpm for 2 min. Repeat | 4<br>4 | _____<br>_____ | 8 |
| 29–37 | Increase HR 5 bpm for 2 min., choice, then decrease HR to bottom of Z4 for 2 min. Repeat | 4<br>4 | _____<br>_____ | 8 |
| 37–45 | From bottom of Z4 increase HR 10 bpm for 2 min., choice, then decrease HR 5 bpm for 2 min. Repeat | 4<br>4 | _____<br>_____ | 8 |
| 45–47 | Decrease HR to bottom of Z4 | 4 | _____ | 2 |
| 47–49 | Decrease HR to bottom of Z3 | 3 | _____ | 2 |
| 49–51 | Decrease HR to bottom of Z2 | 2 | _____ | 2 |
| 51–53 | Warm down | 1 | _____ | 2 |

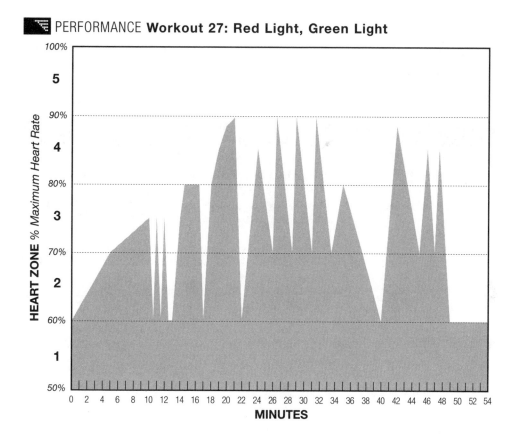

PERFORMANCE **Workout 27: Red Light, Green Light**

## Overview

Ever wish you had a little more "giddy up" to accelerate through the intersection before the traffic light changes to red? How about when a cyclist in a flashy new outfit comes flying past you, catching you off guard, and your inner voice says, "Catch 'er"? Ever have a four-legged piston-driven tandem bike steam by you in a headwind? Catching them and drafting could save you tons of time and effort. Ride the Red Light, Green Light workout as a regular part of your training program, and never again will someone get the jump on you.

## Description

The first half of the workout is a series of timed sprints and accelerations followed by easy-pedal recoveries. The resistance is moderate for a stationary bike, or stay in the small chainring if you are on an indoor trainer. The key is fast cadence with a smooth pedal stroke. The second half of the workout will add more strength and power intervals by adding resistance (large chainring for indoor trainer) and fast cadence. At 35 minutes there is an off-the-bike isometric squat alternative. Squat as if you are about to sit in a chair, keeping your back straight, using your abdominal muscles for support, and looking straight ahead. Hold this position for 1 minute and follow this with a minute of relaxing. Repeat position a total of three times and then it's back on the bike to finish with a series of quick accelerations.

| Stats and Tips for Workout 27: Red Light, Green Light | | | |
|---|---|---|---|
| Zone Number and Name | Minutes in Zone | Heart Zones Training Points | Estimated Calories |
| 5. Red-Line | 5 | 25 | 75–100 |
| 4. Threshold | 20 | 80 | 240–280 |
| 3. Aerobic | 11 | 33 | 99–121 |
| 2. Temperate | 16 | 32 | 96–128 |
| 1. Healthy Heart | 2 | 2 | 6–10 |
| Totals | 54 | 172 | 516–639 |

**Tip:** Alternate lead leg when starting each sprint.

| Sequence for Workout 27: Red Light, Green Light | | | | |
|---|---|---|---|---|
| Elapsed Time (min.) | Workout Plan | Heart Zone | Your Heart Rate (bpm) | Interval Time (min.) |
| 0–5 | Easy-pedal warm-up | 2 | _____ | 5 |
| 5–10 | Increase HR to bottom of Z3 | 3 | _____ | 5 |
| 10–13 | 30 sec. fast cadence with moderate (R) followed by 30 sec. easy pedal (rec). Repeat a total of three times | 3.5 2 | _____ _____ | 3 |
| 13–14 | Easy pedal (rec) | 2 | _____ | 1 |
| 14–17 | 20 sec. very fast cadence with moderate (R) followed by 10 sec. easy pedal (rec). Repeat a total of six times | 4 | _____ | 3 |
| 17–18 | Easy pedal (rec) | 2 | _____ | 1 |
| 18–22 | 5 sec. sprint, 5 sec. (rec), moderate (R) for 4 min. | 4 5 | _____ _____ | 4 |
| 22–24 | Easy pedal (rec) | 2 | _____ | 2 |
| 24–29 | Moderate to heavy (R), steady cadence for 2 min., followed by 30 sec. (rec). Repeat a total of two times | 4.5 3 | _____ _____ | 5 |
| 29–34 | Increase HR to 90%, 120 rpm (12), (R) as needed to reach bottom of Z5 for 2 min. followed by 30 sec. (rec). Repeat a total of two times | 5 3 | _____ _____ | 5 |
| 34–39 | Standing, moderate to heavy (R), comfortable cadence or off the bike, (3) 1 min. isometric squats (holding a squat position) with a 1 min. rest between each | 4 3 | _____ _____ | 5 |
| 39–42 | Easy pedal (rec) back on the bike | 2 | _____ | 3 |
| 42–45 | 5 sec. sprint, 5 sec. (rec), moderate (R) for 3 min. | 4 | _____ | 3 |
| 45–46 | Easy pedal (rec) | 3 | _____ | 1 |
| 46–49 | 20 sec. sprint, 40 sec. (rec), moderate (R). Repeat a total of three times | 4.5 | _____ | 3 |
| 49–54 | Easy-pedal warm-down | 2 | _____ | 5 |

## PERFORMANCE **Workout 28: Spentervals**

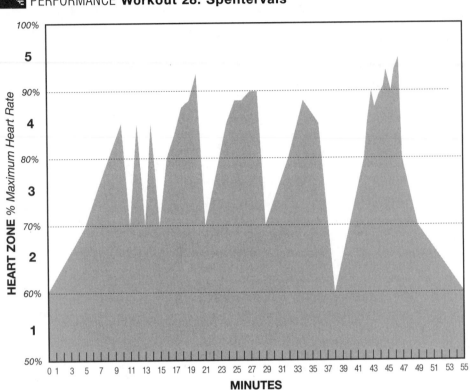

## Overview

If you love to party hard then suffer the next day from the festivities, Spentervals might be your workout. This workout is guaranteed to make you feel totally "spent" when you're done. It truly is a grand tour of five different workouts that melt into one: killer intervals, tempo gusto, speed sprints, Super Spins, and a 5-kilometer time trial to the finish line.

| Stats and Tips for Workout 28: Spentervals | | | |
|---|---|---|---|
| Zone Number and Name | Minutes in Zone | Heart Zones Training Points | Estimated Calories |
| 5. Red-Line | 7 | 35 | 105–140 |
| 4. Threshold | 20 | 80 | 240–280 |
| 3. Aerobic | 16 | 48 | 144–176 |
| 2. Temperate | 12 | 24 | 72–96 |
| 1. Healthy Heart | | | |
| **Totals** | **55** | **187** | **561–692** |

## Description

This ride is pure zone 4 with 50 percent of your riding time there and the other 50 percent in red-hot zone 5. Because it's high and hot, the 48-hour rule automatically goes into effect. That means you need to take a 48-hour break from riding in the high heart zones afterward to allow for adequate between-day or interworkout recovery. The muscle- and fuel-recovery process takes approximately 48 hours, so take a break or do a short active recovery workout in the lower zones.

| Elapsed Time (min.) | Workout Plan | Heart Zone | Your Heart Rate (bpm) | Interval Time (min.) |
|---|---|---|---|---|
| | **Sequence for Workout 28: Spentervals** | | | |
| 0–5 | Warm up to bottom of Z2, easy pedal | 2 | _____ | 5 |
| 5–10 | Increase HR to bottom of Z3 | 3 | _____ | 5 |
| 10–16 | From bottom of Z3 increase HR 30 bpm, hard effort, 100 rpm (10) for 1 min., then (rec) to bottom of Z3 in 1 min., easy pedal. Repeat a total of 3 times | 4<br>3<br>4<br>3<br>4<br>3 | _____<br>_____<br>_____<br>_____<br>_____<br>_____ | 6 |
| 16–17 | From bottom of Z3, 1 min. sprint to bottom of Z4 | 4 | _____ | 1 |
| 17–21 | From bottom of Z4 holding a steady cadence of 80 rpm (8), increase HR 5 bpm every min. for 4 min. Stay seated | 4<br>4<br>4/5 | _____<br>_____<br>_____ | 4 |
| 21–23 | (Rec) to bottom of Z3. Drink water and stretch | 3 | _____ | 2 |
| 23–28 | 10 sec. hard effort, standing, (R), then 10 sec. easy pedal, seated. Repeat interval a total of 15 times or 5 min. total | 4<br>4<br>5 | _____<br>_____<br>_____ | 5 |
| 28–30 | (Rec) to bottom of Z3. Drink more water | 3 | _____ | 2 |
| 30–42 | 30 sec. all-out sprint, then 30 sec. easy pedal (rec). Repeat interval a total of 12 times, alternating standing and seated | 4<br>4<br>4 | _____<br>_____<br>_____ | 12 |
| 42–45 | (Rec) to bottom of Z2. Drink water! Mentally prepare for 5K time trial. | 2 | _____ | 3 |
| 45–50 | 5-min., 5K time trial: Use your imagination and create your own 5 min. race scenario, riding at AT with a final 1 min. sprint to the finish line. | 4<br>4<br>5 | _____<br>_____<br>_____ | 5 |
| 50–55 | Warm down to bottom of Z2 | 2 | _____ | 5 |

**Note:** A time-trial race is you against the clock. Stay motivated by mentally creating the race scenario or use the following imagery: The time trial begins with a fast, hard effort off the starting line for 1 minute to the beginning of the first 1-minute hill. The first 30 seconds of the hill is seated with a fast cadence (120 rpm). The last 30 seconds of the hill is in a standing position with heavy resistance or big gears, powering yourself up and over the top. In the slight downhill that follows, you decrease only 3 bpm every 30 seconds and sustain 80 rpm (adjust resistance or gearing as needed to maintain heart rate). Next is a Super Spin flat section of 120 rpm or faster for 30 seconds. Keep your heart rate at or above your anaerobic threshold with a final all-out 1-minute sprint to the finish line. Once you have crossed the finish line, look at your monitor and don't be surprised if it continues to go up for a few seconds and you reach "peak heart rate" for the workout.

## Outdoor Training and Rides

### Workout 29: Paceline Ride

An important part of outdoor training is the ability and skill of being able to ride a paceline. Paceline riding is not for the beginning cyclist, but as you become more experienced and daring, you will find it's a great way to ride faster with less effort and at lower heart rates. It's as if you are in a wind shadow, and you quickly realize the savings in effort. It does not come without its risks, though, and you will need to weigh the benefits against the occasional mishaps. An excellent chapter on group riding and paceline etiquette by Geoff Drake comes from the *Complete Book of Road Cycling Skills* (1998). Here are a few tips from the chapter:

- As the leader, visualize a string tied between your saddle and the following rider's handlebars. Sudden accelerations will break the string (leaving your pal behind), and quick stops (causing them to overlap your wheel and launch on the tarmac) will make it slacken. Your job is to keep [the string] taut. This doesn't necessarily mean maintaining the same speed. Instead, concentrate on exerting the same pedal pressure. This means that slowing slightly for hills is okay.

- If you must break hard, such as for a dog, announce "stopping!" or "slowing!" Another way to control speed is to sit up and let the wind slow you. In any case, keep pedaling.

- Holding a line. Ride as if you are on rails. On occasion, this means going over a bump that you would otherwise swerve to avoid. Large obstacles, such as parked cars, and road debris merit verbal and hand warnings.

- Climbing. Shift to the next higher gear before standing to compensate for the slower cadence, and maintain pressure on the pedal so your bike doesn't move "backward" relative to the rider behind. The same thing applies when you sit down. Downshift and concentrate on maintaining pedal pressure [to avoid] any abrupt change in speed.

- Following. Never overlap wheels. Stay at least 6 inches behind a smooth, reliable rider and much farther back if you don't know the person. Look through the lead rider, scanning for trouble rather than being mesmerized while staring at the wheel in front of you.

- Handling traffic. Announce an overtaking vehicle, particularly if one of your pals is out in the road too far. A quick "car back" will let those ahead know it's wise to tuck in so traffic can pass.

- Pulling through. In any situation where you are sharing the work by alternating the front position, don't surge. Maintain the same speed as you pull through.

If you want to give paceline riding a try, we suggest you find an experienced and predictable rider that is willing to teach you the ropes—in this case, the string approach to group riding. The more you practice paceline riding, the more comfortable you will become. Never get so comfortable that you forget how quickly things can happen, however. Stay attentive and follow the golden rule of paceline riding: You are responsible for the person behind you.

When riding a paceline, you will find it helpful to have your monitor mounted on the handlebars or somewhere where you won't have to turn or move to see it. If you are drafting correctly, your heart rate will drop significantly.

As a final reminder, always let the rider ahead of you know that you are "on the person's wheel," or in a drafting position. If that person doesn't know you are there, he or she can't lead or respond accordingly.

## Workout 30: Cruisin'

Pick a relatively flat course. This ride consists of three to five intervals between 3 to 12 minutes in duration at an intensity between 60 and 85 percent of your maximum heart rate. The goal is to improve your ability to ride in a relatively big or hard gear at a relatively high cadence for an extended period of time to build muscular endurance.

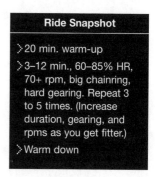

**Ride Snapshot**

⋗ 20 min. warm-up

⋗ 3–12 min., 60–85% HR, 70+ rpm, big chainring, hard gearing. Repeat 3 to 5 times. (Increase duration, gearing, and rpms as you get fitter.)

⋗ Warm down

The work intervals build in intensity from the bottom of zone 2 to the midpoint of zone 4, or from 60 to 85 percent of your maximum heart rate, followed with a recovery to the bottom of zone 2 (60 percent). Once you have recovered to the bottom of zone 2, immediately begin the next interval. Repeat this interval three to five times. Warm down gradually to finish.

## Workout 31: Noodling

Here's your chance to stay in the saddle a little longer, work on some technique, and stay under 65 percent of your maximum heart rate. This is easy riding and can also be used as a recovery ride to give your body a chance to rest.

Pick a distance depending on your fitness level, ranging from 5 miles to 50 miles, or ride for a certain amount of time, from 30 minutes to 3 hours. The goal is to keep your heart rate under 65 percent for most of the time. Try to pick a ride that is relatively flat. If you have hills, use an easy gear and small chainring to spin your way to the top while staying seated. This is a "feel good" ride designed to keep you spinning along and smelling the roses. Simply work on body position, pedal stroke, and tempo. Your legs should feel relaxed as noodles. Don't forget to relax your upper body too. Ride like a noodle, relaxing every muscle in your body, and let your mind go. Do whatever you have to do to stay below 65 percent—though that's easier said than done!

## Workout 32: The Pyramid Scheme

You will think "scheme" as this ride gradually gets more and more challenging. The work intervals increase in time and intensity, and the recovery time is equal to the preceding work interval. Pick a flat to rolling course and begin the pyramid climb after completely warming up (15 to 30 minutes).

The work intervals are 1, 2, 3, 4, 4, 3, 2, 1 minutes and build to more than 90 percent of maximum heart rate. Warm down gradually to the bottom of zone 2 (15 to 30 minutes). The chart shows how the ride proceeds.

Option: You may choose to reach a certain heart rate percentage then drop in intensity instead of continuing to go higher. At this point the pyramid becomes more of a ladder as you increase then decrease intensity. Time remains the same.

| Interval Time (min.) | Percent Max HR | Recovery Time (min.) |
|---|---|---|
| 1 | 60 | 1 |
| 2 | 65 | 2 |
| 3 | 70 | 3 |
| 4 | 75 | 4 |
| 4 | 80 | 4 |
| 3 | 85 | 3 |
| 2 | 90 | 2 |
| 1 | More than 90 | 15–30 warm-down |

# REFERENCES

Baker, Arnie, M.D. *Smart Cycling.* New York: Fireside, 1997.

Blair, Steven, Ph.D., David R. Jacobs, Ph.D., and Kenneth Powell, M.D., M.P.H. Relationships Between Exercise or Physical Activity and Other Health Behaviors. *Public Health Reports, Journal of the U.S. Public Health Service,* vol. 100 (2), 1985.

Brownell, K. D. Obesity: Understanding and Treating in Serious, Prevalent, and Refractory Disorder. *Journal of Consult Clinical Psychology,* vol. 50 (1982), pp. 820–840.

Burke, Ed, and Jacqueline R. Berning. *Training Nutrition.* Carmel, Ind.: Cooper, 1996.

Butterfield, Gail, and Joan Gates, Hershey Foods Corporation. Topic on Nutrition and Food Safety. *Fueling Activity,* 1994.

Drake, Geoff. Group Riding. In Ed Pavelka (ed.), *Bicycling Magazine's Complete Book of Road Cycling Skills.* Emmaus, Penn.: Rodale Press, 1998.

Epstein, L. H., and R. R. Wing. Aerobic Exercise and Weight. *Addict Behavior,* vol. 5 (1980), pp. 371–388.

Foster, Carl, et al. A New Approach to Monitoring Exercise Training. *Journal of Strength and Conditioning Research* 15, no. 1 (2001): pp. 109–115.

U.S. Department of Health and Human Services, *The Surgeon General's Report on Nutrition and Health.* Publication no. 88:50211 Washington, D.C.: Government Printing Office, 1994.

# 7

# Riding and Training to Get Faster and Fitter

*John Saylor played college rugby. After serving in the U.S. Army in Vietnam, he knew he wanted to stay in shape. He continued running sans combat boots and for 20 years found it a meaningful way to stay fit. Realizing his joints were deteriorating, he looked for an alternative form of exercise and stumbled into an indoor cycling class in Seattle. He didn't have a heart rate monitor, so I loaned him one. That was all it took; he was hooked.*

*John's first experience was overwhelming. After almost twenty years of RPE training, he finally had a tool to guide his workout. He worked out, observing his heart rate numbers and comparing them with how he felt. He had very high heart rate numbers while training on a studio bike, which made him think his heart might burst out of his chest. It didn't, of course.*

*What he was observing was the preservation of his maximum heart rate number. John had maintained a high maximum heart rate all these years by maintaining his fitness. As Paul Camerer's experience revealed (see Chapter 4), maximum heart rate won't decline with age if you stay fit.*

*John's first heart zones cycling ride convinced him to buy a low-end monitor, only to regret it later as he learned more about training and wanted more features. He decided to learn everything he could about the application of heart zones technology to his training. He attended seminars, read books, asked questions, and most of all, used himself as a fitness laboratory.*

*As he continued cycling, John found he was no longer exercising but training. After determining his maximum heart rate in class, his next step was to set his heart zones, which was easy. Then he set a training goal. He'd always wanted to complete the Seattle-to-Portland bike ride, commonly known as the STP, which covers 200 miles in two days. He set out by writing down his goal and promising himself a better heart rate monitor if he met his goal to finish the ride in two days.*

*John's goal was to extend the running life of his knees by cross-training using indoor cycling as his method. He went on to set and accomplish his outdoor cycling goal, using his monitor to keep him in his most effective heart zones. When he crossed the STP finish line, he was elated. The ride took him fifteen hours, all in heart zones 3 and below.*

*John then went back to the goal-setting process. This time, the dream was to finish a triathlon, train with his monitor, follow the 10 Steps of Heart Zones Cycling, and most of all, to place in his age group. John had transformed himself from an exerciser to a trainer, from a fitness enthusiast to a cyclist to a triathlete.*

—SALLY EDWARDS

## BEGINNING A TRAINING PLAN

In the preceding chapters, you've been completing the steps, building progressively on each to reach the next. You've learned to set your maximum heart rate, create your heart zones, write a goal, determine how fit you are, and put that into the training wheel. You're now ready to write a training program that best fits you.

Here a few basic principles about the training plan: First, as with your thirty-day training program, this is a plan *you* write. It's based on accepting that you are your own best personal trainer and again recognizing your unique physiological responses to the training experience.

The role of the personal trainer or coach should be to guide and motivate you, teach you how to design a program, and help you psychologically more than physiologically. But you can do this yourself. Relinquishing this personal power in any part of your life, including your fitness, just doesn't work.

Designing your own personal training program will teach you a new skill that will improve with practice, like riding a bike. Perhaps you started with training wheels and a beginner bike. You are now reading a book on how to train more effectively and efficiently. Congratulations! You have come a long way. What you will experience when you first write a training program is powerful. Write your training plan in pencil and be ready to make lots of changes and be flexible.

Creating your riding program can also be a lot of fun. As you look back when you reach your milestones to becoming ever fitter, you'll find many layers of small successes. You also can apply the process to almost every other aspect of your day. The same planning process can help with your finances, personal life, and job. Do this and watch yourself become more confident, self-empowered, and fit.

### STEP 7: *Writing Your Training Plan*

First decide the amount of time needed to reach your riding goal. A weekly training plan is a week's time divided into individual days, with indoor workouts and outdoor rides. Establish the plan for a workable period of time, depending on your goal deadline and training-wheel spokes involved.

## Understanding the Plan

If you're like most riders, you'd like to train less and get more out of every workout. That is what a training plan provides by taking the guesswork out of which workout to do and why. The plan is built around a system of training that integrates principles you've learned. In this way you become your own best trainer, yielding a shorter training time with more benefit. Better still, it's something you can more readily accomplish.

## Filling Out the Training Plan

The best way to fill out your heart cycling plan is to follow these steps in sequence:

1. Write in the starting date.
2. If you anticipate a "rest" or recovery day, note it under the Sports Activities column.
3. Enter under Sports Activities any activities that are already part of your training program, such as a group ride or indoor cycling class.
4. In the same column, note other classes or workouts such as stretching or weight training on their corresponding day.
5. Fill in the rest of your workouts under Sports Activities.
6. Under Type of Ride or Workout, enter the kind of workout in code:

    I = Intervals, S = Short, M = Medium, L = Long, SS = Steady-state,

    B = Bottom of the zone, T = Top of the zone, Mid = Midpoint,

    Multiples = Multiple zones, A = Average heart rate

    You can use codes such as I/S, which would mean that the plan for the workout is short intervals; I/M, medium-length intervals; SS/T if you are going to hold the heart rate steady at the ceiling or top of the zone; or Multiple/SS/T for multiple zones, steady-state, top of the zone. Make up other codes that work for you.

7. Fill in the Total Minutes section next. How many minutes do you have to train that day? If you can include what time of day you're training, you'll find it saves even more time.

# Heart Zones Cycling Training Plan

**Beginning Week:** _____  **Ending Week:** _____  **Number of Weeks:** _____

**Goal:** _____

**Current Training Wheel Spoke:** _____

**Week No.** _____

| Date | Day | Sports Activities | Type of Workout (interval or steady-state) | Total Min. | Time in Z1 | Time in Z2 | Time in Z3 | Time in Z4 | Time in Z5 | Heart Zones Training Points |
|------|-----|-------------------|--------------------------------------------|------------|------------|------------|------------|------------|------------|-----------------------------|
| / / | Mon. | | | | | | | | | |
| / / | Tues. | | | | | | | | | |
| / / | Wed. | | | | | | | | | |
| / / | Thurs. | | | | | | | | | |
| / / | Fri. | | | | | | | | | |
| / / | Sat. | | | | | | | | | |
| / / | Sun. | | | | | | | | | |
| **Number of workouts:** | | | **Totals:** | | | | | | | |
| | | | **Total % by zone:** | | % | % | % | % | % | |

8. Assign those minutes to zones. You should do most of your warm-up and warm-down in zone 1 or zone 2, representing about 10 percent of your total riding time for each. For example, you might want to do all zone 3 training in a 30-minute workout. In that case, plan for 6 minutes in zone 2 for warm-up and cooldown and 24 minutes in zone 3 for the main set of the workout.

9. Calculate the weight or value of the workout by multiplying zone number times minutes. This total is the number of heart zones training points earned for that day. One HZT point is equal to one minute in zone 1. If you were to spend 20 minutes in zone 4, you would record 80 HZT points.

10. Complete the summary section along the bottom of the Heart Zones Cycling Training Plan to determine whether your planned training week matches your goals.

### STEP 8: *Analyzing Your Training Plan*

After writing your first training plan, think for a few minutes. Look at the workouts. Listen to your heart. Will this work? Do I have the time? Am I committed to accomplishing the goal? Do I believe in it?

If you notice your training plan causing you some discomfort, fix it now. People tend to write the ideal plan and then accomplish only half of it because they didn't build in a fudge factor. Interruptions and changes occur that you need to anticipate. There must be room for spontaneous events and changes in other people's schedules that affect yours.

## ADVANCED TRAINING MECHANISMS

Now that you have a basic plan, consider adding a few advanced training mechanisms. A training mechanism is the application of a training principle. The three advanced training mechanisms referred to as the Training Triad can take your training to a new level. As illustrated in the triangular chart, the triad is the application of threshold training, overload-adaptation training, and specificity cross-training.

## The Training Triad

Threshold training is a powerful tool to add to your training toolbox. It relates to getting fitter by training at the heart rate point dividing aerobic and anaerobic metabolism. Muscles contract and use energy in two ways: aerobic metabolism and anaerobic metabolism. Aerobic is derived from a Greek word that means "with oxygen." When you train aerobically, you are at

an intensity low enough to provide plenty of oxygen through your respiratory delivery system to allow the muscles to contract without accumulating an oxygen debt. However, when you exercise too hard, you get shortness of breath. This inability to breathe in enough air is an indicator that you've crossed the threshold into anaerobic training.

The human muscle system is so well designed that when the muscles lack enough oxygen to meet their demands, they can continue to contract but use a different energy pathway called anaerobic metabolism. ("An" in Greek means "without.") Anaerobic metabolism thus functions "without enough oxygen."

You've discovered from your own training experience that you can't sustain an intensity level above your anaerobic threshold. It's a fine place to train for a short time, but then you have to take the intensity down, lowering your training heart rate so you return to the lower zones to recover. This type of anaerobic effort mixed with recovery is another way to describe interval training. Threshold training is one of the best mechanisms to use because it helps you get fitter faster.

## Overload-Adaptation Training

If you overload a muscle group or system, it responds first by tiring. When allowed to rest and recover, the muscle responds by adapting, or getting stronger. The overload-adaptation mechanism works only if you allow adequate recovery time following stress. A positive stress-recovery cycle will cause muscles to adapt positively by improving their work capacity, which will make you fitter.

Negative adaptation due to inadequate recovery means the muscle or system responds by becoming deconditioned, one of the results of overtraining. Overtraining is too much training load without enough recovery time. The charts showing positive and negative training effects will help you understand the difference between overreaching and its positive fitness improvements and overtraining with its negative deconditioning response.

## Optimal Performance Versus Overtraining

Symptoms of overtraining vary and can only be broadly described. They appear to be associated with depressed immune function so that you are at risk for infection and sheer fatigue. They are most commonly associated with high ambient, delta, and resting heart rates plus slow recovery heart rates. These heart rate indicators are some of the best gauges to predict the overtraining syndrome. Other terms for overtraining are chronic fatigue syndrome, exercise-induced immune system dysfunction, and overwork. A shorter group of

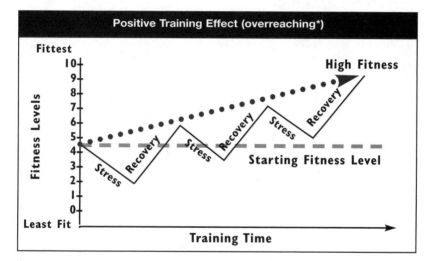

* Overreaching: a type of training marked by temporary fatigue from high training load that results in positive training effect.

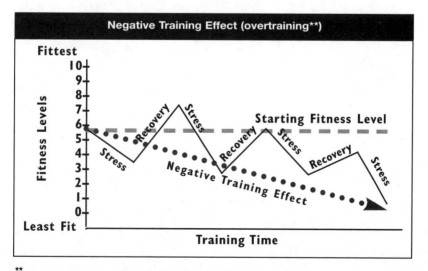

** Overtraining: training in excess of what is healthy, leading to a higher risk of injury, illness, or staleness.

descriptors uses the word "out": burned out, stressed out, and trained out. To prevent overtraining, you must allow for adequate recovery, vary your training program, and do multiple zone training workouts.

Overreaching is an excellent training mechanism for high performance and improved conditioning. This progressive overload-adaptation cycle is planned to combine high training load or high HZT points with recovery workouts and rest.

## Specificity Cross-Training

After finishing second in the 1981 Ironman in Hawaii, Sally Edwards coined the term "cross-training" in the first book written about triathlon training, aptly titled *Triathlon: A Triple Fitness Sport*. Her thesis—that you must cross-train in order to become your fittest—was criticized strongly at the time. Today most exercise scientists and coaches agree with her.

In contrast, specificity training is working in only the specific activity or event in which you plan to perform. The more specific the training program is to a given sport or activity, the greater the improvement in performance. Yet in the world outside the exercise laboratory, people cross-train to improve their single-sport performance.

Since writing the book, Edwards has devised a new training mechanism synthesizing two concepts once considered antithetical. If you want to train for performance, as Jon Ackland noted in *The Power to Perform*, you must always include specificity cross-training.

---

## A Four-Point Guide to Improving Your Racing

- Insufficient base or endurance training
- Monotony in trainizng program

### Point 1. Symptom: Heart Rate Lower during the Race

- Started out too fast at the beginning of the event
- Overtrained
- Poor pre-race tapering
- Insufficient off-season recovery
- Too high a maximum sustainable heart rate (blew up, hit the wall)
- Too much competition in training and racing

### Point 2. Symptom: Heart Rate Higher during the Race

- Insufficient warm-up
- Training periods did not include enough speed or interval workouts and rides
- Cardiac-drift phenomenon occurred from dehydration
- Overtrained: tired, too much training volume, too much training intensity
- Inappropriate amount of general strength training

Good examples of specificity cross-training come from swim training. Swimmers improve in their single events by learning the different swim strokes, not just the one stroke they use to race. Specificity cross-training works for cyclists who indoor cycle, then train for their racing season outside. It works for football players who study dancing to gain the agility they use on the field.

## At-About-Around Your Anaerobic Threshold (AT)

The training mechanism called At-About-Around AT means

*At*: training at your specific anaerobic threshold heart rate number

*About*: training at or about that threshold heart rate number

*Around*: training at, about, and around that threshold heart rate number

This book offers several workouts and tests to determine your current anaerobic threshold heart rate. As you grow fitter, your training heart rates drop because you can do more exercise at a lower heart rate. Your anaerobic threshold heart rate goes up, however, as more exercise stress is required to reach your anaerobic threshold. This is the very definition of fitness: to move your anaerobic threshold as close as you can to your maximum heart rate.

Two nonlaboratory and basic workouts serve as field tests to give you an approximate anaerobic threshold heart rate number. To measure it precisely, invest in an exercise stress test that will determine your anaerobic threshold heart rate more precisely by collecting your expired

* Lifestyle problems: travel, lack of sleep, irregular eating patterns, family commitments, insufficient rest, emotional challenges, too much stress from work, life events, and insufficient successes in achieving goals.

### Point 3. Symptom: Heart Rate Fluctuation

* Chest strap too loose
* Insufficient conductivity (dry skin or electrodes not moist)
* Cross-talk from another participant's monitor
* Interference from other sources

* Rare heart rate abnormality—stop exercising and see a physician immediately

### Point 4. Symptom: Heart Rate Normal

* Training program works—training load is appropriate
* Excellent planning for the peak training spokes in the training wheel
* The energy was right—it was a "good day"

air (measuring your oxygen capacity) or by collecting samples of your blood to measure the lactic acid concentrations. Check with a fitness professional for recommended testing facilities.

Once you know your anaerobic threshold heart rate, training at-about-around it becomes a valuable addition to your weekly training plan.

## RIDING SMART

For many of us, the hardest part of doing anything is simply getting started. John Saylor was lucky because he was committed to a base fitness level and had continued to run and stay relatively fit. Some of us have to start at the beginning or base level of training, but no matter where we start, the key is to start, write down some goals, and dream about them a little.

Hundreds of books discuss how to write, set, and keep goals. Technology and high-speed communication subjects us to reams of information on any subject we desire, and sometimes it's hard to sort out what's best for us. We believe that goals are what keep us on track and training on days we'd rather be elsewhere—differentiating training from exercise, drawing us like magnets closer to our aspirations.

John's smart. He chose cycling to save his joints and learned how to train with a heart rate monitor. When he began his indoor cycling class to escape the wet Seattle weather, he was aware of the indoor cycling craze and figured the class would be a great way to meet new people and work on his cycling skills while waiting out the rain.

What John didn't realize was that indoor training complements outdoor cycling in a variety of ways. Most of his workouts were 50 minutes of interval training in multiple zones, emphasizing good cycling technique to get stronger, faster, and fitter. John got a lot more than he expected: increased fitness in all zones; improved cycling technique; muscles and energy systems to support him across the finish line; a huge jump-start for the outdoor season; and new cycling friends. Last but not least, he met his new best friend and coach, his heart rate monitor.

John reached his goal, taking his friends with him. He wound up bringing all his indoor friends with him on the Seattle-to-Portland bike ride, even though some of them had last ridden a real bike when they were kids or covered a paper route. You can imagine how much fun they had.

That's what's powerful about training smart for high performance. You become committed, and your passion inspires another person, who in turn motivates someone else, and so on down the line.

# WORKOUTS: Indoor Training

HEALTHY HEART **Workout 33: Peekaboo**

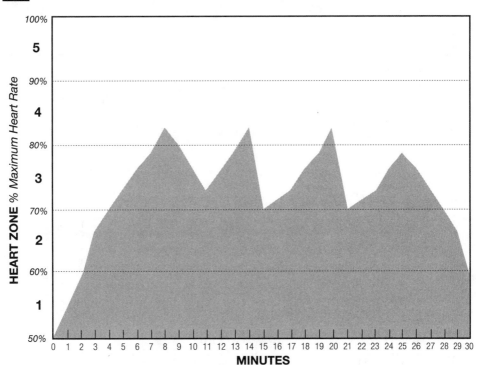

## Overview

Like its name, this workout gives you a chance to "peek" into a higher zone. In addition, you'll get a taste of four heart zones, although most of your workout time will be in zone 3. Three times you take a peek at zone 4, staying just briefly, and then you recover down to the bottom of zone 3.

## Description

In cycling, you must constantly adapt to changing workloads that are thrown at you during the outdoor ride. Some of these changes are environmental and geographical, such as hills, heat, altitude, and wind. This workout gives you constant exposure to changes that simulate those of weather, terrain, and other factors. The intensity changes almost every minute. The ride becomes more challenging as you near the top of zone 3 and peek into zone 4. Working out in these heart zones enhances functional capacity. Improvement in functional capacity comes from increases in the number and the size of blood vessels, an increase in vital capacity, and an increase in the size and strength of your heart.

| Stats and Tips for Workout 33: Peekaboo | | | |
|---|---|---|---|
| Zone Number and Name | Minutes in Zone | Heart Zones Training Points | Estimated Calories |
| 5. Red-Line | | | |
| 4. Threshold | 2 | 8 | 24–28 |
| 3. Aerobic | 22 | 66 | 198–242 |
| 2. Temperate | 4 | 8 | 24–32 |
| 1. Healthy Heart | 2 | 2 | 6–10 |
| Totals | 30 | 84 | 252–312 |

**Tip:** All things change when we do, especially our response to changes as a result of "peeking" at stress and then recovering.

| Sequence for Workout 33: Peekaboo | | | | |
|---|---|---|---|---|
| Elapsed Time (min.) | Workout Plan | Heart Zone | Your Heart Rate (bpm) | Interval Time (min.) |
| 0–2 | Warm up to top of Z1 | 1 | _____ | 2 |
| 2–4 | Easy pedal to midpoint of Z2 (65%) | 2 | _____ | 2 |
| 4–5 | Increase HR to bottom of Z3 (70%) with cadence/rpm | 3 | _____ | 1 |
| 5–9 | From the bottom of Z3, increase HR 5 bpm every min., choice | 3 4 | _____ _____ | 4 |
| 9–11 | Timed (rec) to bottom of Z3, easy pedal, no (R). Count number of bpm dropped in 1 min. | 3 | _____ | 2 |
| 11–15 | From the bottom of Z3, increase HR 5 bpm every min., (R), seated | 3 4 | _____ _____ | 4 |
| 15–17 | Timed (rec) to bottom of Z3, easy pedal, no (R). Count number of bpm dropped in 1 min. | 3 | _____ | 2 |
| 17–21 | From the bottom of Z3, increase HR 5 bpm every min. with cadence/rpm | 3 4 | _____ _____ | 4 |
| 21–23 | Timed (rec) to bottom of Z3, easy pedal, no (R). Count number of bpm dropped in 1 min. | 3 | _____ | 2 |
| 23–26 | From the bottom of Z3, increase HR 5 bpm each min. for 3 min., choice | 3 | _____ | 3 |
| 26–28 | Decrease HR 5 bpm each min. for 2 min. | 3 | _____ | 2 |
| 28–30 | Warm down to bottom of Z2, easy pedal | 2 | _____ | 2 |

## FITNESS **Workout 34: Winner's Circle**

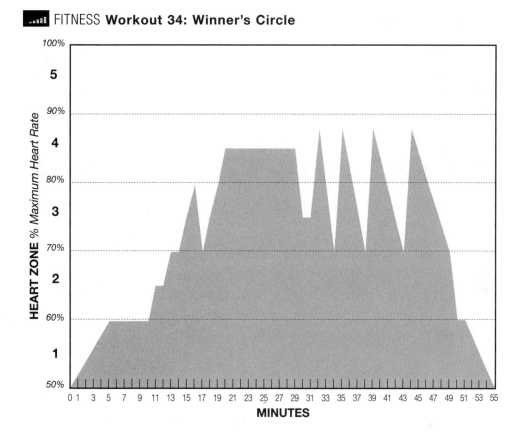

## Overview

Winners use individualized training systems to maximize their fitness in order to attain an "ideal performance state." To accomplish this, winning riders put all of the pieces of training together into a whole, a winner's circle. The winner's circle can be divided into different parts that include at least seven basic governing systems of training: specificity, overload, adaptation, balance, holism, psycho-emotionalism, and variability. Read about these seven parts to a training system in our companion book, *The Heart Rate Monitor Workbook for Indoor Cyclists* (VeloPress, 2000). Practice these different parts of training in the winner's circle by taking on the challenge to ride as many of these 50 workouts as you can.

## Description

This is a great workout for building cycling-specific leg strength and muscular endurance for those long hill rides. Identify a specific heart rate number that you can sustain for an extended period of time. This number should be close to your anaerobic threshold heart rate. Select a heart rate high enough that you must reach to sustain it, but not so high that you can't sustain it for the duration of the work interval. Anaerobic threshold (or lactic acid–threshold) heart rate increases as you become more fit. Isolated-leg training teaches your legs to make smooth circles and also helps in the development of left- and right-leg power output at high cadences. Ultimately, though, getting yourself into your own winner's circle is the goal of training with heart.

| Stats and Tips for Workout 34: Winner's Circle | | | |
|---|---|---|---|
| Zone Number and Name | Minutes in Zone | Heart Zones Training Points | Estimated Calories |
| 5. Red-Line | | | |
| 4. Threshold | 26 | 104 | 312–364 |
| 3. Aerobic | 11 | 33 | 99–121 |
| 2. Temperate | 10 | 20 | 60–80 |
| 1. Healthy Heart | 8 | 8 | 24–40 |
| Totals | 55 | 165 | 495–605 |

**Tip:** Keep a training log or diary of your workouts. It's one of your most important training tools because it's your book, a report of your rides. Refer to the companion log book to this book series titled *The Heart Rate Monitor Log Book for Outdoor and Indoor Cyclists* (VeloPress, 2000) or use the free software sampler, ZONEWare by PC Coach, included with this book.

| Sequence for Workout 34: Winner's Circle | | | | |
| --- | --- | --- | --- | --- |
| Elapsed Time (min.) | Workout Plan | Heart Zone | Your Heart Rate (bpm) | Interval Time (min.) |
| 0–5 | Warm up to bottom of Z2, easy pedal | 2 | _____ | 5 |
| 5–10 | Isolated-leg training[a] (ILT): Right leg for 1 min., then left leg for 1 min. Repeat a total of 2 times. Finish with both legs for 1 min. | 3 | _____ | 5 |
| 10–17 | 60 rpm (6) for 1 min., working on pedal stroke, then 70 rpm (7), for 1 min. and 80 rpm (8) for 1 min., increasing 10 rpm each min. up to 120 rpm (12) for a total of 7 min. | 2 3 4 | _____ _____ _____ | 7 |
| 17–18 | (Rec) to bottom of Z3, easy pedal | 3 | _____ | 1 |
| 18–30 | (R), hard effort, 60 rpm (6) for 45 sec., last 15 sec. increase to 80 rpm (8). Repeat a total of 12 times. | 4 4 | _____ _____ | 12 |
| 30–32 | (Rec) to bottom of Z3, easy pedal | 3 | _____ | 2 |
| 32–34 | Increase HR to just below AT with (R), 80 rpm (8), seated | 4 | _____ | 2 |
| 34–35 | (Rec) to midpoint of Z3 (75%), easy pedal | 3 | _____ | 1 |
| 35–38 | Increase HR to just below AT with (R), 80 rpm (8), seated | 4 | _____ | 3 |
| 38–39 | (Rec) to midpoint of Z3 (75%), easy pedal | 3 | _____ | 1 |
| 39–43 | Increase HR to just below AT with (R), 80 rpm (8), seated | 4 | _____ | 4 |
| 43–44 | (Rec) to midpoint of Z3 (75%), easy pedal | 3 | _____ | 1 |
| 44–49 | Increase HR to just below AT with (R), 80 rpm (8), seated or standing | 4 | _____ | 5 |
| 49–50 | (Rec) to midpoint of Z3 (75%), easy pedal | 3 | _____ | 1 |
| 50–52 | Warm down to bottom of Z2, easy pedal | 2 | _____ | 2 |
| 52–55 | Warm down to bottom of Z1, easy pedal | 1 | _____ | 3 |

[a] Pedaling with one leg at a time, resting the other on a box or stool. You may also choose to keep both feet in the pedals and allow one leg to relax while the other leg does the work.

## ▼ PERFORMANCE **Workout 35: At, About, Around**

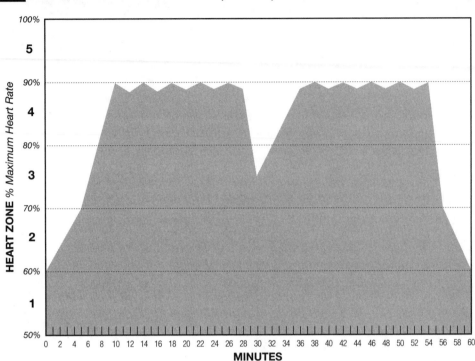

## Overview

Many complex concepts apply in cycle training, and several are so important that they deserve a clearer understanding. At, About, Around is a ride that teaches one of these more difficult training principles. In just one attempt at this ride, you will fully understand why we guarantee that this is probably the most challenging and mentally tough workout of the indoor workouts.

There is a training mechanism that occurs in the body when you work out near your individual and day-specific anaerobic threshold (or crossover) heart rate. When you train above your anaerobic threshold, there is not enough oxygen to sustain your effort for long. When you train at, about, and around this heart rate number, you are at the threshold of burning the maximum amount of fat as well as at a point where training for long periods of time is not possible. The workout occurs "at" your specific anaerobic threshold heart rate number, "about" or close to that number, and "around" or near that number.

## Description

As you improve your fitness, your training heart rate drops because you can do more exercise at a lower heart rate. Your anaerobic threshold heart rate goes up, however, as more exercise stress is required to reach your anaerobic threshold. This is the very definition of fitness: to move your anaerobic threshold as close as you can to your maximum heart rate. One of the best ways to improve your fitness and simultaneously raise your anaerobic threshold is to train at, about, and around that heart rate number. Choose a heart rate number that you think you can train at, about, and around for approximately forty-five minutes. Heads up! This is one tough training ride.

To measure anaerobic threshold heart rate precisely, you must complete an exercise stress test in a laboratory setting where scientists measure your oxygen capacity—the amount of oxygen utilized—or collect blood samples to measure the lactic acid concentrations. Alternatively, you can estimate your anaerobic threshold heart rate by riding the At, About, Around workout. Your highest sustainable heart rate number for this ride will be within 5 bpm of your true and laboratory-tested anaerobic threshold heart rate.

| Stats and Tips for Workout 35: At, About, Around | | | |
|---|---|---|---|
| Zone Number and Name | Minutes in Zone | Heart Zones Training Points | Estimated Calories |
| 5. Red-Line | 20 | 100 | 300–400 |
| 4. Threshold | 20 | 80 | 240–280 |
| 3. Aerobic | 13 | 39 | 117–143 |
| 2. Temperate | 7 | 14 | 42–56 |
| 1. Healthy Heart | | | |
| Totals | 60 | 233 | 699–879 |

**Tip:** Your anaerobic threshold heart rate changes depending on your current level of fitness. Adjust your ride accordingly.

| Sequence for Workout 35: At, About, Around | | | | |
|---|---|---|---|---|
| Elapsed Time (min.) | Workout Plan | Heart Zone | Your Heart Rate (bpm) | Interval Time (min.) |
| 0–5 | Warm up to bottom of Z2 (60%) | 2 | _____ | 5 |
| 5–10 | Increase HR to bottom of Z3 (70%) | 3 | _____ | 5 |
| 10–12 | Increase HR to AT estimate plus 5 bpm | 5 | _____ | 2 |
| 12–14 | Decrease HR 5 bpm to AT | 4 | _____ | 2 |
| 14–16 | Increase HR 5 bpm | 5 | _____ | 2 |
| 16–18 | Decrease HR 5 bpm | 4 | _____ | 2 |
| 18–20 | Increase HR 5 bpm | 5 | _____ | 2 |
| 20–22 | Decrease HR 5 bpm | 4 | _____ | 2 |
| 22–24 | Increase HR 5 bpm | 5 | _____ | 2 |
| 24–26 | Decrease HR 5 bpm | 4 | _____ | 2 |
| 26–28 | Increase HR 5 bpm | 5 | _____ | 2 |
| 28–30 | Decrease HR 5 bpm | 4 | _____ | 2 |
| 30–36 | Decrease HR to midpoint of Z3 (75%), easy pedal | 3 | _____ | 6 |
| 36–56 | Repeat minutes 10–30 | | | 20 |
| 56–58 | Decrease HR to bottom of Z3 (70%) | 3 | _____ | 2 |
| 58–60 | Warm down to bottom of Z2 (60%), easy pedal | 2 | _____ | 2 |

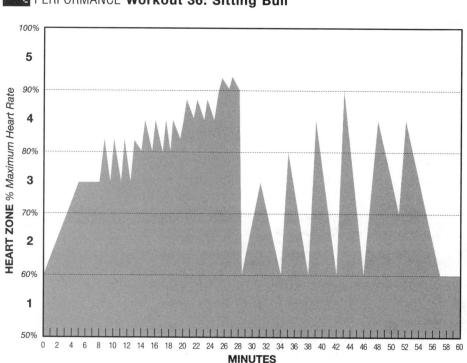

PERFORMANCE **Workout 36: Sitting Bull**

## Overview

This workout has nothing to do with the great Indian chief Sitting Bull but rather a very tired
cyclist who after seventy miles in the heat and wind refused to ride any farther at the last food
stop. He instead rested cross-legged in the shade of a pine tree, content to call it a day. But

| Stats and Tips for Workout 36: Sitting Bull | | | |
|---|---|---|---|
| Zone Number and Name | Minutes in Zone | Heart Zones Training Points | Estimated Calories |
| 5. Red-Line | 6 | 30 | 90–120 |
| 4. Threshold | 24 | 96 | 288–336 |
| 3. Aerobic | 14 | 42 | 126–154 |
| 2. Temperate | 16 | 32 | 96–128 |
| 1. Healthy Heart | | | |
| **Totals** | **60** | **200** | **600–738** |

**Tip:** Elevate your legs against a wall for 5 to 10 minutes afterward to let pooled blood and
metabolic waste drain away.

alas, what are great friends for but to give you a lot of "bull"—get you back on the bike and through the finish line.

## Description

This is a "bullish" workout that matches your rpm or cadence with your heart rate percentage. You will work your way up the ladder in intensity and cadence starting at 75 rpm and 75 percent of maximum heart rate followed by 80 rpm and 80 percent of maximum heart and so on. This is a great way to train your aerobic system and save your leg muscles for later. To challenge yourself, try the first half of the workout sitting and the second half standing.

| Sequence for Workout 36: Sitting Bull | | | | |
|---|---|---|---|---|
| Elapsed Time (min.) | Workout Plan | Heart Zone | Your Heart Rate (bpm) | Interval Time (min.) |
| 0–8 | Easy-pedal warm-up to Z3 | 3 | _____ | 8 |
| 8–14 | 30 sec., 75 rpm (7.5), (75%) followed by 1 min., 95 rpm (9.5). Repeat interval a total of 4 times | 3 | _____ | 6 |
| 14–20 | 30 sec., 80 rpm (8), increase HR to bottom of Z4 (80%) with (R) followed by 1 min., 95 rpm (9.5). Repeat interval a total of 4 times | 4 | _____ | 6 |
| 20–26 | 30 sec., 85 rpm (8.5), increase HR to midpoint of Z4 (85%) with (R) followed by 1 min., 95 rpm. Repeat interval a total of 4 times | 4 | _____ | 6 |
| 26–29 | 30 sec., 90 rpm (9), increase HR to bottom of Z5 (90%) with (R) followed by 1 min., 95 rpm. Repeat a total of 2 times. | 5 | _____ | 3 |
| 29–32 | 3 min. easy pedal (rec) | 2 | _____ | 3 |
| 32–36 | Increase HR to 75%, 75 rpm, use (R) as needed, standing, followed by 1 min. (rec) | 3<br>2 | _____<br>_____ | 3<br>1 |
| 36–40 | Increase HR to 80%, 80 rpm, use (R) as needed, standing, followed by 1 min. (rec) | 4<br>2 | _____<br>_____ | 3<br>1 |
| 40–44 | Increase HR to 85%, 85 rpm, use (R) as needed, standing, followed by 1 min. (rec) | 4<br>2 | _____<br>_____ | 3<br>1 |
| 44–49 | Increase HR to 90%, 90 rpm, use (R) as needed, standing, followed by 2 min. (rec) | 5<br>2 | _____<br>_____ | 3<br>2 |
| 49–57 | Increase HR to between 80% and 90%. 20 sec. hard effort followed by 40 sec. (rec), 30 sec. hard effort, 30 sec. (rec), 40 sec. hard effort, 20 sec. (rec), 1 min. (rec). Repeat a total of 2 times | 4<br>2<br>4<br>2 | _____<br>_____<br>_____<br>_____ | 3<br>1<br>3<br>1 |
| 57–60 | Warm down | 2 | _____ | 3 |

## Outdoor Training and Rides

### Workout 37: Need for Speed

Sprinting is not something most recreational cyclists practice because they see no need for it. In reality, we use it more than we think. How about those bursts of speed to hold your place in traffic or make it through the intersection before the light turns red? Or those unfriendly dogs that come raging out of yards, when your best defense is quick acceleration?

Interval training helps you ride faster and develops your aerobic and anaerobic capacity. The Need for Speed ride emphasizes acceleration and leg speed. Your heart rate will vary according to the effort and length of the interval. The idea is to give it your best effort, which will be as hard as you can ride followed by enough time for a complete recovery.

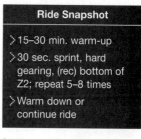

**Ride Snapshot**

> 15–30 min. warm-up
> 30 sec. sprint, hard gearing, (rec) bottom of Z2; repeat 5–8 times
> Warm down or continue ride

Warm up for at least 15 to 30 minutes (or you can even add this interval set to the middle or end of an existing ride). Do five to eight sprints of up to 30 seconds each with a full recovery (bottom of zone 2). Use gears that you won't completely spin out in. Choose to do some of the sprints standing, focusing on good form and technique. After several weeks of incorporating these sprints into your rides, you will notice a significant improvement in your top-end speed and your ability to hold that intensity longer.

### Workout 38: Spitfire

A little spit on the road and a lot of fire in your quads will get you through this "buns of steel" workout. If you have knee problems, avoid this ride, because all the climbing is done at low rpms in the large chainring and in a seated position. For others, this is an excellent strength workout to plug into your training program.

Ready? After warming up, find a quarter-mile-long hill that you can't ride in 53/14 gearing without standing (that's steep, in case you're wondering). From a standstill, start your watch (chronograph) and begin climbing in the hardest gear you can maintain while seated. Try to keep your cadence no more than 50 rpms. Note your heart rate during the climb. At the top, check your heart rate and elapsed time, then spin easily as you descend. Repeat the climb once your heart rate has recovered to the bottom of zone 1 (50 percent). Note your heart rate and elapsed time on each hill repeat. Stop the hill repeats when your elapsed climbing time is more than 15 seconds over your first climb. As you get stronger, several things will happen:

- Your climbing time will decrease (more strength and power).
- You will be able to ride a bigger gear at the same cadence (getting stronger).
- You will be able to do more hill repeats before fatigue sets in (developing muscular endurance).
- Your climbing heart rate will decrease (more "power" to you).
- Your recovery time will decrease (your heart is getting fitter).

> **Ride Snapshot**
>
> ⟩ Warm up 20–30 minutes in zone 2
> ⟩ Number of steep hill climbs @ 50 rpm (seated)
> ⟩ Zone 1 recovery between climbs
> ⟩ Warm down or easy-pedal ride home in zone 2

## Workout 39: Head for the Hills

To manage hilly terrain successfully, you must minimize your fatigue while climbing and become more efficient in your pedaling stroke. Spinning or pedaling at a high cadence (90-plus rpm) uses your aerobic system instead of your muscles. A prime example of someone who uses this method is Lance Armstrong. In the 1999 Tour de France, with 7 kilometers to go on the 11-kilometer climb to Sestriere, Lance unloaded his cadence and power and surged ahead of the lead riders. As broadcaster Phil Liggett exclaimed, "He's ripped their legs off." Lance won the stage by over 30 seconds.

You will want to warm up at least 30 minutes at an easy pace before doing this series of cadence surges. Find a nice long, gradual hill or a series of gradual hills. Pick a gear in which you can ride at 70 rpm and 75 percent of maximum heart rate for 30 seconds, then accelerate hard, stay seated, and increase your cadence to 95 rpm for 1 minute as you continue to climb. Slow your cadence back to 70 rpm and repeat the interval once your heart rate has recovered to 75 percent. Continue these surges until you can't maintain 95 rpm for the 1-minute cadence surge. Initially you may only be able to do a few surges on the hills, but keep trying. The hills will get easier as you get fitter. Spin home at an easy pace for 20 to 30 minutes.

> **Ride Snapshot**
>
> ⟩ Warm up 30 minutes easy pedal in zone 2
> ⟩ 30 sec. @ 70 rpm and heart rate 75 percent, surge 1 min. @ 95 rpm
> ⟩ Recover to 75 percent and repeat number of times possible
> ⟩ Warm down or ride home in zone 2

## Workout 40: Steady Eddie

On a relatively flat course, ride continuously at 70 percent of your maximum heart rate without recovery and at a cadence between 75 and 95 rpm. Avoid roads that have heavy traffic and stop signs. Start with 30 minutes and build to 60 minutes or more. This ride may be done several times a week as a part of your endurance-training spoke, or drop down to 60 percent of your maximum heart rate and use this as a recovery ride. The purpose of this ride is to build your muscular endurance.

## REFERENCES

Ackland, Jon, with Brett Reid. *The Power to Perform: A Comprehensive Guide to Training and Racing for Endurance Athletes*. Auckland, New Zealand: Reed Books, 1994.

Wilmore, Jack, and David Costill. *Physiology of Sport and Exercise*. Revised. Champaign, IL: Human Kinetics, 1999.

Duane Reed, an "Ironman," doing a standing sprint, sometimes called a standing run.

# 8
# Environmental Challenges for Riders

*The date was July 14, the temperature 90 degrees. My elapsed cycling time was eight hours, at an altitude of 8,700 feet, and I was on the last few meters of a 12 percent grade on Ebbets Pass in the California Sierras. Sally Edward's voice was ringing in my ears. A couple of months before, I had mentioned to her I was training for the California Death Ride and that in the history of the ride they had never lost a rider. She smiled because she had done the ride and said, "Yeah, but it's sure put some really good riders in wheelchairs." Sally's comment should have been my first clue that this ride was tough and not to be taken lightly.*

*It is difficult to train for high altitude, heat, and range cattle in Seattle. Yes, California has big cattle and bone-rattling cattle guards across the road on steep, fast descents. My friends Abbie and Scott had spent three and a half months training for this ride of 129 miles, 16,000 vertical feet, and five mountain passes. Even Mt. Rainier in Washington State and Hurricane Ridge in the Olympic Mountains couldn't prepare us for what the Sierras had in store for us on that day.*

*The best three words to describe the Death Ride are high, hot, and hard. We were prepared for the hard but not for the high and hot. We managed to ride four out of the five passes before calling it a very long day. It was a pretty good effort for the first time but not wholly satisfying when we knew that fifth pass was lurking out there calling our names.*

*Our goal next year is to return not only better trained for heat and altitude but also able to ride smarter and fuel our bodies better. That's because I ended up taking an ambulance ride to the South Lake Tahoe hospital after twelve hours on the bike.*

*Athletes read and hear a lot about drinking water and staying hydrated, but they often don't pay as much attention to the importance of maintaining sodium levels in the blood during*

Sally Reed (left) and Abbie Morris (right) summiting Ebbets Pass during the California Death Ride.

endurance events. Low concentrations of sodium in the blood is called "hyponatremia." It usually occurs during long or ultradistance races in the heat, but it may occur anytime. It is estimated that approximately 30 percent of the finishers of the Hawaii Ironman are both hyponatremic and dehydrated. The longer the race, the greater the risk of hyponatremia.

During the ride, I thought everything was going according to plan. I was drinking tons of water and eating at all the food stops. I had an energy drink on board and was drinking it along with water the entire time, but after eight hours, water was the only thing that didn't taste too sweet. For the next four hours, I drank only water so I wouldn't dehydrate in the heat and altitude. My heart rate was averaging 75–80 percent on the climbs, and all was well until that fourth mountain pass. The effort required getting to the top was like climbing Mt. Everest. If it hadn't been for my friend Abbie encouraging me and literally talking me up the last mile, I would have passed out under the shade of a ponderosa pine, never to be seen again. The rest is history, and the Death Ride became my near-death experience.

What happened? The simple answer is that what I lost in sweat (salt and water) was being replaced by ingested water (no salt). This diluted the sodium in my bloodstream, and hyponatremia *resulted. During the ride I lost more salt through sweat per hour than I replaced by food and fluids, including my energy drink. The human body can tolerate a degree of imbalance for a short period but can't sustain it for too long.*

*Aspirin, ibuprofen, and other nonsteroidal anti-inflammatory agents may interfere with kidney function and contribute to the development of hyponatremia. Under tough conditions, your kidneys need to function at 100 percent. I was taking three ibuprofen every three hours just to take the edge off the muscle aches.*

*In short, I was an accident waiting to happen.*

*The worst part of the experience was waking up in the hospital twenty-four hours later complaining that I was a starving cyclist who had been to hell and back but all the staff would give me was chicken broth and Jell-O.*

*What would I do differently next time? Train more in heat and altitude, eat salty foods several days before and during the ride, drink more electrolyte replacements during and after the ride, and reward my five-pass finish with a big, salty burger and salty fries.*

—SALLY REED

## MANAGEABLE CONDITIONS

Some conditions in our lives we can control. Some control us. The best we can hope to achieve is to manage both types. Consider the following conditions to see how you can readily manage them.

## Bike Fit

Working to achieve your optimal bike fit not only makes you a better cyclist but also keeps your heart rate lower as you cycle faster. Finding the right bike fit requires experience and guidance from a bike-fit specialist.

Fitting a bicycle depends on a number of factors. When you have it right, you'll immediately know the difference in both comfort and performance. You'll love riding your bike when it's a good match.

Starting with the right frame size and geometry is paramount to choosing outdoor bikes. Before you select the frame, decide what type of riding you prefer. Road and mountain bike frames are based on function; downhill bikes differ from time trial or criterium bikes. All-around bikes are the first choice for a beginner, but as you evolve, investigate special bikes for special purposes.

Studio bikes are all the same size, and to compensate for different-size riders, the components, not the frame, are adjustable. Spend the time to make adjustments to get a better fit. Tinker with your bike fit until you find what truly works. Make minor changes until you have a finely tuned bike fit.

| Ten Tips on Bike Fit | |
|---|---|
| 1 | When you're seated on the bike, knees should have a gentle bend when the cranks are vertical (6 o'clock position). |
| 2 | Saddle nose should be level (or tilted slightly downward). |
| 3 | When you're standing next to the bike, saddle should be at or near the hipbone. |
| 4 | A seat that is too far forward may cause discomfort in the front of the knee. |
| 5 | A seat that is too far back may cause discomfort in the lower back and excessive flexion at the hip as well as compromise muscular efficiency. |
| 6 | If the handlebars are too close, the back may overcompensate and create an excessive curve in the lower back, yielding pain and/or discomfort. |
| 7 | An overly stretched-out position will cause you to lean too far forward on the bike and place tension on the neck and shoulders, overextension of the lower back, discomfort of the pelvis, and/or undue pressure on the wrists. |
| 8 | Generally, handlebars should be at or higher than saddle height. |
| 9 | At the top of your pedal stroke, you should have at least two fingers of clearance between the handlebars and the thighs. |
| 10 | The overall goal of proper bike fit is to achieve optimum comfort, maximum power, overall efficiency, and balance and coordination on the bike. |

Courtesy of Paul Swift and Joan Wenson, *LeMond RevMaster Instructor's Manual (2000)*. Used by permission.

## Fuel

By now you know that what, when, and the way you eat can greatly affect your performance. Which fuels you burn and how quickly they are metabolized are directly affected by your exercise intensity and your heart training zones. Following are four factors that influence fuel usage. Manipulating these four variables is a management skill that you can use to improve your performance.

- The ratio of carbohydrates, proteins, and fats in your normal diet
- What you eat before and during the ride
- How hard you are riding
- How long you ride

In an extensive study conducted in 1985 on high-performance athletes, Sally Edwards took part in an endurance research project at Temple University in Philadelphia. Researchers measured her body fat, aerobic capacity, threshold points, metabolic rates, and heart rates. They wired her body and installed blood-testing devices. She was asked to simulate swimming for an hour with an arm crank, then hop on a stationary bike for five hours, and follow that with three hours on the treadmill. During the test, technicians scraped off sweat, measured the amount and type of calories consumed, drew blood and analyzed it for its chemical composition, measured quality and quantity of her urine, counted calories expended, determined oxygen consumed, and analyzed hydration.

Researchers concluded—not surprisingly—that they needed to do more studies with more controls because athletes are highly individual, especially in the fuel ratios they burn. Whereas Sally chose and metabolized carbohydrates at a high rate, other subjects who were fat-burning athletes preferentially chose foods higher in fat and burned a higher ratio of fat to carbohydrates.

Properly balanced nutrition is a manageable variable in achieving efficient and performance-oriented cycling. You need to eat what you can effectively metabolize, understanding that the conditions under which you eat will also affect your performance. Finally, the heart zone in which you ride is key to the ratio and total amount of calories burned.

## Jet Lag

Some cyclists travel extensively. The result of traveling, especially by jet, is a disruption of their normal sleep and training patterns caused by changes in time zones. For those who travel to high altitudes, physiological responses when cycling are affected by the low partial pressure of oxygen forcing the heart to pump harder and faster and the lungs to work harder for the same riding effort. In contrast, traveling from higher altitudes to lower ones causes little noticeable effect on heart rate and lung capacity.

Everyone responds to the effects of travel differently. Your heart rate monitor is an excellent tool to measure those effects on yourself. You'll note the change when you ride after a particularly difficult travel schedule or any other similar stress. For most cyclists, the best way to deal with jet lag is to arrive several days in advance of an event to allow time to adjust to the effects of travel.

## Rest and Recovery

The higher your heart rate intensity in training, the more rest and sleep your body needs. Again, your monitor will tell you when you aren't allowing adequate rest and recovery between workouts. If you have a choice between getting a full night's rest or training more, choose sleep so that your body can restore itself—can repair and recover. If you forgo sleep, your next workouts may be of less benefit to you, and you'll sacrifice positive training improvements.

The quality of your sleep also affects your ability to get fitter and enjoy your workouts. Many studies show that sleep disruptions impair the benefits you gain from sleep.

Adequate recovery from riding also is critical. Measuring your resting heart rate is an excellent assessment to ensure that you allow enough time between rides to recover sufficiently. Other potentially helpful recovery techniques include taking massage, saunas, and whirlpool baths; stretching; engaging in meditation or prayer; listening to music; and spending quality time with friends and loved ones.

## Illness and Injury

Most illnesses such as colds and flu weaken your body's immune system. Likewise, you can erode your immune system in various ways; one frequently experienced by cyclists is called the "too high, too hot" syndrome. Riding in too high of a heart zone for too long a period of time compromises the immune system.

Illnesses and injuries are a double negative. They not only force you into periods of sustained inactivity but also cause you to lose opportunities for rides that could lead to improvements. You then must undertake a rebuilding phase to return to your pre-illness riding level.

Injuries are caused mainly by either traumatic experience or overtraining. Too long, too hot, and burnout usually results from inadequate rest and response to your body's messages of weakness. Overtraining typically is expressed as pain, lack of sleep, or decrease in your riding capacity. Athletes will say, "I'm training harder than ever and getting slower. What's wrong?" This usually means their anaerobic threshold has been suppressed by their training for too long in zones 4 and 5.

If you experience chronic or persistent pain when you ride, stop or change your riding. It takes careful attention to train through an injury, although it's possible if you cross-train or change your training pattern substantially.

## Stress

You have significant control over other manageable phenomena, such as rapid weight loss and inadequate nutrition and hydration. Stress from other parts of your life—whether personal, financial, spiritual, or professional—impacts your riding and your performance, yet can be managed to a degree. All of these stresses have a cardiac response that is measurable on your heart rate monitor.

Resting or awakening heart rate is one of the best ways for you to assess the impact of stress. If your heart rate exceeds its average by more than five beats per minute, you should either drop your training heart zone by at least one level and shorten the training time, or cancel the workout for the day. Rest and recovery will make you fitter than will one more training ride.

Some riders always have an excuse for poor performance. For them, everything just goes wrong: hot day, storm and freezing cold, then hot again, hills, wrong gears, too little water, no food, got lost, wind, flat tire, no pump, glasses fogged, wrong glasses, wrong clothes, no night-light, sunburn, and/or scratched paint on frame. All of these external conditions, especially those not anticipated, affect heart rate. Your anxiety goes up, or maybe depression sets in, or you respond with anger, and as a result, enthusiasm evaporates.

You can see the benefits of preparation and maintenance in managing stress and improving riding conditions. To promote trouble-free riding, try these tips:

- Clean your bike
- Make regular bike tune-ups
- Lighten your bike
- Improve your bike equipment
- Adjust your bike to fit you
- Change your riding position
- Match your bike frame to your riding events
- Replace your headlight batteries regularly
- Carry a map when you ride in a new area
- Use sunscreen
- Check tire pressure before riding
- Carry spare tubes
- Carry two water bottles
- Carry saddle bag with your identification, money for telephone call, and all tools for changing a flat tire or to deal with mechanical problems
- Carry ointment to prevent or soothe saddle sores

# The Five Emotional Heart Zones

By Dan Rudd, Ph.D.

Emotional heart zone training is a way to listen to your heart by becoming aware of your emotional state and consciously shifting to a healthier zone, particularly if you happen to be in a toxic emotional zone. Just as the body is designed to heal itself, the emotions can be used to guide us from a condition of stress and disease to a state of peace, health, and compassion.

The field of psychoneuroimmunology (psycho = mind, neuro = body's nervous system, immunology = the body's natural ability to defend and heal itself) teaches us about the connection between our thoughts and what happens in our bodies. Our emotions and perceptions of what is happening in our world cause our heart and brain to send messages that stimulate physiological responses in our body. Our emotional states trigger reactions in our body that affect heart rate, blood chemistry, and the activity of every cell in the body.

Emotional heart zones training is designed to help you stay conscious of what emotional zone you are in. Many people get "stuck" in a particular emotional zone without conscious awareness. When we are agitated, angry, or stressed, the stress hormones continue to flood our bodies like a chemical bath. We need to know how to turn them off.

There are five emotional heart zones. As you read the descriptions, notice which of these zones is most familiar to you and where you tend to spend your time.

## The Emotional Heart Zones

| Zone Number | Emotional Zone | Zone Description | Zone Benefit |
|---|---|---|---|
| 5 | Red Zone | Out of control, frantic, total panic, disconnected, emergency | Toxic |
| 4 | Distress Zone | Worried, anxious, angry, scattered, fearful, reactive | Cautious alert |
| 3 | Performance Zone | Focused, in the flow, positive stress, fulfillment, completion | Achievements |
| 2 | Productive Zone | High concentration, effective, energetic, prolific | Results |
| 1 | Safe Zone | Meditative, relaxed, affirming, regenerative, comfortable, compassionate, peaceful | Energizing |

### Zone 1. Safe Zone

The Safe Zone is where we go to recharge our batteries, calm ourselves, get peaceful, and refocus our energy. The Safe Zone is very personal, and it is important for you to design your own safe place. For some, this zone will have a prayerful or meditative focus. For others, certain music or sounds of nature will create a peaceful inner feeling. A visual memory of a beautiful place, a remembrance of a special moment, or thoughts of compassion toward a loved one may put your heart at peace. Just as exercise is one of the best things for your physical heart, a well-developed Safe Zone is the greatest gift you can give to your emotional heart.

### Zone 2. Productive Zone

The Productive Zone is where you may spend much of your time at home, work, or play. In this zone, you are getting things done and feeling pretty good. You are relatively peaceful and focused, going about your day-to-day responsibilities. In zone 2, you have complete access to your emotions and your thoughts.

### Zone 3. Performance Zone

The Performance Zone has all the features of zone 2 except it is also characterized by greater focus, concentration, positive intensity, and accomplishment. You would probably be in zone 3 when you are doing something you really love, whether it be work, play, or relationships.

### Zone 4. Distress Zone

The Distress Zone is a state where the bad stuff starts to happen. It is characterized by feelings of fear, worry, anger, anxiety, depression, guilt, and helplessness. This is where the stress response is triggered and physiological changes begin to affect heart rate, blood chemistry, and activity in all the cells and organs within the body. The ability to think clearly declines, and the emotions begin to take over. In zone 4 we become much less productive in our work and much more destructive in our relationships.

### Zone 5. Red Zone

The Red Zone is a place you never want to go. This zone involves out-of-control behavior, raw emotion with no rational thought. It is characterized by aggression, violence, and hysteria. Abusive and destructive behavior happens. It is highly toxic to the person in zone 5 as well as anyone else nearby.

To put your heart back into your life, we all need to train and condition both our physical and our emotional hearts. Learning to use your emotional and physical heart zones together leads to more energy and less stress in your life.

*Dan Rudd, Ph.D., is the president of Blitz, Business Leadership in the Zone. Together with Sally Edwards, he teaches organizations and companies how to put the heart back into their business for increased profitability. Reprinted by permission.*

## NATURAL ENVIRONMENT

The natural environment can be your best friend or your worst enemy. Unfortunately, you can't control the environment, but to a certain degree you can manage how it affects you if you know what to anticipate.

## Wind and Heat

Tailwinds are gifts from the heavens, but headwinds can quickly turn an exhilarating ride into a grind. Crosswinds can keep your hands vice-gripped to your handlebars.

Wind is a part of the cycling experience. You learn how to be low and narrow when riding into the wind and be tall and wide like a sail when the wind is at your back. The best way to handle wind is to prepare for it mentally. In a strong headwind, you can say to yourself, "This is good. The wind is my friend; it's making me stronger and better." One open-water swimmer likens it to swimming in seaweed: You can't get angry at the seaweed or it will overcome you. The same holds for wind. As with all challenges, your success is in how you handle them.

Heat is rarely a cyclist's friend, even if you have acclimatized and stay properly hydrated. Nearly all record-breaking endurance performances have been set under cool conditions. Hot environments and a high rate of internal heat production from muscle metabolism doubles thermal stress. The cardiovascular system is trying to meet the demands by shunting blood from the organs and supplying it to the skin while simultaneously trying to supply oxygen to the working muscles. In mild air-temperature conditions, body temperature is more easily regulated, and heat is dissipated mostly by sweat evaporation as more blood oxygen is directed to the muscles. Heart rate goes up in hot ambient conditions. On average, your heart rate increases one beat for every two to three degrees increase in temperature above 70 degrees Fahrenheit. Your ability to generate power (except for short sprints) will be reduced. (Note that extreme cold weather decreases not only power but heart rate as well.)

According to one study, "Acclimatization to heat typically requires 10–14 days in the warmer environment, and 75 percent of the adaptation is believed to have occurred within 5 days" (Sparling and Millard-Stafford 1999).

If you're not accustomed to heat, your initial rides should be shorter and at a lower heart rate intensity (zones 2 to 3), building to longer rides and higher intensity over subsequent days and weeks. In order to minimize body-heat storage and enhance sweat evaporation, wear breathable clothing that wicks away perspiration.

Staying properly hydrated is important because dehydration retards heat acclimatization and increases demands on your cardiovascular system. Fluid ingestion during cycling in the heat reduces body temperature, dehydration, and cardiovascular strain; increases performance; and decreases average heart rate.

The general recommendation is that your rate of fluid ingestion during prolonged exercise should match fluid losses from sweating, or about 5 to 10 ounces every 15 minutes. The typical bike water bottle holds roughly 24 ounces, so one water bottle lasts an average of 30–45 minutes. Remember, however, that higher intensities and higher environmental temperatures require a higher fluid intake.

Sweat-loss rate may give the best approximation of individual fluid requirements. Sweat loss is easily estimated by measuring the difference between pre- and post-exercise body weight. For every pound lost, you need one to two cups of fluid. A mere 2 percent decrease in body weight from water loss can negatively impact performance.

Historically, plain water was thought to be the ideal fluid to drink during riding. However, recent studies indicate that 6 to 8 percent carbohydrate-electrolyte sports drinks are well tolerated during exercise in the heat and can improve endurance. Solutions greater than 12 percent carbohydrate, such as fruit juices and soft drinks, may cause gastrointestinal distress and impair warm-weather performance.

Drinking a lot of water (hyperhydration) before cycling in hot weather is another recommended strategy. The current guideline is to ingest 15 to 20 ounces of fluid two hours before competition; the rationale is that gastric emptying is enhanced when the stomach is full.

After you cycle in heat, sodium replacement may maximize rehydration. Recovery requires both higher fluid volume replacement and higher sodium content.

Following are some tips for riding in wind and heat:

- Stay low and narrow into the wind. Be willing to grind it out. Stay positive.
- Initial rides in heat should be short and at lower intensities, as it takes 10 to 14 days to acclimatize to heat.
- Choose clothing that breathes and wicks away perspiration.
- As a substitute for water, ingest at least 1 liter or 34 ounces of a 6 to 8 percent carbohydrate-electrolyte drink every hour to maintain hydration and increase performance during long (an hour or more) rides.
- Stay fully hydrated to improve acclimatization.
- Drink more fluids when cycling at higher intensities and higher temperatures.

## Salt and Endurance Cycling

Water is the most abundant substance in your body. Losing just 2 percent of your body's water can negatively affect your cycling performance. However, the corresponding loss of sodium from sweating can be even more dangerous than losing water. If you are only consuming water during your ride, you run the risk of diluting the sodium concentration in your blood, a condition called hyponatremia, or water intoxication.

In hot, humid conditions, large amounts of sweat are lost. If the lost sweat (salt and water) is replaced by ingested water (no salt) only, the bloodstream becomes diluted and hyponatremia results.

When your body loses sodium through sweat, it also loses some of its ability to move water, which eventually leads to dehydration even if you are drinking plenty of water. Without sodium, the water you drink will not be distributed properly throughout your body, and you will feel bloated, nauseous, and unable to perform at your best. The symptoms can range from mild to severe and include headaches, muscle cramps, extreme fatigue, disorientation, and slurred speech. If these symptoms go unattended, they can lead to seizures, coma, brain damage, and even death.

Longer rides carry a greater risk of hyponatremia because of the total amount of sweat lost. During rides in the heat, more salt is lost per hour than is usually replaced by food and fluids, including sport drinks. The goal is to know how to maintain sodium balance during your training and racing. Rehearse your hydration, eating, and salt strategy when you train. Know what your needs are before the race. Remember that there are many variations between individuals and there are no absolute right answers.

Here are some suggestions on how to avoid hyponatremia:

Drink frequently to stay hydrated.

For a long, hot ride, aim for a total sodium intake of approximately 1 gram per hour, as recommended by Doug Hiller, M.D., from his experience with the Hawaii Ironman. (This may not be appropriate for everyone; check with your doctor.)

Increase your salt intake three to four days prior to the race by eating salty foods.

Avoid aspirin, ibuprofen, or other anti-inflammatories, and acetaminophen during exercise, especially during the race. These drugs interfere with kidney function, and under tough race and exercise conditions your kidneys need to function at 100 percent.

If you don't think your food and sport drink are providing enough sodium, then consider salt tablets. Be cautious, however, because it's easy to take in too much sodium when using them. Read the label carefully and make sure you know how much you are taking.

Sodium-rich foods also aid in the recovery process by reestablishing your electrolyte balance.

Check with your doctor to see if you have any health problems.

- After cycling in heat, replace sodium to maximize rehydration.
- The fitter you are, the quicker you will adjust to heat. Get fitter.

## Rain

It's only logical that two cyclists from Seattle should write about rain. Rain is inevitable if you are a cyclist—a matter of when, not if. The rule of the ride is to be prepared.

Buy a breathable rain jacket that repels water while allowing body heat to dissipate and sweat to evaporate. Check with your local bike shop or the Internet and become familiar with the latest inclement-weather apparel. Consider wearing performance-fabric cycling tights or rain pants to keep your legs dry and your knees warm.

Most cyclists wouldn't choose to start a ride in the rain unless it was a race or sponsored event, so most of the time, it rains at some point during your ride, which means thinking ahead. Conditions can change quickly for the worse, so you will need to use your best judgment in determining whether it's safe to continue.

Since water creates a slick surface, rain can make the road slippery for turning and braking. Give yourself more time to maneuver and stop. Watch out for puddles that can grab your wheel and reduce your control. What looks like a puddle might be a ten-inch-deep pothole. Slow down and be more cautious, realizing that your brakes may not work as usual. If the road is very slick, underinflate your tires slightly to get more surface area and traction.

As visibility decreases drastically for both you and motorists, you should wear brightly colored clothing so you can be seen. Dark glasses should be replaced with clear or amber lenses.

Keep your core body temperature up, as rain can bring cooler temperatures. If you become wet either from rain or sweat, your body temperature can drop quickly and your ride can become not only miserable but dangerous.

While Sally Reed was riding in RAMROD (Ride Around Mount Rainier in One Day) in 1998, a thunderstorm hit near the top of an eight-mile climb up a steep mountain pass. Mountain thunderstorms can be one of the scariest events on the planet. You are helpless and exposed to their awesome power. As Sally neared the top of the climb, the air was thick and energized with electricity. Lightning bolts flashed, and crackling thunder created a giant din. The support crew waited anxiously ten minutes away with rain gear, but by then, Sally didn't care about getting wet; she just wanted to get off the mountain.

By the time Sally reached the top, put on her rain gear, and started her descent, her body temperature had dropped dangerously, and she had begun to shiver uncontrollably. If it hadn't been for planning and a great support crew waiting with dry clothes and a warm car, her RAMROD experience would have been over.

Always keep in mind that cycling weather can be unpredictable, so prepare for all likely conditions, and most important, use common sense. Here are some tips for managing the effect of riding in rain:

- Use clear or amber-colored lenses.
- Allow extra time for slowing down, stopping, and braking.
- Be alert for standing water and puddles.
- If you have to draft, ride off to the side to avoid the "rooster tail" and mud.
- Maintain core body temperature by dressing properly and stopping often to warm up.
- Wear bright yellow or orange-colored clothing for visibility.
- Underinflate tires for more traction.

After the ride, wipe down your bike, lubricate the chain, and use a water-dispersing spray on all cables, housings, and pivot points of the brake and gear systems. Make sure no water has gotten inside your frame.

## Altitude

As altitude increases, the percentage of oxygen remains relatively stable, but the barometric pressure changes. You find yourself breathing rapidly in order to take in more oxygen. Maximum heart rates decrease about one beat for every 1,000 feet of increased elevation.

Athletes who have trained at sea level experience higher heart rates at higher elevation. As elevation increases, performance decreases. The good news is that thin air provides less resistance. Here are some tips for handling the effects of altitude:

- Dehydration occurs rapidly at high altitude, so drink more than usual.
- Give yourself time to adapt to higher elevation. Take it easy for the first few days if possible.
- Avoid caffeine and alcohol, as they lead to dehydration.
- If you have symptoms of altitude sickness, such as headache and nausea, descend quickly.

## WORKOUTS: Indoor Training

HEALTHY HEART **Workout 41: Talk Is Cheap**

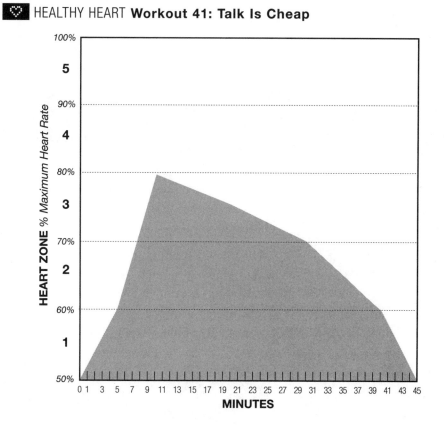

### Overview

Some of us talk aloud, speaking on the outside. Others have a stream of conversation running on the inside, in our minds. Some of us do both simultaneously. Buddhists call the inside talk "monkey mind." This workout is about letting your monkey mind out by training at your talk-threshold heart rate, or what Heart Zones Cycling riders call the TTHR. Training at your TTHR is typically within the Aerobic Zone (zone 3), so you not only have the reward of releasing the internal stream of mental thought, but you also consume lots of oxygen and calories at the same time.

### Description

Your talk-threshold heart rate, or TTHR, is a very narrow range of heartbeats perched on the heart rate threshold where talking concedes to your need for air for breathing. At this heart rate point, you feel you can still talk, but you don't want to exert yourself any harder. Note the heart rate in beats per minutes (bpm) that closely resembles this point, and chart it in your log. As you get fitter, your TTHR changes; the heart rate number increases, and you can maintain a conversation at a higher working heart rate. If you can let your monkey mind go at the same time, you will discover the bliss of riding.

| Stats and Tips for Workout 41: Talk Is Cheap | | | |
|---|---|---|---|
| Zone Number and Name | Minutes in Zone | Heart Zones Training Points | Estimated Calories |
| 5. Red-Line | | | |
| 4. Threshold | 10 | 40 | 120–140 |
| 3. Aerobic | 20 | 60 | 180–220 |
| 2. Temperate | 7 | 14 | 42–56 |
| 1. Healthy Heart | 8 | 8 | 24–40 |
| Totals | 45 | 122 | 366–456 |

**Tip:** Every time you check your monitor, talk. If you can say a couple of sentences and still breathe easiily, you are at the correct TTHR.

| Sequence for Workout 41: Talk Is Cheap | | | | |
|---|---|---|---|---|
| Elapsed Time (min.) | Workout Plan | Heart Zone | Your Heart Rate (bpm) | Interval Time (min.) |
| 0–5 | Warm up, easy pedal, to bottom of Z1 | 1 | _____ | 5 |
| 5–10 | Increase HR with faster cadence/rpm to top of Z2 | 2 | _____ | 5 |
| 10–20 | Increase HR to 5 bpm above estimated TTHR and sustain, choice | 3/4 | _____ | 10 |
| 20–30 | Decrease HR to TTHR and sustain, choice | 3/4 | _____ | 10 |
| 30–40 | Decrease HR to 5 bpm below TTHR and sustain, choice | 3 | _____ | 10 |
| 40–42 | Decrease HR to bottom of Z2, easy pedal | 2 | _____ | 2 |
| 42–45 | Decrease HR to Z1, warm down, easy pedal | 1 | _____ | 3 |

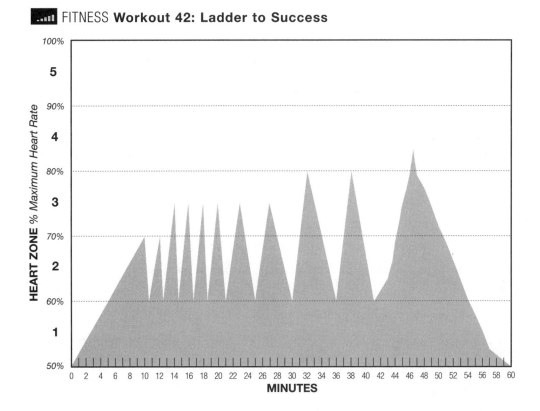

FITNESS **Workout 42: Ladder to Success**

## Overview

Most of us ride and train for personal reasons. For some of us, exercise reduces stress, improves outlook, and gives us more energy. Identifying those reasons helps to keep us on the bike.

| Stats and Tips for Workout 42: Ladder to Success | | | |
|---|---|---|---|
| Zone Number and Name | Minutes in Zone | Heart Zones Training Points | Estimated Calories |
| 5. Red-Line | | | |
| 4. Threshold | 7.5 | 30 | 90–105 |
| 3. Aerobic | 14.5 | 43.5 | 130–160 |
| 2. Temperate | 28 | 56 | 168–224 |
| 1. Healthy Heart | 10 | 10 | 30–50 |
| **Totals** | **60** | **140** | **418–539** |

**Tip:** The first pedal stroke up the Ladder to Success is that of change. The first pedal stroke of change is learning.

While you are training on the bike, set your mind to answering the question "What's on those top few rungs of my ladder to success?" Revisit this ride and this question until you can verbalize a clear statement of the reasons you ride and train.

## Description

This workout is a series of spin sprints, hill climbs, and a fast-paced pyramid climb into zone 4 and back down, followed by a challenging yet controlled recovery. The goal of this workout is to increase your leg speed and muscle power and train your body to adapt as workload increases. The 30-second interval sprints test how quickly you can raise your heart rate as well as how quickly you can recover. The heavy-resistance intervals simulate a series of hills, each one steeper and longer. This pattern tests your muscular strength and endurance along with your mental toughness to hang in there. The pyramid climb develops your physiology to adapt to changes in power demands every 30 seconds. As a result, your cardiovascular system improves as you adapt to this progressive overload.

| Sequence for Workout 42: Ladder to Success | | | | |
|---|---|---|---|---|
| **Elapsed Time (min.)** | **Workout Plan** | **Heart Zone** | **Your Heart Rate (bpm)** | **Interval Time (min.)** |
| 0–5 | Warm up to bottom of Z1, easy pedal | 1 | _____ | 5 |
| 5–10 | Increase HR with rpm to bottom of Z2 | 2 | _____ | 5 |
| 10–20 | (5) 30 sec. sprints with 30 sec. (rec). Sprints start at the bottom of Z3 and go to the midpoint of Z3 (75%) then (rec) to bottom of Z2 (60%) | 3<br>2 | _____<br>_____ | 10 |
| 20–32 | From bottom of Z2 increase HR with heavy (R) to midpoint of Z3 (75%) in 1 min. then (rec) to bottom of Z2 in 2 min. Repeat a total of 4 times | 3<br>2 | _____<br>_____ | 12 |
| 32–43 | Hill 1: 4 min., standing, heavy (R), rpm above 60 (6) to bottom of Z4 then a 2 min. (rec) to bottom of Z2. Hill 2: 3 min., standing, heavy (R), rpm above 60 (6) to bottom of Z4 then a 2 min. (rec) to bottom of Z2. | 4<br>2 | _____<br>_____ | 11 |
| 43–47 | Pyramid climb[a] from the bottom of Z2 into Z4. Increase HR with (R) 5 bpm every 30 sec., steady tempo (cadence) | 2<br>3<br>4 | _____<br>_____<br>_____ | 4 |
| 47–60 | From Z4 decrease HR 5 bpm every min. Mental focus! Controlled (rec) | 4<br>3<br>2<br>1 | _____<br>_____<br>_____<br>_____ | 13 |

[a] Incremental increases and decreases in time and intensity. Think of climbing a hill with a steady tempo or cadence and adding resistance or gearing to increase your heart rate.

PERFORMANCE **Workout 43: The Zipper**

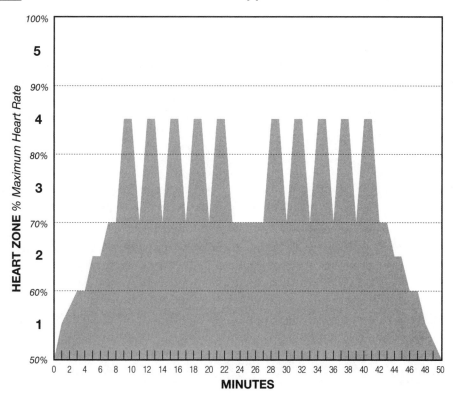

## Overview

You are about to experience a "workout wonder." The primary wonder in this workout is to decide which hurts more, your legs burning or your lungs sucking air from the highest and hottest heart zones. Just like the teeth on a zipper, this ride might eat you up because it's close to a Red-Line experience. Check out the workout profile and match its zipper shape with repeated high, hot intervals.

## Description

The purpose of the Zipper workout is lactic acid–tolerance training, or developing your physiology to train through the high blood acidosis that results from anaerobic metabolism. When you train at high heart rates, lactic acid concentrations build up in the specific muscles being worked and result in a sensation of "burn" in them. Beware: Tomorrow you may be tired and sore—it's called delayed muscle soreness. You will also wonder why only a few intervals done at high intensity are so fatiguing. All lactic acid–tolerance training sessions stress you to near your max, and that's simply tough on the body. Nevertheless, your lactic acid tolerance will increase if you do this workout periodically, so enjoy zipping through this high, hot, and hard workout.

| Stats and Tips for Workout 43: The Zipper | | | |
|---|---|---|---|
| Zone Number and Name | Minutes in Zone | Heart Zones Training Points | Estimated Calories |
| 5. Red-Line | | | |
| 4. Threshold | 20 | 80 | 240–280 |
| 3. Aerobic | 18 | 54 | 162–198 |
| 2. Temperate | 8 | 16 | 48–64 |
| 1. Healthy Heart | 4 | 4 | 12–20 |
| Totals | 50 | 154 | 462–562 |

**Tip 1:** If ten intervals are too hard in the beginning, start with five and build up to ten. Change body position frequently.

**Tip 2:** Increase intensity to 90 percent for a Red-Line experience or performance training.

| Sequence for Workout 43: The Zipper | | | | |
|---|---|---|---|---|
| Elapsed Time (min.) | Workout Plan | Heart Zone | Your Heart Rate (bpm) | Interval Time (min.) |
| 0–2 | Warm up to bottom of Z1, easy pedal | 1 | _____ | 2 |
| 2–7 | Warm up, easy pedal, steadily to midpoint of Z2 | 2 | _____ | 5 |
| 7–9 | Increase HR with cadence/rpm to bottom of Z3 (70%) | 3 | _____ | 2 |
| 9–24 | First set: Increase HR to midpoint of Z4 (85%) and sustain for 2 min. followed by 1 min. (rec) to bottom of Z3 (70%). Repeat a total of 5 times, alternating standing and seated | 4 3 | _____ | 15 |
| 24–28 | Easy pedal (rec) to the bottom of Z2 and sustain | 2 | _____ | 4 |
| 28–43 | Second set: Repeat above work/recovery interval a total of 5 times. Change body position, cadence, and (R) each interval | 4 3 | _____ | 15 |
| 43–50 | Warm down by gradually decreasing HR, easy pedal | 2 | _____ | 7 |

## PERFORMANCE **Workout 44: Salty Dog**

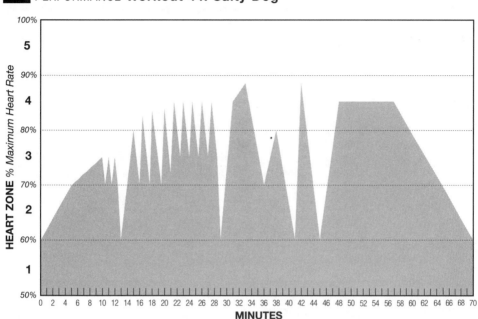

## Overview

In hot, humid conditions, you lose a large amount of sweat, which can disturb sodium and water balance. Adequate hydration and sodium (salt) intake—either via sports drinks or food—becomes vitally important during long rides or races. The "Death Ride," also known as the Tour of the California Alps, is just such a ride. It's 16,000 vertical feet of mountain-pass climbing in high altitude and extreme heat. High, hot, and hard is the best description of this one-day trek. This ride takes some serious training and proper planning for a prolonged effort in heat and high altitude. That means determining how to maintain your sodium balance during and after the ride. For more information, see the sidebar "Salt and Endurance Cycling" earlier in this chapter.

## Description

This is an intense 70-minute workout with a little bit of everything from fast spinning to high-cadence climbing to steep strength-building hills. Tucked in the middle of the workout is a high-cadence, high-intensity standing interval called the Lance Dance. For 5 minutes you visualize yourself as Lance Armstrong climbing out of the saddle at a very fast cadence as if you are dancing on your bike. The last 20 minutes is for building power with quick accelerations and two tough hill climbs.

| Stats and Tips for Workout 44: Salty Dog | | | |
|---|---|---|---|
| Zone Number and Name | Minutes in Zone | Heart Zones Training Points | Estimated Calories |
| 5. Red-Line | | | |
| 4. Threshold | 41 | 164 | 492–574 |
| 3. Aerobic | 10 | 30 | 90–110 |
| 2. Temperate | 19 | 38 | 114–152 |
| 1. Healthy Heart | | | |
| Totals | 70 | 232 | 696–836 |

**Tip:** Drink a sports drink within 15 min. after finishing; eat 200–400 calories of high-carbohydrate food within 30 min.

Heart Bra

Bike Computer

Heart Rate Monitor
with Speed and Distance Sensor

Tools of the Trade

| Sequence for Workout 44: Salty Dog | | | | |
|---|---|---|---|---|
| Elapsed Time (min.) | Workout Plan | Heart Zone | Your Heart Rate (bpm) | Interval Time (min.) |
| 0–10 | Easy-pedal warm-up to bottom of zone 3 | 3 | _____ | 10 |
| 10–13 | 30 sec. moderate (R) followed by 30 sec. easy pedal. Repeat a total of 3 times | 3.5 | _____ | 3 |
| 13–15 | Easy pedal (rec) | 2 | _____ | 2 |
| 15–29 | 20 sec. moderate (R), 20 sec. hard (R), 20 sec. very hard (R) followed by 30 sec. easy pedal (rec). Repeat a total of 8 times | 4/4.5 | _____ | 14 |
| 29–31 | Easy pedal (rec) | 2 | _____ | 2 |
| 31–36 | Lance Dance, 90 to 95 rpm, standing | 4/4.5 | _____ | 5 |
| 36–38 | Easy pedal (rec) | 2 | _____ | 2 |
| 38–41 | From 70 rpm increase cadence 10 rpm every 10 sec. to 120 rpm. Repeat 1 min. sequence a total of 3 times | 4 | _____ | 3 |
| 41–42 | Easy pedal (rec) | 2 | _____ | 1 |
| 42–48 | 110 rpm (11) for 3 min. with the most sustainable (R) followed by a 3 min. (rec) | 4 2 | _____ _____ | 6 |
| 48–51 | Standing, accelerate 10 sec. with smooth efficient pedal stroke followed by a 50 sec. seated (rec). Repeat a total of 3 times | 4 | _____ | 3 |
| 51–57 | 1 min. moderate (R) hill climb followed by 30 sec. heavy (R) followed by 30 sec. easy pedal (rec). Repeat a total of 3 times | 4 | _____ | 6 |
| 57–63 | 1 min. heavy (R) followed by 30 sec. standing run followed by 30 sec. easy pedal (rec). Repeat a total of 3 times | 4 | _____ | 6 |
| 63–70 | Easy-pedal warm-down | 2 | _____ | 7 |

## Outdoor Training and Rides

### Workout 45: Rock 'n' Roll

You can make this ride as long and as tough as you want. The idea is to repeat work and rest intervals every 15 seconds for 5 minutes. "Rock" for 15 seconds, then easy "roll" for 15 seconds. Rest and recover for 5 minutes, then repeat the work/rest, rock 'n' roll interval again. Repeat this 5-minute interval as many times as you like. You may choose to do your 15-second "rock"

> **Ride Snapshot**
>
> ⟩ 15 sec. On (rock), 15 sec. Off (roll) for 1–5 min., (rec) for 5 min.; repeat 1–5 times
> ⟩ Warm down or continue ride

interval at any intensity above 70 percent. Your "roll" heart rate should increase in recovery beats the fitter you become. The only requirement is to keep your cadence high. If you are giving an all-out effort for 15 seconds, your heart rate will be in zones 4 and 5. The Rock 'n' Roll workout will help your pedaling efficiency and leg speed at whatever intensity you choose.

### Workout 46: Saturday Night Fever

As you crawl out of bed Sunday morning to meet your riding partners, have you ever questioned why you did what you did Saturday night, or better yet, why you didn't do what you should have done Saturday night?

This speed interval can be incorporated into your ride when you are ready to focus on the task at hand: speed work.

The basic way to develop fast, smooth leg speed is to spin easy to moderate gears at a high rpm or cadence. Choose a relatively flat section of road. After a 15- to 30-minute warm-up, start with your normal riding cadence. That could be anywhere from 75 to 95 rpm. Gradually increase your cadence until your legs lose coordination and you are bouncing on the saddle. Ease off about 5 rpm and sustain for 5 to 15 seconds. Repeat several times. This is not a high-intensity heart rate interval. Most of these repeats will be in zones 3 and 4. After a few times,

your maximum cadence and smoothness will be much better. You can also stay in easy gears on the downhills, letting gravity help turn your legs.

> **Ride Snapshot**
>
> ⟩ 15–30 min. warm-up
> ⟩ 75–95 rpm, moderate gearing, gradually increase cadence to 120-plus, ease off 5 rpm, sustain up to 1 min., zones 3–4; repeat several times
> ⟩ Continue ride

Stay in the small chainring in front and move to harder gears in the back, increasing your cadence to 120 rpm and trying to sustain for 1 minute. Focus on relaxing, keeping your upper body quiet and arms loose. All the motion happens in your legs. Keep your head still and think "smooth and fast."

Your legs should be a blur as if they were in a cartoon strip. As you develop your leg speed and get smoother and more efficient, your heart rate should be lower during these intervals.

## Workout 47: Five-by-Five

This ride is very similar to the indoor ride in Chapter 4 called Five-by-Two. The purpose is to teach your cycling-specific muscles and cardiovascular system to adapt to a changing workload every 5 minutes. It will be entirely your choice on how you want to increase your heart rate. Pick a course that is flat to moderately rolling hills with no traffic or stop signs. This ride will take approximately 60 to 70 minutes depending on warm-up and warm-down time.

Warm up adequately to your maximum heart rate minus 50 beats. For example, if your maximum heart rate is 180 bpm, you would warm up to 130 bpm. Increase your heart rate 5 bpm every 5 minutes until you reach the highest heart rate you think you can sustain for 5 minutes. Your heart rate number may be anywhere from 75 to more than 90 percent of your maximum heart rate. You decide the highest percentage you want to ride to and sustain for 5 minutes, then decrease your heart rate 5 bpm every 5 minutes until you reach your original starting heart rate number (in the example, 130 bpm).

Finish the ride by warming down gradually.

## Workout 48: Hill-Billy

Grab your training partner and head for the hills. This high-cadence climb is good two to three times a week if you want to develop more power. Power will let you ride the big chainring for those short, steep climbs.

Warm up for 20–30 minutes of easy zone 2 riding. Pick a hill that takes about 10–15 seconds to climb. Approach the hill with momentum and maintain 100 rpm all the way to the top. Shift to an easier gear if necessary to maintain cadence. Spin easily for one minute, then repeat. Alternate standing and sitting. Do a total of three repeats, then spin easily in zone 2 for 5 minutes. Do three more hill repeats or until you can't hold 100 rpm. Finish with an easy-pedal zone 2 ride home. As you get stronger, you should be able to ride bigger gears at the same heart rate and get there quicker. Note these factors about heart rate:

### Ride Snapshot

> Warm up 20–30 min.

> 3 x 15 sec. @ 100 rpm with 1 min. recovery in between (alternate standing/sitting)

> 5 min. zone 2 recovery

> 3 x 15 sec. @ 100 rpm with 1 min. recovery in between (alternate standing/sitting)

> Easy-pedal recovery

- Your heart rate will typically go up when you're standing.
- A higher cadence will increase heart rate, training the aerobic system and saving your legs.
- Shifting to a bigger gear and maintaining cadence will increase heart rate.
- There are three ways to increase heart rate on a bike: increasing cadence, increasing resistance, and changing position (standing).

## REFERENCES

Below, P. R., R. Mora Rodriquez, J. Gonzalez-Alonzo, J. Fluid and Carbohydrate Ingestion Independently Improve Performance During One Hour of Intense Exercise. *Medical Science Sports Exercise*, vol. 27, no. 2 (1995): pp. 200–210.

Jenkins, Mark A. The Sports Med Web, 1997.

Kregel, K. C., P. T. Wall. Effects of Ingesting Carbohydrate Beverages During Exercise in the Heat. *Medical Science Sports Exercise*, vol. 18, no. 5 (1986): pp. 568–575.

Millard-Stafford, M., P. B. Sparling, L. B. Rosskopf. Carbohydrate-Electrolyte Replacement Improves Distance-Running Performance in the Heat. *Medical Science Sports Exercise*, vol. 24, no. 8 (1992): pp. 934–940.

Rudd, Dan, Ph.D., and Sally Edwards. *More Energy, Less Stress*. Sacramento, CA: Heart Zones Publishing, 2001.

Sparling, P. B., and M. Millard-Stafford. Keeping Sports Participants Safe in Hot Weather. *The Physician and Sports Medicine*, July 1999.

Swift, Paul, and Joan Wenson. *LeMond RevMaster Instructor's Manual*. Kirkland, WA: StairMaster Health and Fitness Products, 2000.

# 9

# The ABCs of Heart Rate Monitors

*I used a heart rate monitor in my first triathlon without knowing how, except for the training we had done in Heart Zones Cycling class. I knew nothing about thresholds or cardiac drift. I just looked at the numbers and hoped my heart wouldn't blow up. During the bike leg of my first Danskin Triathlon, I correlated the numbers with what I had seen on an indoor studio bike, but during the swim and run, the numbers didn't have much meaning. My training partners were all in the same boat. Before the race, Sally Edwards teased us about being "club-trained triathletes" because we swam indoors in a 50-meter pool, rode studio bikes in an air-conditioned room, and ran on treadmills with towels and water bottles handy.*

*We realized after our first race that we needed to know more about what the numbers on our monitors were telling us. We decided to test our anaerobic threshold heart rates in the swimming pool, on the track, and on the bike. All of us wanted to do better next year and knew our heart rate monitor would be the key.*

*With a big hug and a signed triathlon book from Sally, I was armed for my year of training. What Sally didn't know was that she gave me the best racing advice and motivation possible. Inside the front cover of* Triathlons for Women *she wrote, "Read this and win your age group!" I immediately thought, "She thinks I can do it." She believed in me more than I did. It's a common theme in life and in races. We have people who believe in us and inspire us to do what we think are extraordinary feats.*

*I followed Sally's directive to write a race plan laying out my goals for my second Danskin. I set predictions of split times and average heart rate numbers for each leg of the race. Through specific training my anaerobic threshold heart rate had increased about five beats in each event, and I knew exactly what heart rate number was sustainable. I didn't win as Sally had said, but I also didn't read all of her book! Second place was the motivation I needed for the next year, along with turning fifty and "aging up."*

*For the third Danskin Triathlon, I convinced my riding partners to start seriously using their monitors, and when they got faster, so did I. It's amazing how that works. We mounted one heart monitor on our handlebars and a second one on our wrists so we could easily monitor our heart rate.*

*This continuous information made all the difference in the race. It gave me the confidence to push hard, knowing that I had trained at these heart rate numbers and my heart wasn't going to blow up. A half mile before the finish line, as Lynn Brooks (twenty-time Ironman finisher) passed me, I looked down and my heart rate had dropped. At that moment, second place didn't seem appealing, so I did what I had heard Sally Edwards say so many times: "You reach down deep, throw away your heart rate monitor, and run with your emotional heart." A true red-line finish never looked so good! No, I didn't catch Lynn, but I had given it my best shot. If that meant second place, it was okay. I still didn't know how my good friend Sue Dills had done, because she had started in the wave five minutes ahead of me. In short, third place might be a reality.*

*When the age-group winners were announced, I heard my name over the loudspeaker. Not for third place, not for second place—but for first! How could that be? Lynn clearly passed me, unless I was seeing things (strange things happen at high heart rates). I learned that both Lynn and Sue were in the wave before me. If Lynn hadn't provided me with that last half mile of motivation, it may well have been a different story.*

*When you help your friends train using heart rate monitors, it's easy to joke about giving away all your training secrets. The best secret is that when your friends and training partners get faster, so do you.*

—SALLY REED

## THE HEART RATE MONITOR, YOUR NO. 1 TOOL

Your heart rate monitor is more than your friend, coach, and tool. It's difficult to describe what it can do emotionally and physically to help you do your best. It's a hardworking, durable device that keeps on ticking, storing data, and giving you continuous information about the most important muscle in your body, your heart.

In a tool chest of key sports-performance equipment, the heart rate monitor would occupy an established place. To interpret your heart muscle in relation to so many other events, activities, and cycles within the body, it must possess special powers. Here is a description of some of them:

*Motivation.* For a boost of energy to keep you training, turn to your monitor for motivation to complete a workout or improve a training session. Strap it around your handlebars or wrist. When you drift above a set heart rate number, the alarm sounds to let you know. Conversely, when you lose focus and slow down, it sounds the alarm to tell you to pick it up. It keeps you fresh by objectively assessing your performance.

*Biofeedback.* Because the monitor reads your heart's frequency of contraction, the data it provides are more precise than the perceived-exertion (RPE) scale. The delicate range of heartbeats surrounding the anaerobic threshold heart rate zone can be measured with much greater accuracy using a monitor.

*Braking.* If you're a high achiever who loves to train in high zones, you can use your monitor for getting faster by having it slow you down or hold you back. This is useful when you must conserve your energy supply to finish a final climb with energy left to do it well.

*Computing.* High-end monitors feature accessory software and download capability, allowing you to use them with your computer to interpret data on a more sophisticated level. Some software programs also have analysis capabilities; others include training programs tailored to your current fitness level.

*Diagnosis.* Undertraining, overtraining, and overreaching are all phases of training that can produce different outcomes in your overall plan. You can use a monitor to assess your body's response to a dosage of exercise. For example, awakening heart numbers as well as ambient and delta heart rate values all have direct application to diagnosing the current status of your working muscle groups. Changes in these values are critical in evaluating your ability to train for improvement.

*Quantification.* The Heart Zones Cycling system uses the monitor as a prescription tool that aids in determining the recommended quantity of training. This system is explained in more detail in Chapter 3. In an ideal world, the best quantification tool would be a power meter that measures energy output on a bike.

## WORKINGS OF A HEART RATE MONITOR

Today's portable and wireless heart rate monitors measure the number of beats the heart contracts in one minute. Extremely accurate compared with laboratory-quality devices, they are relatively inexpensive and readily available. Basically, a heart rate monitor measures exercise intensity or cardiac demand.

A heart rate monitor consists of three different parts. A washable, adjustable elastic band circles your upper torso at chest level to attach the transmitter to the front or back area of the body. The signal detection unit or electrodes form the transmitter. A plastic casing holds two separate rubber electrodes, which must touch the skin for the unit to operate. The electrodes detect the electrical potential of each heartbeat and pass this electrical current through signal, noise, and data processing. The transmitter unit also contains a copper-coiled radio-like transmitter and a battery that powers the signal transmission to the receiver. Transmission power is predetermined; most monitors project unidirectionally for 32 to 36 inches from the transmitter.

The watch-like device is the receiver, and it displays the heart rate as a number. Inside the receiver unit is an application-specific integrated circuit masked with prescribed actions that coordinate the inner workings of the monitor, including the external buttons used to program it.

## HOW TO BUY A HEART RATE MONITOR

When buying a monitor, you'll find a long list of features that you should consider aside from the five basic types discussed earlier. Since more than two dozen manufacturers worldwide produce heart rate monitors, it's impossible to list here all features and models. However, here's a short list of some features:

*Heart zones.* Allows you to program the range, top and bottom, of at least one heart zone and provides an audible signal or visual display telling you if you are within, above, or below that range. Advanced features include time in zone, which at the end of your ride gives you the amount of time you spent in the zone or zones you programmed. More advanced monitors can provide this information for multiple heart zones.

*Watch.* Shows the time of day. Usually includes an alarm function.

*Percentage of maximum heart rate.* Displays at what percentage of your maximum heart rate you are performing at that moment.

*Memory.* Stores information throughout the ride for later review or downloading. Also known as the recall function.

*Stopwatch.* Records the elapsed time during your ride. May provide lap functions that include heart rate with the lap.

*Average heart rate.* When you start your stopwatch, records the time and heart rate to later provide you with your average during that time period.

*Computer interfaceable.* Monitors that download heart rate data through several different transmission methods to enable manipulation by computer software for advanced information.

Almost all monitors today are water-resistant, mount easily on your handlebars, and offer backlighting. The technology for heart rate monitors is rapidly changing. Some models display calories burned; provide fitness testing, analysis, and improvement; and help you determine your heart training zones on a daily basis.

There are many features to consider, but the basic continuous-read model can work well for the beginning cyclist. This monitor has no buttons, no programs, no time of day or alarms. It merely tells you your heart rate, and it is inexpensive. A monitor with too many features can be overwhelming. Purchase one with features that meet your needs.

## THE CHALLENGES OF TECHNOLOGY

A heart rate monitor is not the holy grail, although some athletes live, breathe, and swear by theirs. They never work out without one, and if they were forced to train without it, their symptoms would be similar to those of addicts in withdrawal. Following are a few problems you should recognize as you use a monitor so you can maximize its effectiveness.

*Inconsistency.* Your heart rate has a great deal of beat-to-beat as well as minute-to-minute variability because it's controlled as much by the involuntary nervous system as by the volitional one. Day-to-day variability is also sizable, influenced by environmental factors such as stress, ambient temperatures, altitude, hydration, sleep patterns, nutrition, and training intensities. If you see variations in your heart rate numbers, don't be surprised. It's not the monitor; it's you.

*Research.* Exercise scientists and coaches generally agree that training with a heart monitor improves performance, but research verifying this principle is lacking. The term "going naked" refers to intentionally shunning the use of a monitor, and the practice has become popular in a number of sports by athletes who insist they perform equally well without the technology as with it.

*Laboratory versus the real world.* Exercise physiologists agree that oxygen utilization ($VO_2$) is directly related to heart rate, but they disagree about relying on that same relationship when athletes perform in competitive situations versus the results obtained in laboratory settings. It appears that heart rates during performance far exceed those predictable from laboratory testing, especially at intensities above 85 percent of maximum heart rate. A few experts thus question whether heart rate is a valid measurement tool for exercise intensity.

## Heart Rate Monitor Buyers' Guide

| Type of Monitor and Corresponding Features | Monitor Selection Based on Cyclist's Level | | |
|---|---|---|---|
| | Beginning/ Basic | Recreational/ Fitness | Advanced/ Performance |
| **Continuous-Read Monitors** | | | |
| Heart rate | √ | √ | √ |
| Time of day | | √ | √ |
| Water-resistant | √ | √ | √ |
| **Zone and Memory Monitors** | | | |
| Programmable zones | | √ | √ |
| Peak heart rate | | √ | √ |
| Stopwatch | √ | √ | √ |
| Time in zone | | √ | √ |
| Time above/below zone | | √ | √ |
| Out-of-zone alarm | | √ | √ |
| Average heart rate | √ | √ | √ |
| Wake-up alarm | | | √ |
| Percentage of maximum heart rate | √ | √ | √ |
| Countdown timer | | | √ |
| Backlight | | √ | √ |
| Calorie counter | | √ | √ |
| Time in 5 zones | √ | √ | √ |
| Calculates Heart Zones Training points | | √ | √ |
| **Downloadable Monitors** | | | |
| Manual | | √ | √ |
| Direct: Sonic link, infrared, USB Port | | | √ |
| **Bike Monitors** | | | |
| Cycle functions: speed, distance, odometer, cadence (optional) | √ | √ | √ |
| Altitude | | | √ |
| Temperature | | | √ |
| Power output (watts) | | | √ |

*Comprehension.* In advanced models of heart rate monitors and their companion software programs, the programming of the hardware and understanding of the software are beyond the

# Ten Tips to Get the Most from Your Heart Rate Monitor

### 1. Select Your Heart Rate Monitor Carefully

There are many models of heart rate monitors, but they can be broken down into five types.

*Continuous-read monitors.* These are very basic and simple. They only tell you your current heart rate. They are easy to identify; they have no buttons. They have a large, easily read display. Great for walking or swimming.

*Zone monitors.* These allow you to know which zone you are working in. You can program in one or more zones and the monitor may beep to let you know if you are at, above, or below your selected range.

*Memory monitors.* These are more high-tech because they store different types of information such as time in zone and average heart rate, and you later play back the data for recording. They don't allow you to interface with a computer, but at least you have some information for analysis and recording purposes. They are sometimes referred to as "programmable" monitors because you can program them to record various data.

*Downloadable monitors.* Without a doubt, these monitors offer you the most. They store heart rate samples or other data for downloading later, manually or into a PC. If you wish to invest in an interface box and software program, you can transfer the data for interpreting. Several companies such as the Heart Zones Company (www.heartzone.com) have developed new software programs that allow you to enter the data manually from a downloadable monitor into a computer. This avoids the expense of the interface unit that some manufacturers sell, but you still have the ability to retrieve the information and analyze it for your fitness management.

*Bike monitors.* These are a new breed of monitor. They are two monitors in one—a bike computer and a heart rate monitor. On most models, you can see both bike information like cadence and speed on the same screen as you can read heart rate. If you love numbers as much as we do, this is your best choice for a heart rate monitor to use on your bike.

The more you spend, the more you get. There is a direct correlation between the price of the monitor and the amount of information it provides. It may be cheaper in the long run to spend a little more up-front. There is a direct cost-benefit ratio. If you invest a few more dollars in your first purchase, you may not need to upgrade later as you do with computer technology.

When selecting a heart rate monitor, choose the features that match your personal needs. Monitors range from $50 for a basic continuous-read model to $250 for one that is downloadable into your computer.

## 2. Read the Manual

This is indeed the most important tip. It is worth taking the time to learn to use your monitor. You may wish to keep your manual with you for the first week so you can refer to it as often as you like. After you have worked with the monitor and the manual together for a while, you will find it easy to get all of the information you want.

## 3. The One-Week Rule

If you are new to heart zone training, don't expect to grasp how to make your heart rate monitor work for you the very first day. It takes time. Monitors are technology. Be patient with yourself. Give yourself a week of wearing your monitor, and you'll find that you fall in love with the power of the information it provides.

## 4. Be Sure Your Transmitter Belt Is Tight Enough

Erratic numbers often occur if your chest strap is too loose. As a rule of thumb, start by fitting it around your waist. At this point there should be approximately a six-inch separation between the two end pieces of the chest strap. This allows you to lift it up around your chest and then tighten it from there. Replace the elastic strap periodically because it does wear out. Replacement straps usually sell for about $10. A transmitter belt that fits well will be more comfortable to wear, as well as more accurate.

## 5. Monitor by the Heart Numbers

Learn what the numbers mean. The monitor tells you the intensity at which your heart is working, measured in beats per minute. When your heart rate increases, usually it's because the intensity applied to the heart has increased, which requires more blood to be pumped. Be aware, however, that not only exercise increases your heart rate. Other factors such as temperature, altitude, dehydration, type of exercise, state of health, or psychological stress can affect your heart rate.

## 6. Believe the Monitor

We often hear stories from individuals who think their monitor is broken. Typically, women say their monitor doesn't work because the number is too low. Men say theirs are broken because the numbers are too high. The monitor's numbers are almost always accurate. Why this misunderstanding? It's usually because of how hard individuals perceive they are training. Men typically train too hard and women too easy. Set your individual goals and zones, design an appropriate training program, and believe your monitor.

## 7. Use Your Monitor as a Management Tool, Not a Speedometer

Many people use their heart rate monitor to tell them if they are at, above, or below a designated heart rate. However, you can get greater benefit out of less training time if you use it systematically to train in an effort to accomplish a goal. Use it to "manage" your heart rate training program. Think of it as a training partner, coach, or a high-tech safety device. Heart rate monitors are also great tools for those wanting to manage their weight (see Chapter 11).

### 8. Don't Press the Buttons Under Water

Your monitor is pressure-sealed when it leaves the factory. If you push the buttons and allow water to seep inside, you may damage it. Be careful in heavy rain as well.

### 9. Don't Change the Battery Yourself

Changing the battery is a task best left to the manufacturer. Your manual will tell you where to send the monitor to have this done. Again, the unit is sealed under pressure, and when you reassemble it yourself, you probably won't get the same quality of seal that the manufacturer can using special tools. Some units do allow you to change the battery yourself, but they will clearly state this in the manual.

### 10. Accessories Are Useful

There are many useful items that will help you fully enhance and enjoy your monitor. Two key ones are books and heart application programs. It is essential that you know how to apply this piece of fitness hardware to your life. How do you best use your monitor when cycling, or for stress reduction, weight loss, or general fitness? These are types of applications. To select the best books, go to our website (www.heartzones.com) where you'll find many titles that will help you make it easy and fun to use your monitor as a training tool. There are also newsletters and links that will keep you informed on how to get the most from your monitor and your training.

Another accessory you may find useful is a mount that allows you to attach the receiver to a bike or treadmill. Also, you can find sports bras that have a slot to hold your transmitter, eliminating the elastic strap and possible chafing. Some people prefer to change the watchband, depending on the style it came with. You may find one that fits your wrist more comfortably. These are only a few of the accessories available that can help you match your needs to your monitor.

expertise of most coaches and athletes. The accompanying owner manuals for many of the monitors are likewise difficult and laborious. Many athletes find they suffer information overload from downloaded monitor information. For those who can interpret the data correctly, the final step—how to use the data to change the training dosage—may also pose a challenge.

*Response time.* Heart rate monitors use complicated algorithms, or mathematical equations, to calculate the number displayed on the face of the watch-like device. There is some lag time in both the heart's response to a change in exercise intensity and the monitor's algorithmic calculation (3- to 5-second lag time on monitor) of that number. For example, if you were warmed up and sprinted 100 yards on your bike, you might be breathing at maximum respiratory and heart rate, but your monitor would not read that absolute number because of the lag time in both heart rate and the nature of how heart rate monitors collect and process the heart rate numbers.

*Group training.* Have you ever tried to do your workout with a training partner and a couple of heart rate monitors? Have you noticed that at first it's a struggle to decide whose heart rate and whose pace to follow? That's because in group training situations, it's hard to do your own workout and not the group's. This is most often true in cycling. If you're riding in a group and you don't feel comfortable riding in close proximity to others who are riding fast, using a heart rate monitor has limited application. When riding in a pack in a race, bike-handling skills and drafting to maintain bike speed are more important than staying at the right heart rate.

*Fixation.* Some riders stare at their heart rate monitors more than they watch for road conditions or obstacles such as cars. In one Danskin race, a racer was so fixated on her bike monitor that she hit a parked car. Common sense should tell you that knowing your heart rate number is less important than riding safely on your bike.

## TEN COMMON HEART RATE MONITOR CONCERNS AND MISTAKES

Everyone makes mistakes, so it's always helpful to learn from those made by others. Here are Sally Edwards's responses to common concerns about heart monitors to help you in your training:

## 1. My Heart Rate Monitor Is Broken; the Numbers It Displays Are Too High.

I hear this comment from those who love to train in the high, hard heart zones—cyclists who know only how to hammer on their bike, constantly pushing the pace, and who are unfamiliar with recovery riding. Usually I find that the heart rate monitor works fine; the cyclist needs to slow down to get fitter and faster.

## 2. The Longer I Ride at the Same Speed, the Higher My Heart Rate Soars.

This common phenomenon is called cardiac drift. When you ride, especially in the heat, dehydration decreases your blood volume, increasing your heart rate unless you drink fluids to stay hydrated. Replenishing fluid lost through sweat is an important factor in avoiding cardiac drift.

## 3. When I First Start to Ride, My Heart Rate Jumps Above 150 bpm, but I Don't Perceive That I Am Riding at That Heart Rate.

This phenomenon is difficult to explain. I often ride with others who share that same experience. Try to eliminate mechanical problems with the monitor such as a chest strap that is too loose. Riding too close to others so that the monitors "cross-talk" can sometimes add the individual heart rate numbers together. Be patient and give your monitor a few minutes to adjust to the activity.

## 4. Sometimes I Can't Get a Reading.

Usually this is caused by a problem with your transmission range. The monitor and chest strap must be within 32 inches of each other for the connection to be strong enough for the monitor to sense. If you use aerobars and your monitor is on your wrist more than 32 inches from your chest, the monitor will go blank because it is too far from the chest strap.

## 4. I Can't Push the Right Buttons for the Right Functions.

We all get frustrated with learning how to program our heart rate monitor. The answer is to spend the time to read your owner's manual and memorize your monitor's functions. For the most complicated monitors, you may need up to three hours of reading the booklets and practicing with the monitor to learn the proper use of the buttons. It takes a good week of wearing the monitor to feel confident using it.

## 6. I Want to Get Only My Average Heart Rate.

People ask, "I know my average heart rate during my training interval, but the reading includes my warm-up and warm-down heart rates, so how do I get my average without having it distorted by these lower values?"

My suggestion is that you wear a sports watch on your wrist and put your bike or heart rate monitor on your handlebars. Use the sports watch to measure elapsed time; start the stopwatch function on the monitor when you begin the main part of your workout. Since the monitor is averaging every heartbeat, it records only when the stopwatch is running, giving you only the data you want. If this is too much trouble, invest in a higher-end monitor that allows you to see separate averages for your warm-up, warm-down, and intervals.

## 7. Is Using My Heart Rate Monitor the Same as Measuring Power Output?

It would be valuable to know how many watts of power you generate when you ride. To measure this, you need a special gauge, sometimes mounted inside the rear hub of your wheel. These devices are expensive, around $600–$1,000. However, a heart rate monitor, particularly if it's a bike monitor (altitude, heart rate, distance, and speed) will furnish most of the information needed to quantify your training experience.

## 8. I Bought a Monitor That's Too Difficult for Me to Figure Out.

Most people find that a monitor has certain features they appreciate. The problem is that when you buy one for the first time, you don't know what those features will be. Most of us want to wear our monitor as a watch, but it wasn't until recently that manufacturers reduced the size and electronics to make monitors comfortable for all-day wear and cosmetic appeal. Read the owner's manual and experiment with your monitor to see if you can't increase your understanding of its functions. Also remember that you don't immediately have to master features you might not need right away.

## 9. I Notice a Great Deal of Daily Variation in My Heart Rate.

Your heart rate monitor is telling you about your physical and emotional stress at a particular moment. Your heart rate varies a great deal as your body subtly responds to ambient changes. Examples of factors that will affect your heart rate are if you take medication, if you are in a different climate, or if you change altitude or diet or sleep patterns.

## 10. I Download Information from My Monitor to My Computer, but I Don't Know What It Means.

You certainly aren't alone. Sometimes computer software is difficult to understand. Engineers tend to create software based on what a piece of hardware can do, regardless of whether the user needs that information. Keep track of only the information that's important and significant to accomplishing your goals. Ignore the rest.

## HISTORY AND THE FUTURE OF HEART RATE MONITORS

Monitoring the heart has been a common practice for thousands of years. The early Chinese physicians first used the technique for diagnosing health. Accurate measurements of heart rate taken manually—called manual pulse palpation—are less reliable and accurate than those from a monitor. For purposes of training, testing, and biofeedback research, accuracy is extremely important in heart rate monitoring.

Monitoring the heart with a heart rate monitor first began in 1978 when Tunturi, a Scandinavian equipment manufacturer, released the Pulser monitor, developed by Polar Electro Oy. This primitive grandparent to today's sleek, small watch-like monitors was hardwired from the chest strap to the wrist monitor. It was big and bulky, but it worked.

Five years later, Polar introduced to the world the first wireless monitor called the PE 2000. Manufactured in Hong Kong by Dayton Industries and developed at the Department of Electronics at the University of Oulu, these early monitors were targeted for coaches, athletes, and researchers to enhance their knowledge, skills, and performance. The medically accurate and fragile Holter monitors and the portable but unwieldy electrocardiogram (ECG) apparatus were impractical to use. Today, the use of heart rate monitors has been expanded and used for health, fitness, and wellness applied in dozens of ways, such as

- Physical and health education classes in schools
- Training of racing and performance horses
- Weight management to stay in the fat-burning range
- Health professionals: doctors and physical therapists
- Cardiac rehabilitation
- Stress management
- Athletic clubs: embedded in exercise equipment
- Corporate fitness and training programs for improved emotional well-being
- Sports disciplines: running, triathlon, basketball, tennis, and cycling
- General fitness training

This slow growth of heart rate monitor training, known today as heart zone training, is in part due to the complexity of the technology. Interestingly, the first consumer monitor was also one of the most complex to program and use. Because of its intricate electronics and functions, acceptance of heart rate monitors was extremely slow. It took nearly a decade for an easy-to-use, consumer-friendly monitor to appear on the market.

The first wireless heart rate monitors were microcomputers like the Polar Sports Tester PE 2000. It was hard to program and bulky but accurate. By 1989, Polar introduced in Europe the Sports Tester PE 3000 and the first computer downloadable monitor. It was equipped with a computer interface that transmitted via magnetic fields. The retail price was nearly $500, and few were bought in the United States because of its high price and complicated functions. Both models were extremely accurate and reliable. This monitor was in competition with models produced by other manufacturers who had now developed early technology.

Simultaneously, monitors that measured blood flow using photoelectric sensors and not the electrical activity of the heart muscle were growing in popularity. These early pulse monitors were easy to use and less expensive but not as accurate as electrode sensors measuring the electrical activity of the heart.

In the early 1990s two factors affected the market and the developing technologies: increased competition and falling prices. As new technologies and features developed with new manufacturers such as Cardiosport, Sports Instruments, Cat Eye, Nike, Sensor Dynamics, Reebok, and Specialized, the popularity of using a heart rate monitor increased.

Convergence was the buzzword of electronics in the last decade of the twentieth century. Different technologies came together, converged, and became available in one product. Convergence happened with heart rate monitors as well. The sports watch, the heart rate monitor, the stopwatch, and the bike computer all combined into one piece of sports equipment: the Polar CycloVantage. It had all the functions of a bike computer—speed, cadence, time, distance, and capability for being downloaded into a computer. Subsequent convergence has resulted in the bike monitor, which also includes altitude and is manufactured by Specialized and others.

But the market didn't want more technology or features and functions; it was demanding lower prices and simplicity. Consumers wanted plug-and-play, easy-to-use heart rate monitors and watches. The first buttonless, read-only heart rate monitors hit the market in 1992, and they came from numerous manufacturers with prices under $100 for the first time. Finally, the market started to simmer. A broad range of consumer applications and acceptance of the technology grew.

Polar's innovation in heart rate monitoring continues today to lead the field in technology. By 1995 the company had introduced the Vantage NV, which included more firsts such as coded transmission. Each monitor had its own unique signal eliminating interference known as cross-talk. Next Polar introduced a monitor that had R-to-R recording, which measures the time between each individual heartbeat. The Vantage NV came with sophisticated Microsoft Windows analysis software. Recently, the Finland-based company has added even more technology and features in different models that are designed to help individuals with measurement and motivation as follows:

- Caloric expenditure estimations
- Training zone estimates
- Estimations of fitness improvements
- Estimations of oxygen consumption

Here are just a few of the innovative heart rate technologies that were first introduced by Polar Electro Oy:

1977 The first battery-operated fingertip pulsemeter

1978 The first hard-wired heart rate monitor: Tunturi Pulser

1983 The first wireless heart rate monitor: Sport Tester PE 2000

1984 The first heart rate monitor that downloads into a computer

1985 The first computer software that works with a personal heart rate monitor

1986 The first heart rate analysis software for the computer

1987 The first heart rate monitor that calculates time in zone

1990 The first wireless bike computer and heart rate monitor: The Cyclovantage

1992 The first integrated one-piece transmitter unit

1991 Introduction of low-priced heart rate monitors (under $100)

1994 Nightvision in heart rate monitors

1995 First monitor with coded transmission and with R-R recording and analysis: Polar Vantage NV

1997 First heart rate monitor to use R-R recordings to estimate training zones and calorie consumption

1999 First heart rate monitor to estimate oxygen consumption and fitness improvement

2000 The convergence of heart rate, altitude, and bike functions (such as power output) into one unit. The first monitor to use "sonic link" for downloading into PC Coach software

2001 More than twenty manufacturers and one hundred models available to consumers. Heart rate applications available on mobile PDA devices

What does the future hold for heart rate monitor manufacturing? Here are several predictions for the next decade:

- New advances by Polar and other manufacturers that continue to drive new product innovation and technology
- Market forces continuing to drive down price, resulting in fewer manufacturers
- New applications for heart rate technology within other technologies
- Development of wearable heart rate monitors that use automatic synchronization technologies, such as Bluetooth web-based applications and cell phone integration
- Plug-and-play features that make using a monitor easier
- Price competition and new manufacturers
- Performance monitors that use a new sensor technology eliminating the need for a chest strap
- Single-appliance monitors that include all bio-information: blood pressure, cholesterol, heart rate, body composition, and more

What does the future hold for heart zones training, the application of heart rate monitoring? Here are several predictions for the next decade:

- Manufacturers becoming more involved in the development of applications for their products
- Enhanced applications such as heart zone training used for diagnosing diseases, helping the aging population, aiding individuals with special needs
- Mass and universal acceptance of the technology for both its cosmetic appeal and its functional use
- Development of powerful monitors that measure psychological stress and its commensurate biofeedback power
- Web-based applications for heart rate
- Enhanced software that powers both client and server applications
- Sport-specific applications and monitors for tennis, rowing, aerobics, step walking, and other unique events

The future looks promising. More than thirty years ago, cartoon character Dick Tracy wore a watch telephone on his wrist. Today, Finland's Nokia is finally catching up with Dick Tracy. Only twenty years ago, wristwatch heart rate monitoring and heart zones training began. Today, Finland's Polar is manufacturing leading-edge heart rate monitor technology. Can the two converge with a digital, wireless, telephone heart rate monitor that communicates with you via the Internet? Probably.

## STEP 9: Logging Your Workouts and Rides

As you start to practice the habits of the Ten Steps to Heart Zones Cycling, you may find that keeping a diary of your rides can be one of the most enjoyable parts of training because it's a chance to record the event. As you record information about your ride, the process and the words can become motivational. It gives you a way to compare your riding plan from Step 7 with the actual rides in Step 9. By recording these quantifying characteristics, you'll be able to maximize your workouts and rides and fine-tune your riding program, as well as eliminate certain rides and workouts that don't help you achieve your goals.

You'll quickly discover you like to record certain information. It might be average heart rate because it's useful for measuring improvement—or just because you like numbers.

It takes less than five minutes a day to fill out a log sheet, but the information you record can be used for a lifetime. Furthermore, a well-kept log is far superior to relying on sheer memory when you want to recall a training period that led to achieving a goal. Share your log with others and ask them for their support and evaluation.

If you've never kept a log, now is the time. Copy the blank pages provided, use software, or purchase *The Heart Rate Monitor Log Book for Outdoor and Indoor Cyclists* (VeloPress 2000).

## STEP 10: Reassessing Your Fitness Level

Measuring progress and improvement may be one of the most valuable uses of your heart rate monitor. By performing biweekly and monthly fitness tests, you will know if your training program is working or if you are overtraining. Perform these assessments and workouts both on and off the bike on a regular basis, then record the results in your training log.

**Off the Bike (every two to four weeks)**

1. Resting Heart Rate
2. Ambient Heart Rate
3. Delta Heart Rate

| Date | Sport Activity | Distance | Time | TIME IN ZONE | | | | |
|---|---|---|---|---|---|---|---|---|
| | | | | Zone 1 | Zone 2 | Zone 3 | Zone 4 | Zone 5 |
| | | | | | | | | |
| | | | | | | | | |
| | | | | | | | | |
| | | | | | | | | |
| | | | | | | | | |
| | | | | | | | | |
| | | | | | | | | |
| | | | | | | | | |
| | | | | | | | | |
| | | | | | | | | |
| | | | | | | | | |
| | | | | | | | | |
| | | | | | | | | |
| | | | | | | | | |
| | | | | | | | | |
| | | | | | | | | |
| | | | | | | | | |
| | | | | | | | | |
| | | | | | | | | |
| | | | | | | | | |
| | | | | | | | | |
| | | | | | | | | |
| | | | | | | | | |
| | | | | | | | | |
| | | | | | | | | |
| | | | | | | | | |
| Weekly Summary | | | | | | | | |
| | | | | | | | | |
| | | | | | | | | |
| Year-to-Date Summary | | | | | | | | |
| | | | | | | | | |
| | | | | | | | | |
| Notes: | | | | | | | | |
| | | | | | | | | |
| | | | | | | | | |

| Key Workout Type | Average Heart Rate | Rating A+ to F or 1 to 10 | Strength Training Time | Stretching Time | % Fat/ Body Weight | A.M. Heart Rate | Altitude Changes | Total HZT Points |
|---|---|---|---|---|---|---|---|---|
| | | | | | | | | |
| | | | | | | | | |
| | | | | | | | | |
| | | | | | | | | |
| | | | | | | | | |
| | | | | | | | | |
| | | | | | | | | |
| | | | | | | | | |
| | | | | | | | | |
| | | | | | | | | |
| | | | | | | | | |
| | | | | | | | | |
| | | | | | | | | |
| | | | | | | | | |
| | | | | | | | | |
| | | | | | | | | |
| | | | | | | | | |
| | | | | | | | | |
| | | | | | | | | |
| | | | | | | | | |
| | | | | | | | | |
| | | | | | | | | |
| | | | | | | | | |
| | | | | | | | | |
| | | | | | | | | |

**Notes:**

| Date | Sport Activity | Distance | Time | Zone 1 | Zone 2 | Zone 3 | Zone 4 | Zone 5 |
|------|----------------|----------|------|--------|--------|--------|--------|--------|
| | | | | | | TIME IN ZONE | | |
| 3/15 | Swim | 1,000 yd | 30 min | 3 min | 15 min | 12 min | — | — |
| | | | 1:00 | | | | | |
| 3/16 | Bike | 8 mi | 1:30 | — | 10 min | 60 min | — | — |
| 3/17 | Rest Day | | | | | | | |
| 3/18 | Bike | 18 mi | 1:15 | — | 9 min | 41 min | 25 min | 6 min |
| 3/19 | Run | 5 mi | 45 min | 9 min | 12 min | 28 min | — | — |
| 3/20 | Bike | 20 mi | 1:15 | — | 15 min | 60 min | — | — |
| 3/21 | Rest or alternate activity | | | | | | | |
| Weekly Summary | Swim | 1,000 yd | :30 | 3 min | 15 min | 12 min | — | — |
| | Bike | 38 mi | 3:30 | — | 24 min | 1:21 | 25 min | 6 min |
| | Run | 5 mi | :45 | 9 min | 12 min | :28 | 0 min | — |
| Year-to-Date Summary | Swim | 8,500 yd | 12:30 | 42 min | 6:45 | 8:42 | — | — |
| | Bike | 380 mi | 20:30 | — | 8:45 | 14:00 | 8:00 | 6:00 |
| | Run | 190 mi | 30:10 | 4:30 | 6:45 | 10:58 | 10:30 | — |

**Notes:** *I am really enjoying this training period. The feeling of getting fitter is wonderful.*

| Key Workout Type | Average Heart Rate | Rating A+ to F or 1 to 10 | Strength Training Time | Stretching Time | % Fat/ Body Weight | A.M. Heart Rate | Altitude Changes | Total HZT Points |
|---|---|---|---|---|---|---|---|---|
| | | | | | | | | |
| Interval | 157 | B | 15 min | 20 min | 27% | 63 | 1,000' | 69 |
| | | | | | 154 lb | | | |
| Interval | 149 | A | 0 | 15 min | 27% | 61 | 1,500' | 200 |
| | | | | | 155 lb | | | |
| | | | | | | | | |
| | | | | | | | | |
| | | | | | | | | |
| | | | | | | | | |
| | | | | | | | | |
| | | | | | | | | 271 |
| | | | | | | | | |
| | | | | | | | | |
| Steady- State | 152 | A– | 15 min | 10 min | 28% 155 lb | 62 | 500' | 230 |
| | | | | | | | | |
| | | | | | | | | 210 |
| | | | | | | | | |
| | | | | | | | | |
| | | | | | | | | |
| | | | | | | | | |
| | | | | | | | | |
| | 151 | A- | 30 min | 45 min | 155 lb | 62 | 3,000' | 980 |
| | | | | | | | | |
| | | | | | | | | |
| | | B | | | | | | 26,222 |
| | | | | | | | | |

**Notes:** *Happy with consistency. Followed my training plan. Earned a B+, which keeps me motivated.*

*Weight is steady.*

**Indoor Training (every two to three months)**

1. Recovery Intervals Workout (Chapter 5, workout 17)

2. Two-by-Twenty Anaerobic Threshold Test (Chapter 5, workout 20)

**Outdoor Rides (every one to three months)**

1. Recovery Interval Ride (Chapter 4, workout 15)

2. Distance Improvement Ride (Chapter 5, workout 21)

3. Anaerobic Threshold Ride (Chapter 5, workout 22)

4. Aerobic Time Trial (Chapter 5, workout 23)

5. All-Out Time Trial (Chapter 5, workout 24 )

6. Spitfire (Chapter 7, workout 38)

7. Head for the Hills (Chapter 7, workout 39)

8. Hill-Billy (Chapter 8, workout 48)

## WORKOUTS: Indoor Training

### 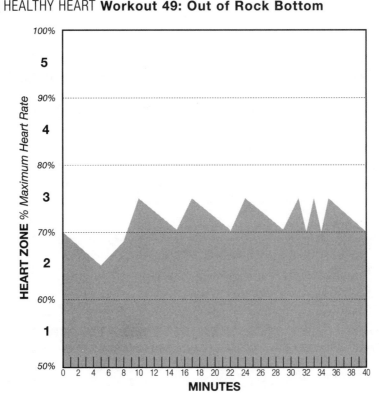 HEALTHY HEART **Workout 49: Out of Rock Bottom**

### Overview

We've all had days when we've gone to the depths, hit our rock bottom. From down in those black pits, the struggle to get out engages the heart. One of the best ways out of rock bottom is to climb out step by step, pedal stroke by pedal stroke. Even Tigger in *Winnie the Pooh* couldn't bounce out of his rock bottom in one leap. When you crest the top and climb out of the hole, you can look down and feel the accomplishment of being out. Next time, avoid riding the road that took you there.

One way to avoid rock bottom is to train with your heart. That's what this workout is about.

### Description

This workout strengthens your cardiovascular system by pushing you to 75 percent of your maximum heart rate, or the midpoint of your Aerobic Zone (zone 3), with four challenging intervals. The first two intervals develop your sprint capability, and the second two concentrate on leg strength and power. It might surprise you how fast forty minutes will pass. That's because climbing out of rock bottom is a movement in the right direction; it is toward the positive. The Japanese expression *kaizen* is pertinent to this workout: Try making small, constant improvement. *Kaizen* your ride by improving 1 percent a hundred times to equal a 100 percent improvement.

| Stats and Tips for Workout 49: Out of Rock Bottom | | | |
|---|---|---|---|
| Zone Number and Name | Minutes in Zone | Heart Zones Training Points | Estimated Calories |
| 5. Red-Line | | | |
| 4. Threshold | | | |
| 3. Aerobic | 18 | 54 | 162–198 |
| 2. Temperate | 22 | 44 | 132–176 |
| 1. Healthy Heart | | | |
| Totals | 40 | 98 | 294–374 |

**Tip:** Riding is a positive experience that can help you recover from personal challenges that negatively pull you toward rock bottom.

| Sequence for Workout 49: Out of Rock Bottom | | | | |
|---|---|---|---|---|
| Elapsed Time (min.) | Workout Plan | Heart Zone | Your Heart Rate (bpm) | Interval Time (min.) |
| 0–5 | Warm up to bottom of Z2 | 2 | _____ | 5 |
| 5–8 | Increase HR to midpoint of Z2 (65%) with cadence/rpm | 2 | _____ | 3 |
| 8–10 | Increase HR 5 bpm from midpoint of Z2, cadence/rpm | 3 | _____ | 2 |
| 10–24 | Increase HR gradually to midpoint of Z3 (75%) by the following: 10 sec. sprint/50 sec. (rec), 15 sec. sprint/45 sec. (rec), 20 sec. sprint/40 sec. (rec), 25 sec. sprint/35 sec. (rec), 30 sec. sprint/30 sec. (rec), (Rec) to bottom of Z2, 2 min. Repeat a total of 2 times | 3<br><br><br><br>2 | _____<br><br><br><br>_____ | 14 |
| 24–29 | Increase HR to midpoint of Z3 (75%) by performing the following 1 min. interval: 45 sec. moderate (R) 15 sec. increase rpm. Repeat a total of 5 times | 3 | _____ | 5 |
| 29–31 | (Rec) bottom of Z2 | 2 | _____ | 2 |
| 31–36 | Ups and Downs:[a] Increase HR from bottom of Z2 to midpoint of Z3, then (rec) to bottom of Z2 and begin interval again. Count number of times up to midpoint of Z3 and down to bottom of Z2 in 5 min. | 3<br>2 | _____<br>_____ | 5 |
| 36–40 | Warm down to bottom of Z2 | 2 | _____ | 4 |

[a] Count the number of times you increase heart rate and recover in a set period of time.

## FITNESS **Workout 50: Fast Lane**

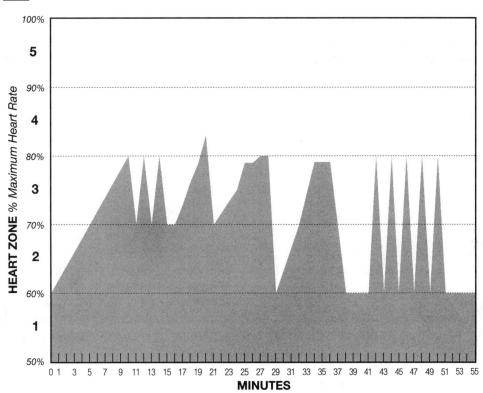

## Overview

Life can be ridden in the fast lane. For most cyclists, this is the place to be. The Fast Lane workout is an expressway to getting faster and stronger as you look back just long enough to appreciate where you started.

## Description

This workout is designed to enhance the functional capacity of the heart, lungs, and vascular system. You will push yourself through the Aerobic Zone and into the anaerobic Threshold Zone. You will get a brief taste of training with less oxygen and with an increased feeling of acidosis from the accumulation of lactic acid in your bloodstream and in your cycling-specific muscles. You'll enjoy your time spent in Zone 3 because you can release both emotionally and physically some of your stored-up toxins. Training in zone 3 also builds resistance to fatigue and increases cardiovascular efficiency. Fast-lane riding trains the metabolic pathways to spare carbohydrates and instead metabolize fatty acids. Some riders get almost addicted to the Fast

Lane workout, not just because it's fun but because of those wonderful, natural, mood-altering endorphins that are produced so plentifully in zones 3 and 4.

| Stats and Tips for Workout 50: Fast Lane | | | |
|---|---|---|---|
| Zone Number and Name | Minutes in Zone | Heart Zones Training Points | Estimated Calories |
| 5. Red-Line | | | |
| 4. Threshold | 11 | 44 | 132–154 |
| 3. Aerobic | 24 | 72 | 216–264 |
| 2. Temperate | 20 | 40 | 120–160 |
| 1. Healthy Heart | | | |
| Totals | 55 | 156 | 468–578 |

**Tip:** During hard pedaling, allow your foot to fall (float) without exerting force every three or four strokes. This helps delay muscle fatigue.

| Sequence for Workout 50: Fast Lane | | | | |
|---|---|---|---|---|
| Elapsed Time (min.) | Workout Plan | Heart Zone | Your Heart Rate (bpm) | Interval Time (min.) |
| 0–10 | Warm up gradually to bottom of Z2 | 2 | \_\_\_\_\_ | 10 |
| 10–16 | From bottom of Z2 add approximately 30 bpm to midpoint of Z3 in 1 min., then (rec) to the bottom of Z2 in 1 min. Repeat a total of 3 times | 3 2 | \_\_\_\_\_ \_\_\_\_\_ | 6 |
| 16–21 | From the bottom of Z2 add 5 bpm each min. for 5 min. using (R) and 80 rpm (8) | 3 4 | \_\_\_\_\_ \_\_\_\_\_ | 5 |
| 21–24 | (Rec) to the bottom of Z2 | 2 | \_\_\_\_\_ | 3 |
| 24–29 | 5 min. interval—alternate 10 sec. "on"[a] and 10 sec. "off"[b]—standing and seated | 3 4 | \_\_\_\_\_ \_\_\_\_\_ | 5 |
| 29–32 | (Rec) to the bottom of Z2 | 2 | \_\_\_\_\_ | 3 |
| 32–38 | 6 min. interval—30 sec. super spin[c] and 30 sec. easy pedal (rec). Repeat a total of 6 times | 3 | \_\_\_\_\_ | 6 |
| 38–42 | (Rec) to bottom of Z2 | 2 | \_\_\_\_\_ | 4 |
| 42–52 | From bottom of Z2 increase HR to the bottom of Z4 in 1 min. all-out effort. (Rec) to Z2 in 1 min. Repeat a total of 5 times | 4 2 | \_\_\_\_\_ \_\_\_\_\_ | 10 |
| 52–55 | Gradually warm down to Z2 and Z1 | 2 1 | \_\_\_\_\_ \_\_\_\_\_ | 3 |

**Note:** For a performance workout, increase to 90 percent of maximum heart rate.

[a] Work interval (hard pedal) for specific amount of time.
[b] Recovery interval (easy pedal) for specific amount of time.
[c] Controlled pedaling or spinning above 120 rpm.

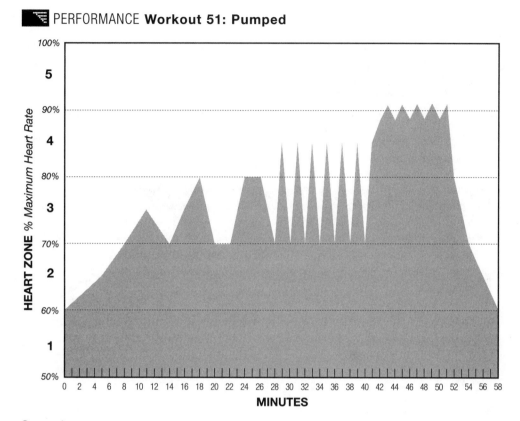

PERFORMANCE **Workout 51: Pumped**

## Overview

Circuit training is a highly effective way of exercising. Circuit skill training on a bike—such as is done in the Pumped workout—is a specific application of the circuit training system. During each of five tough interval sets, you will work on a simulated circuit station, each featuring one of five specific cycling skills, with a recovery between each station. The benefit of training this way is that you improve your cycling skills, add variety to your workout, and get a great heart-pumping workout.

## Description

There are five different stations in the Pumped circuit training workout:
- Interval 1: Strength circuit station
- Interval 2: Tempo circuit (steady-state) station
- Interval 3: Power circuit station
- Interval 4: Cadence circuit station
- Interval 5: Anaerobic threshold circuit station

During each interval, focus on the training method that applies to that interval. For example, when you are doing the fourth interval, stay in the mind-set throughout the 3-minute stress period of pedaling at a very high cadence. During the recovery period that follows each interval, stay in the relaxation and active-rest mind-set to lower your heart rate as quickly as possible. One way to stay in the moment is to focus on the numbers on your monitor, which should be mounted on your handlebars. Your heart rate monitor will show how your energy level is pumped when you finish this workout.

| Stats and Tips for Workout 51: Pumped | | | |
|---|---|---|---|
| Zone Number and Name | Minutes in Zone | Heart Zones Training Points | Estimated Calories |
| 5. Red-Line | 5 | 25 | 75–100 |
| 4. Threshold | 20 | 80 | 240–280 |
| 3. Aerobic | 23 | 69 | 207–253 |
| 2. Temperate | 10 | 20 | 60–80 |
| 1. Healthy Heart | | | |
| Totals | 58 | 194 | 582–713 |

**Tip:** Maximum sustainable heart rate is one of the best predictors of racing success.

| Sequence for Workout 51: Pumped | | | | |
|---|---|---|---|---|
| Elapsed Time (min.) | Workout Plan | Heart Zone | Your Heart Rate (bpm) | Interval Time (min.) |
| 0–5 | Warm up to bottom of Z2, easy pedal | 2 | \_\_\_\_\_ | 5 |
| 5–8 | From bottom of Z2, increase HR 10 bpm, 90 rpm (9) | 2 | \_\_\_\_\_ | 3 |
| 8–14 | Increase HR to bottom of Z3 and sustain for 3 min., then increase HR 10 more bpm for 3 min. | 3 | \_\_\_\_\_ | 6 |
| 14–24 | Isolated-leg training[a] (ILT), changing legs every min., at 60 rpm (6) beginning at bottom of Z3 and increasing HR gradually by adding (R) to bottom of Z4 | 3 4 | \_\_\_\_\_ \_\_\_\_\_ | 10 |
| 24–26 | Pedal with both legs 60 rpm (6) to midpoint of Z4 | 4 | \_\_\_\_\_ | 2 |
| 26–28 | Super spin[b] at 120+ rpm (12), sustain at bottom of Z4 | 4 | \_\_\_\_\_ | 2 |
| 28–29 | Easy pedal (rec) to bottom of Z3 | 3 | \_\_\_\_\_ | 1 |
| 29–37 | From a slow easy pedal, 1 min. fast, hard effort to midpoint of Z4 with heavy (R), followed by 1 min. easy pedal (rec) to bottom of Z3. Repeat a total of 4 times | 4 3 | \_\_\_\_\_ \_\_\_\_\_ | 8 |
| 37–42 | From bottom of Z3, heavy (R) standing, 60 rpm (6), increase HR to midpoint of Z4 and sustain for 1 min., then easy pedal (rec), seated, to bottom of Z3, 90 rpm (9). Repeat a total of 3 times | 3 4 | \_\_\_\_\_ \_\_\_\_\_ | 5 |
| 42–43 | Increase HR to AT and sustain for 1 min. | 4 | \_\_\_\_\_ | 1 |
| 43–53 | Increase HR to 5 bpm above AT and sustain for 1 min., then decrease HR 5 bpm for 1 min. Repeat 5 bpm interval a total of 5 times | 4–5 | \_\_\_\_\_ | 10 |
| 53–54 | Decrease HR to bottom of Z4 | 4 | \_\_\_\_\_ | 1 |
| 54–58 | Decrease HR to bottom of Z3 for 2 min., then warm down to bottom of Z2 | 3 2 | \_\_\_\_\_ \_\_\_\_\_ | 4 |

[a] Pedaling with one leg at a time, resting the other on a box or stool. You may also choose to keep both feet in the pedals and allow one leg to relax while the other leg does the work.

[b] High rpm or pedaling cadence. Usually 120 rpm or higher, keeping the pedal stroke smooth and efficient. Pedal only as fast as you can stay in control.

## PERFORMANCE **Workout 52: Seattle Ridge**

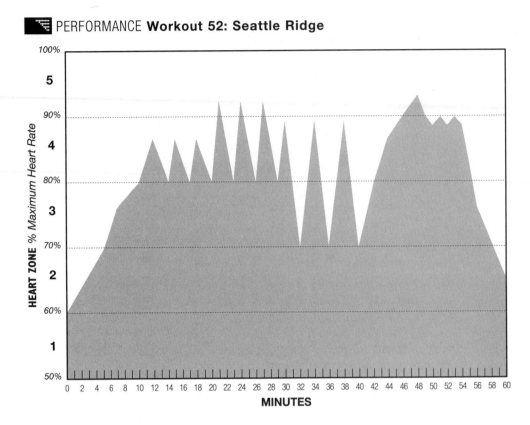

## Overview

Seven hills dot sea-level Seattle, Washington, one of the homes of Heart Zones Cycling. None of them, however, is named after Chief Seattle, the Native American who first encountered the white settlers of the Northwest. Rather, Seattle Ridge, a popular ski run, is located high in the mountains of Sun Valley, Idaho. Therefore, this is an appropriate name for a ride that will make you feel you are pedaling at high altitude with a low concentration of the food that lungs crave—oxygen. If you feel the acidic taste of too much Red-Line time, then you will have ridden this workout with total commitment. Baldy, Sun Valley's largest ski mountain, is over 9,000 feet high, and this workout gives you the sensation of climbing it from bottom to top more than once.

## Description

Most riders love the Seattle Ridge workout because one-third of the riding time is in the Threshold and the Red-Line Zones—zones 4 and 5. Every rider pays a price for hanging out in such high and hot zones. That price is totally individual—so watch for the symptoms of too much high-intensity training. As you ride Seattle Ridge's 20- and 40-bpm intervals, choose between using speed or resistance to ascend and descend each one. For an even harder ride, raise your front wheel 4 to 6 inches off the ground by putting a support underneath the wheel or the bike frame. The result resembles the more acute feeling of climbing steep hills.

| Stats for Workout 52: Seattle Ridge | | | |
|---|---|---|---|
| Zone Number and Name | Minutes in Zone | Heart Zones Training Points | Estimated Calories |
| 5. Red-Line | 12 | 60 | 180–240 |
| 4. Threshold | 28 | 112 | 336–392 |
| 3. Aerobic | 12 | 36 | 108–132 |
| 2. Temperate | 8 | 16 | 48–64 |
| 1. Healthy Heart | | | |
| Totals | 60 | 224 | 672–828 |

**Tip:** Overreaching is a way of exercising at high training loads but without reaching a point of damage as in overtraining. For even more information on overtraining, an excellent resource is Ackland 1996 (pp. 133–140).

| Sequence for Workout 52: Seattle Ridge | | | | |
|---|---|---|---|---|
| Elapsed Time (min.) | Workout Plan | Heart Zone | Your Heart Rate (bpm) | Interval Time (min.) |
| 0–5 | Warm up to bottom of Z2 (60%), easy pedal | 2 | _____ | 5 |
| 5–10 | Increase HR gradually to midpoint of Z3 (75%) with cadence/rpm | 3 | _____ | 5 |
| 10–14 | **10 bpm interval:** Increase HR to the bottom of Z4 for 2 min.,steady cadence, increase (R). Increase HR to midpoint of Z4 (85%) for 2 min., steady cadence, increase (R). Seated | 4 4 | _____ _____ | 4 |
| 14–20 | (Rec) to bottom of Z4 for 1 min., easy pedal, then increase HR to midpoint of Z4 for 2 min. using (R), steady cadence. Repeat | 4 4 | _____ _____ | 6 |
| 20–29 | **20 bpm interval:** Increase HR from bottom of Z4 to bottom of Z5 in 2 min., using (R), steady cadence. (Rec) to bottom of Z4 in 1 min., easy pedal. Repeat a total of 3 times | 5 4 | _____ _____ | 9 |
| 29–43 | **40 bpm interval:** Increase HR to bottom of Z5 in 2 min., sprint with (R). (Rec) to bottom of Z3 in 2 min., easy pedal. Repeat a total of 3 times | 5 3 | _____ _____ | 14 |
| 43–44 | Increase HR to bottom of Z4, choice | 4 | _____ | 1 |
| 44–46 | Increase HR 10 bpm to midpoint of Z4, choice | 4 | _____ | 2 |
| 46–48 | Increase HR to bottom of Z5, choice | 5 | _____ | 2 |
| 48–49 | All-out sprint for peak HR | 5 | _____ | 1 |
| 49–55 | Decrease HR to bottom of Z5 for 1 min., then decrease HR 5 bpm more for 1 min., then increase 5 bpm for 1 min. Drop 5 bpm for 1 min., add 5 bpm for 1 min., and finally drop 5 bpm for 1 min. | 5 4 | _____ _____ | 6 |
| 55–60 | Decrease 10 bpm every minute as warm-down into Z2 | 2 | _____ | 5 |

## Outdoor Training and Rides

### Workout 53: SOS

Spin, optimal power, and sprint (SOS) are the three intervals to remember for this ride. In fact, maximum sustainable power is really the second interval, but we've called it optimal power to help you remember what to do on the ride. These three interval sets can be worked into almost any ride you are doing. For the first interval spin, you will want to be completely warmed up and have picked a nice long, flat stretch in the road. The purpose is to work on your pedal stroke by increasing your cadence 10 rpm every 10 seconds starting with 70 rpm and finishing at 110 rpm. Start in an easy gear (small chainring) and keep your pedal stroke smooth and round. Pedal in the shape of circles rather than squares, concentrating on the image of scraping mud off the bottom of your shoe as the pedal goes around at the bottom of the stroke. Recover to the bottom of zone 2 and immediately begin another set. Repeat five times total.

| Ride Snapshot |
|---|
| ➢ 20–30 min. warm-up |
| ➢ Spin 70 rpm, easy gearing (small chainring), increase cadence 10 rpm every 10 sec. for 1 min., (rec) bottom of Z2. Repeat a total of 5 times. |
| ➢ Optimal power 110 rpm, biggest gear you can ride for 1 min., zone 4, followed by 1 min. (rec). Repeat a total of 2 times. |
| ➢ Sprint 1–5 min., easy gear, high cadence, 10–20 miles per hour, 10 sec. standing, 10 sec. seated (rec), zone 4. Build up toward a total of 5 minutes. |
| ➢ Warm down or continue ride |

Cyclists train to develop power and to sustain a high power output. This next interval set will help to do just that. Again, you will need a fairly flat stretch of road where you can ride for at least 10 minutes without interruptions or hills. Choose the biggest gear you can ride in at 110 rpm. Sustain this cadence and gearing for 1 minute followed by a 1-minute recovery. Repeat one more time. As you get fitter, work your way up to sustaining this interval for 3 minutes with a 3-minute recovery and then repeat. This will take you well into zone 4 if you do the ride correctly. As you get fitter, you will notice your recovery heart rate dropping faster because your heart is getting stronger. You will also be able to push a bigger gear at the same cadence, which means your muscles are getting stronger.

The third interval is a sprint. These sprints are all done in a standing position, which will help your balance and confidence. Look for another 10-minute flat stretch in the road. In an easy gear, bring your speed up to 10 to 20 miles per hour. Come out of the saddle in a standing position for 10 seconds at a high cadence or pedal speed, then sit down and recover for 10 seconds. Repeat as many times as you can, building toward a total of 5 minutes. Finish by recovering down to zone 2 with an easy pedal. This interval set will get your heart rate well into zone 4.

Remember, SOS is a ride to improve your overall fitness.

## Workout 54: Sign Here, Press Hard

This is a fun game to play and one that my friend Duane loves to include when things get a little slow. He will pick out a sign anywhere from 200 to 300 yards away and challenge anyone to beat him to it. Ready, set, go! It's the pedal to the metal and a fun way to work on your sprints and fast starts. If you are only slightly competitive, you will want to make the game the best three out of five sprints. Duane always catches me off guard on the first one, and I like to think I get smarter and faster as the game goes on. Just make sure the signs aren't stop signs, and give yourself plenty of recovery between sprints. Plan on seeing some high heart rate numbers on this workout, especially if the sprints are longer than 300 yards.

## Workout 55: Hill Sprints

Hills are our friends. Like headwinds, they make us stronger. It's all a matter of attitude and what your training goals are. If you want to be stronger, then sooner or later hills will be in your plan. You can expect your heart rate to go well into zone 4 and even zone 5 if you are giving it your best effort. It also will depend on the length of the hill. The longer the hill for these sprints, the higher the heart rate.

| Ride Snapshot |
| --- |
| ⟩ Fast cadence halfway up the hill, shift to big chainring, sprint over the top, zones 4–5, (rec) to bottom of zone 2. Repeat 2 to 5 times. |
| ⟩ Warm down or continue ride |
| ⟩ Tip—How to measure the steepness of a hill. The inclination, or the ascent or descent gradient, of a hill is determined by the following: Each 1 foot of elevation gain over a distance of 100 feet equals a 1 percent gradient. One hundred feet is about the length of two semitrucks. |

Find a gradual hill 200 to 400 yards long. Spin halfway up, then shift into the big chainring and sprint over the top. Try two to five repeats with complete recovery between efforts. As you get stronger over time, shift to harder gears in the back and stay with your big chainring in the front. Always try to finish strong on your last repeat, as if you were sprinting for the finish line.

## Workout 56: Snookie

When I (Sally Edwards) was growing up, my family had a dog named Snookie. He was the best and most loyal dog any kid could ever want. Throw him a stick day or night, and he would fetch it faster than greased lighting. Wherever my friends and I were, Snookie was there too. Even when we were riding our bikes, Snookie was always just behind, ears flopping, tongue dragging, and tail wagging. Are you like that—giving it your all? This ride will build that Snookie-type of persistence to help you power and train your anaerobic threshold.

Warm up in zone 2 for 20 to 30 minutes. Find a flat road about 5 to 6 miles long. Begin by riding in a 53/18 gear at an rpm you can sustain for 3 to 5 minutes. Keep your heart rate around 75 percent. Shift to a harder gear, such as 53/16, and an rpm you can sustain for 3 to 5 minutes. Keep your heart rate around 80 percent. Shift to a harder gear, 53/14, and an rpm you can sustain for 3 to 5 minutes. Keep your heart rate around 85 percent. Shift to your hardest gear, 53/12, and an rpm you can sustain for 3 to 5 minutes. Keep your heart rate at or just below 90 percent. Easy-pedal recovery in zone 2 for the next 5 minutes.

| Ride Snapshot |
| --- |
| ⋗ Warm up 20–30 min. |
| ⋗ 3–5 min. @ 53/18 (75%) |
| ⋗ 3–5 min. @ 53/16 (80%) |
| ⋗ 3–5 min. @ 53/14 (85%) |
| ⋗ 3–5 min. @ 53/12 (90%) |
| ⋗ 5 min. (rec) zone 2 |
| ⋗ 20-sec. big-gear sprints, 5 times, with 1 min. (rec) between sprints |
| ⋗ Ride home zone 2 |

In a big gear, do five 20-second sprints with a 1-minute recovery between each sprint. Ride home in zone 2 to recover and warm down.

# REFERENCES

Ackland, John. *Power to Perform: A Comprehensive Guide to Training and Racing for Endurance Athletes.* Auckland, NZ: Reed Publishing, 1996.

# 10
# Your Training Ride Program: The 10 Steps

*As you've heard repeatedly, training is an individual process. You'll now apply this principle as you journey through the ten steps to training with your heart monitor. On one level, the ten steps are quite simple; on another level, they take you into the individual process of riding at your best.*

*Richard Elstine was captivated by this potential. A forty-eight-year-old mathematically minded man, Richard struggled constantly with the limits of time. He had only thirty minutes a day to ride and squeezed the most out of every training heartbeat. He completed more than 1,000 heart zones training sessions, all on an indoor cycle, with a manually downloadable heart rate monitor.*

*The significance wasn't Richard's ability to persist and keep track of five years of workouts with his monitor and remain totally motivated, but that with only thirty minutes of daily workout—2.5 hours of training time a week—every year he got fitter. Furthermore, Richard could measure and prove it using his monitor.*

*At first I questioned whether such improvement was possible when he invested so little time, but after seeing the graphs and analyzing his data, I was convinced Richard's fitness levels were progressively improving. His intensive recording and analysis occasionally astonished me, but the process worked for Richard. Using his monitor made him happy. He was excited about writing goals, tracking changes, and sharing his work with others.*

*Richard preferred to keep his records in pencil and place them in binders. (Other people like to record them in the companion log to this book,* The Heart Rate Monitor Log Book for Outdoor and Indoor Cyclists, *or use a software program.) Recently, he outlined a new hypothesis he'll test for a year. His goal is to prove that the heart zones are progressive. He believes that by training entirely in heart zones 3 through 5, he will get the benefits of all five zones.*

—SALLY EDWARDS

## THE TEN STEPS

It's time now to extract from earlier chapters the information to assemble your training program. You've already done the work; this is where you'll put it together. You might be tempted to skip this section; please don't. Finish the brief process of putting together the ten steps. Invest the effort now, and it will pay off in improved fitness and a sense of accomplishment. Indeed, the ten steps are the beginning of a lifetime journey.

### STEP 1. *Estimating Your Maximum Heart Rate*

_____ bpm

### STEP 2. *Choosing Your Goals*

Goal writing is an important step, because if you haven't set a clear destination, it's difficult to get there. Most of us ride and train to accomplish something new. Review your goals and again list them briefly here.

Short-term goals: _____

_____

Long-term goals: _____

_____

_____

### STEP 3. *Setting Your Heart Zones*

| Zone Number and Name | Percentage of Maximum Heart Rate | Your Heart Zones |
|---|---|---|
| 5. Red-Line Zone | 90–100% | _____ bpm |
| 4. Threshold Zone | 80–90% | _____ bpm |
| 3. Aerobic Zone | 70–80% | _____ bpm |
| 2. Temperate Zone | 60–70% | _____ bpm |
| 1. Healthy Heart Zone | 50–60% | _____ bpm |

### STEP 4. *Creating Your 30-Day Program*

To get fit, you need to ride in different zones on different rides. Some days your ride will be high-intensity, in high heart zones. Other days will be for recovery. It's this variability—this commitment to taking the monotony out of your rides—that will stimulate your effort to achieve increased fitness.

Take the total time you have committed to riding and break it down into minutes to assign to the different heart zones.

### STEP 5. *Determining Your Training Spokes*

Fill out your training wheel (see the sample in Chapter 5).

### STEP 6. *Assessing Your Current Level of Fitness*

Determine how fit you are now. You can find your current fitness level by taking some training rides and measuring a few parameters. Where on the training wheel are you currently?

### STEP 7. *Writing Your Training Plan*

Make a plan to accomplish the goals you set in step 2. Your success will bring a sense of accomplishment and improved self-esteem.

### STEP 8. *Analyzing Your Training Ride Plan*

Is your plan realistic? If so, it will keep you on your bike, motivated, and getting faster. Beginners should use the following sample 12-week training program as a guide:

| Sample 12-Week Training Program for Fitness | | | | | |
|---|---|---|---|---|---|
| **Weekly Time in Zone (min.)** | | | | | |
| **Week** | **Zone 1** Healthy Heart | **Zone 2** Temperate | **Zone 3** Aerobic | **Zone 4** Threshold | **Zone 5** Red-Line | **Total Workout** Time (min.) |
| *Base Training* | | | | | | |
| 1 | 30 | 30 | 0 | 0 | 0 | 60 |
| 2 | 55 | 65 | 0 | 0 | 0 | 120 |
| 3 | 40 | 140 | 0 | 0 | 0 | 180 |
| 4 | 30 | 140 | 30 | 0 | 0 | 200 |
| 5 | 20 | 160 | 50 | 0 | 0 | 230 |
| *Endurance Training* | | | | | | |
| 6 | 15 | 175 | 80 | 0 | 0 | 270 |
| 7 | 0 | 190 | 90 | 0 | 0 | 280 |
| 8 | 0 | 180 | 110 | 0 | 0 | 290 |
| 9 | 0 | 170 | 130 | 0 | 0 | 300 |
| 10 | 0 | 160 | 155 | 0 | 0 | 315 |
| *Strength Training* | | | | | | |
| 11 | 0 | 170 | 140 | 20 | 0 | 330 |
| 12 | 0 | 180 | 150 | 30 | 0 | 360 |

### STEP 9. *Logging Your Workouts and Rides*

All the tools for recording your workouts are provided here. You'll author a book about your-self and riding your bike, filling it with a year's worth of riding information and impressions of your growth and development as an athlete. (See the sample log pages in Chapter 9.)

### STEP 10. *Reassessing Your Fitness Level*

You've now come full circle. One of your early steps was to determine how fit you were on your bike. If your training program is working, it's easy to measure your success with a heart rate monitor and possibly a bike computer. Repeat the fitness assessments listed in Chapter 7, and use your monitor and your body in your own personal exercise laboratory. We're interested in your progress. It's easy to reach us at www.HeartZone.com.

## RIDING INTO THE FUTURE

Isn't there always one last point to make? Think about the possibility of riding and staying fit the rest of your life. The road to sustainable wellness is right here, in the form of your individual plan.

## *Heart Zones Training Is a Universal System*

Heart zones training is an approach that you can incorporate into any cardiovascular workout discipline. The system described here applies to cross-country skiing, conditioning for team and individual sports—basketball, soccer, volleyball, bowling, football—in-line skating, tennis, golf, and most other activities.

Judy Stansbury, Robert Kerr, and Deve Swain read Sally Edwards's original heart rate monitor book and decided to apply the principles to their area of interest, schoolchildren. They've designed school-based programs for children to study in health classes, physical education classes, and fitness courses. This new approach to a school-based application has gotten kids excited about exercise and technology, about themselves and their self-esteem, because it's an individualized approach to learning.

Horse training is being revolutionized through application of heart zones training to equine fitness. Endurance, race, and performance horses are being conditioned using heart rate monitor technology. Mike Nunnan of Pursuit Performance in Australia has trained thoroughbred horses that are winning the big-prize purses in cash and breeding rights. Mike shares this information in his book *Heart Rate Training for Horses* and on his website, www.PursuitPerformance.co.au.

Heart Zones Training has an international base. The technology, finally more affordable, is sold

Think about riding into the future as a long-term commitment. For competitive riders, this is called an annualized approach. For a fitness rider, it's called riding forever, one year at a time. In this approach, you take a full year and divide it into its different logical parts. For most riders, this is based on the seasons—in the cold months we tend to train more indoors, and in the warmer periods we ride more outside. Group rides and races are based on the seasons of the year, so building your training on a seasonal annualized system makes the most sense.

An annualized approach provides for different phases, or blocks or periods, of training—building your base, strengthening, getting faster for longer rides, and then enjoying a recovery phase on the bike. It's for you to decide how many phases are in your training system.

The annualized approach adds variety to your training. As we've discussed, variety stimulates improvement, so the more variety you can include in your training program—different bike modes, indoor/outdoor, new routes, changing training partners, food options, new equipment—the more these changes can lead to enhanced fitness. They provide a positive stimulus and a positive response that leads to the all-important training effect.

in virtually every country. Seminars and conferences attended by exercise scientists and fitness enthusiasts are being held in countries such as Switzerland and South Africa to inform the world about the heart rate monitor's applications as a stress monitor, fat-burning monitor, and physical-performance monitor.

Psychotherapists are applying heart zones training to help clients become happier and solve their problems. Dan Rudd, Ph.D., writes in his forthcoming book *More Energy, Less Stress: A Ten-Week Program to Health and Fitness* that "a heart rate monitor gives you the tool to be more loving with yourself through care of your physical and emotional heart."

Most Olympic athletes train with a heart monitor. Almost all high-level cyclists train with biofeedback data that their monitor provides to them or their coaches. Six-time Hawaii Ironman champion Mark Allen, who admits to high dependence on his monitor, says, "I've used the monitor in almost every running and cycling workout over the past eight years, and I love it." Five-time Tour de France winner Miguel Induráin used his monitor in each of his training workouts; his coaches downloaded the data every day. Lance Armstrong's coach, Chris Carmichael, relies on heart rate data as an integral part of Lance's training.

Although the monitor itself is only a tool, its application is powerful. Heart zones training works with any heart rate monitor, any model, for any sport or activity, every time you use it. Heart Zones Training is the intellectual software of the monitor hardware. The system is universal in every sense of the word.

Exercise scientist and researcher Darvin McBrayer of Baylor University coined the term "functional wellness" to describe the body's ability to function on a higher level of health. To Darvin, that means, in part, increasing your metabolic rate, the number of calories you are burning by being alive. In assessing you, he would measure your blood chemistry to see if your stress byproducts are at healthy levels. Ultimately, whether you are a beginner or a competitive rider, isn't this the true goal—to live a happier and healthier life with more energy and less stress?

The road to this paragraph may seem like a long one, because you've learned so much. You understand a new and different way of riding that involves the emotional and physical parts of training. You have all the tools you need to take your heart, your most important muscle, on an incredible life journey on your bike. When you put your two hearts together—the heart that pumps blood and the heart that enhances the joy of riding—you've found the road to lifetime wellness. That's the road to ride.

## WORKOUTS: Indoor Training

### HEALTHY HEART **Workout 57: Lancelot**

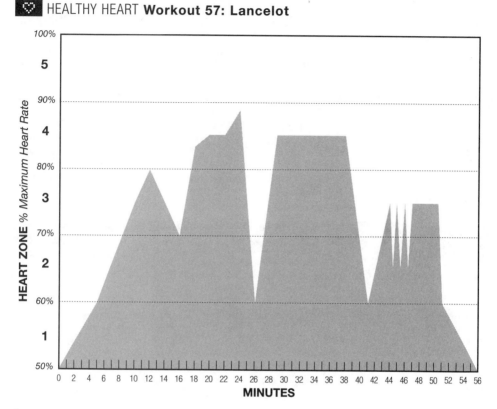

## Overview

This workout is named after one of America's greatest male cyclists, Lance Armstrong. His amazing comeback from cancer and his determination to beat the odds have provided inspiration for many people. Lance is "one in a million" physiologically, but we average folks can still take advantage of his training techniques to reach our own personal training goals.

## Description

There are four major goals in this ride. The first is to develop muscular strength and endurance with a low rpm and moderate to heavy resistance or gearing. Next is to do power starts from a standing position to practice that quick, powerful start or jump at which Lance is such an expert. Third, learn to sustain faster bike speeds by training at your anaerobic threshold. Thus, pick the highest sustainable heart rate for a 12-minute period (the higher the percentage of maximum heart rate, typically the fitter you are). The fourth goal is to train those neurological pathways with high-rpm speed work.

| Stats and Tips for Workout 57: Lancelot | | | |
|---|---|---|---|
| Zone Number and Name | Minutes in Zone | Heart Zones Training Points | Estimated Calories |
| 5. Red-Line | | | |
| 4. Threshold | 22 | 88 | 264–308 |
| 3. Aerobic | 11.5 | 34.5 | 103–126 |
| 2. Temperate | 14.5 | 28.5 | 87–116 |
| 1. Healthy Heart | 8 | 8 | 24–40 |
| Totals | 56 | 159 | 478–590 |

**Tip:** Training is individual and dependent on your genetics combined with your physiological capacity.

| Sequence for Workout 57: Lancelot | | | | |
|---|---|---|---|---|
| Elapsed Time (min.) | Workout Plan | Heart Zone | Your Heart Rate (bpm) | Interval Time (min.) |
| 0–5 | Warm up in Z1 | 1 | \_\_\_\_ | 5 |
| 5–10 | Easy pedal to bottom of Z2 | 2 | \_\_\_\_ | 5 |
| 10–16 | Increase HR 10 bpm every 2 min. with (R), steady cadence/tempo, 50–60 rpm (5–6) | 2 3 3 | \_\_\_\_ \_\_\_\_ \_\_\_\_ | 6 |
| 16–18 | Sustain HR at bottom of Z3 | 3 | \_\_\_\_ | 2 |
| 18–26 | Standing power starts[a] with 10 sec. heavy (R) all-out effort sprint from a slow spin followed by a 20 sec. easy pedal (rec). Repeat a total of 16 times | 4 | \_\_\_\_ | 8 |
| 26–29 | Easy pedal (rec) to bottom of Z2 | 2 | \_\_\_\_ | 3 |
| 29–41 | Anaerobic threshold (AT) training[b] at highest sustainable HR | 4 | \_\_\_\_ | 12 |
| 41–44 | Easy pedal (rec) to bottom of Z2 | 2 | \_\_\_\_ | 3 |
| 44–47 | Spin ups[c] from 70 rpm (7) to 120 rpm (12) in 30 sec. with a 30 sec. easy pedal (rec). Repeat a total of 3 times | 2–3 | \_\_\_\_ | 3 |
| 47–51 | Spin ups with isolated leg training[d]: 30 sec. spin up with left leg, 30 sec. easy pedal (rec), then switch to right leg spin up 30 sec. with a 30 sec. easy pedal (rec). Repeat a total of 4 times | 3 | \_\_\_\_ | 4 |
| 51–56 | Warm down easy pedal to Z2 then Z1 | 2 1 | \_\_\_\_ \_\_\_\_ | 5 |

[a] In a standing position and from a slow spin or roll, expend all-out effort for 10 seconds by using heavy resistance or hard gearing followed by 20 seconds of recovery or easy pedaling. Alternate lead foot.
[b] Riding at, about, or around your estimated anaerobic threshold. Typically this is the highest heart rate number you can sustain for an extended period of time.
[c] Increasing cadence or rpm 5 to 10 rpm at regular intervals while keeping the pedal stroke smooth and efficient.
[d] Pedaling with one leg at a time, resting the other on a box or stool, or simply keep your feet in the pedals and allow one leg to relax while the other leg does the work.

## ▎▎▎▎ FITNESS **Workout 58: A Positive Spin**

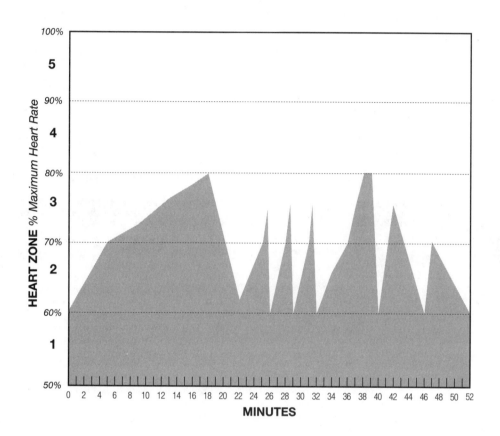

## Overview

Approaching any workout—whether physical or mental—with a positive attitude and positive self-talk builds confidence. Confidence connected with core values breeds a winning attitude that can lead to success. That's just what Positive Spin is guaranteed to provide for you—a workout on the pathway toward physical self-improvement.

## Description

This workout provides the opportunity to visualize your goals and adopt a positive spin with a positive grin as a way to achieve them. The Positive Spin workout integrates the three components of strength, power, and leg speed by using interval training. The riding goals are to finish this workout with a grin and feel positive about your effort.

| Stats and Tips for Workout 58: A Positive Spin | | | |
|---|---|---|---|
| Zone Number and Name | Minutes in Zone | Heart Zones Training Points | Estimated Calories |
| 5. Red-Line | | | |
| 4. Threshold | 11 | 44 | 132–154 |
| 3. Aerobic | 25 | 75 | 225–275 |
| 2. Temperate | 16 | 32 | 96–128 |
| 1. Healthy Heart | | | |
| Totals | 52 | 151 | 453–557 |

**Tip:** Feel the pressure against the top of your shoe when doing isolated-leg training.

| Sequence for Workout 58: A Positive Spin | | | | |
|---|---|---|---|---|
| Elapsed Time (min.) | Workout Plan | Heart Zone | Your Heart Rate (bpm) | Interval Time (min.) |
| 0–5 | Warm up to bottom of Z2 | 2 | \_\_\_\_\_ | 5 |
| 5–10 | Increase HR to bottom of Z3 | 3 | \_\_\_\_\_ | 5 |
| 10–22 | Pyramid climb[a] at 30–30 [30 sec. sprint, 30 sec. (rec)], 60–30, 90–30, 120–30, 90–30, 60–30,30–30. Keep HR in Z3 and Z4 | 3 3 4 4 | \_\_\_\_\_ \_\_\_\_\_ \_\_\_\_\_ \_\_\_\_\_ | 12 |
| 22–25 | (Rec) to bottom of Z2 | 2 | \_\_\_\_\_ | 3 |
| 25–34 | A 3 min. interval broken down into a 30 sec. fast pedal to bottom Z3 followed by 30 sec. moderate to heavy (R) to midpoint of Z3 followed by a 2 min. (rec) to bottom of Z2. Repeat a total of 3 times | 3 2 | \_\_\_\_\_ \_\_\_\_\_ | 9 |
| 34–42 | From the bottom of Z2 add 10 bpm for 2 min. From midpoint of Z2 add 10 bpm, moderate (R) for 1 min. Add 10 bpm, fast spin for 1 min. Add 10 bpm, heavy (R), for 1 min. Sustain 80% standing for 1 more min. Finish with a 2 min. (rec) to bottom of Z2 | 2 2 3 4 4 2 | \_\_\_\_\_ \_\_\_\_\_ \_\_\_\_\_ \_\_\_\_\_ \_\_\_\_\_ \_\_\_\_\_ | 8 |
| 42–46 | Isolated-leg training[b] (ILT) 2 min. each leg, 60 rpm (6), heavy (R) | 3 | \_\_\_\_\_ | 4 |
| 46–47 | Easy pedal both legs to bottom of Z2 | 2 | \_\_\_\_\_ | 1 |
| 47–50 | Spin ups[c] from 60 rpm (6) to 140 rpm (14) in 1 min., increasing 10 rpm every 10 seconds. Repeat a total of 3 times | 3 2 | \_\_\_\_\_ \_\_\_\_\_ | 3 |
| 50–52 | Warm down to bottom of Z2 | 2 | \_\_\_\_\_ | 2 |

[a] Incremental increases and decreases in time and intensity. Think of climbing up and then down a mountain. In this workout the work-interval durations increase and then decrease, whereas the recovery-interval duration stays at 30 seconds. The pattern is 30–30, 60–30, 90–30, and so on.

[b] Pedal with only one leg; rest the other on a box or stool. You may also rest it on the bike frame if you are riding a spin bike or simply keep your feet on the pedals and allow one leg to relax while the other does the work.

[c] Increase the cadence progressively by 5 to 10 rpm at regular intervals. Keep your legs under control. Concentrate on smooth pedaling and no bouncing.

## PERFORMANCE **Workout 59: Happy Feet**

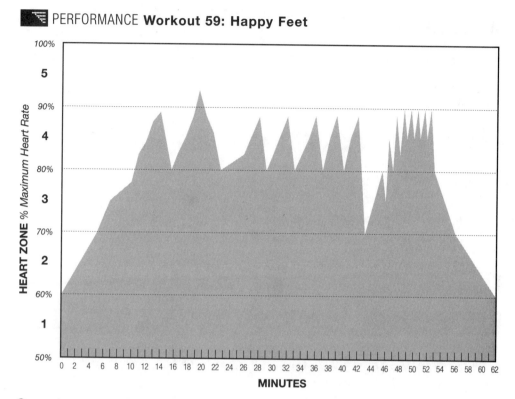

## Overview

This workout will make you feel as if you have a new pair of shoes—it makes your feet care-free! That's because when your feet are spinning and your heart is pumping, your heart rate monitor is displaying high, happy numbers on its face. Happy Feet is full of variety and opportunities to use your imagination. Mentally take yourself outdoors to ride steep hills and fast descents. Focusing on small incremental differences in heart rate will make the time fly by and your feet even happier.

## Description

Your goal is to raise your heart rate by using a smooth, fast spin as you concentrate on a quiet upper body and streamlined position. The heavy-resistance hill climbs should be done at 60 rpm or faster in the biggest gear in which you can ride and hold your cadence. The hill training develops muscular strength in either a standing or seated position. Ride the sprint intervals one of two ways: The first is a high-cadence, low-resistance approach, working on leg speed. The second is a slower-cadence, heavy-resistance (bigger gear) approach. Either way, keep those feet happy and pedaling.

| Stats and Tips for Workout 59: Happy Feet | | | |
|---|---|---|---|
| Zone Number and Name | Minutes in Zone | Heart Zones Training Points | Estimated Calories |
| 5. Red-Line | 6 | 30 | 90–120 |
| 4. Threshold | 30 | 120 | 360–420 |
| 3. Aerobic | 17 | 51 | 153–187 |
| 2. Temperate | 9 | 18 | 54–72 |
| 1. Healthy Heart | | | |
| Totals | 62 | 219 | 657–799 |

**Tip:** Use your heart rate monitor to diagnose your training rides. For example, if your heart rate stays high during recovery periods, it means something, but what it means depends on a number of factors that you will have to analyze. It might be a symptom that you are overtrained, did not warm up adequately, are not hydrated sufficiently, or perhaps have an impaired immune system.

| Sequence for Workout 59: Happy Feet | | | | |
|---|---|---|---|---|
| Elapsed Time (min.) | Workout Plan | Heart Zone | Your Heart Rate (bpm) | Interval Time (min.) |
| 0–7 | Warm up gradually to bottom of Z3 | 3 | \_\_\_\_ | 7 |
| 7–10 | Increase HR to midpoint of Z3 | 3 | \_\_\_\_ | 3 |
| 10–15 | From midpoint of Z3 increase HR 5 bpm every min. for 5 min. by increasing cadence/rpm. Add (R) as needed | 3 3 4 4 4 | \_\_\_\_ \_\_\_\_ \_\_\_\_ \_\_\_\_ \_\_\_\_ | 5 |
| 15–16 | Decrease HR to the bottom of Z4 for 1 min. | 4 | \_\_\_\_ | 1 |
| 16–26 | From the bottom of Z4 add 5 bpm every min. using (R) and steady tempo. Once you reach Z5 decrease HR 5 bpm every min. to bottom of Z4 | 4 4 | \_\_\_\_ \_\_\_\_ | 10 |
| 26–38 | Three-hill series: From bottom of Z4 increase HR 5 bpm with cadence for 2 min., then increase HR 10 bpm more with heavy (R) for 1 min. Decrease HR to bottom of Z4 for 1 min. Repeat a total of 3 times | 4 4 4 | \_\_\_\_ \_\_\_\_ \_\_\_\_ | 12 |
| 38–44 | Two-hill series: From bottom of Z4 increase HR 10 bpm with heavy (R) for 1 min., then increase HR 5 bpm more with fast cadence for 1 min. Decrease HR to the bottom of Z4 for 1 min. Repeat | 4 4 4 | \_\_\_\_ \_\_\_\_ \_\_\_\_ | 6 |
| 44–45 | (Rec) to bottom of Z3 for 1 min. | 3 | \_\_\_\_ | 1 |
| 45–53 | (8) 30 sec. sprints with 30 sec. (rec) starting from bottom of Z3 gradually increasing HR to bottom of Z5 | 3 5 | \_\_\_\_ \_\_\_\_ | 8 |
| 53–62 | Warm down to bottom of Z2, easy pedal and stretch | 2 | \_\_\_\_ | 9 |

## PERFORMANCE **Workout 60: Knock Your Socks Off**

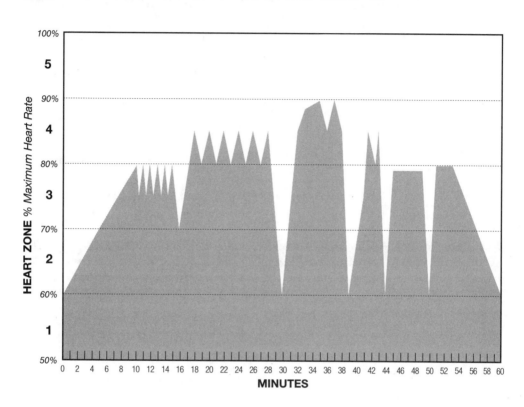

## Overview

You've probably heard the expression "Knock their socks off"! It's a common phrase in the service business when staffers really want to impress—want to exceed customers' expectations, not just meet them. The service is so exceptional that customers are stunned and want to come back. This workout will knock your socks off and keep you coming back for more.

## Description

The first half of the workout trains your cardiovascular system at three different heart rate levels: 10 bpm *below* anaerobic threshold, *at* anaerobic threshold, and *just above* anaerobic threshold. If you don't know what your threshold is you can (1) use your best guess from previous training, (2) ask yourself what is the highest heart rate you can sustain for 5 minutes or, (3) do the Two-by-Twenty Anaerobic Threshold Test in Chapter 5.

The second half of this workout is a combination of fast sprints and a long standing hill climb at a comfortable cadence concentrating on form and correct body positioning.

| Stats and Tips for Workout 60: Knock Your Socks Off | | | |
|---|---|---|---|
| Zone Number and Name | Minutes in Zone | Heart Zones Training Points | Estimated Calories |
| 5. Red-Line | | | |
| 4. Threshold | 32 | 128 | 384–448 |
| 3. Aerobic | 11 | 33 | 99–121 |
| 2. Temperate | 17 | 34 | 102–136 |
| 1. Healthy Heart | | | |
| Totals | 60 | 195 | 585–705 |

**Tip:** Keep your body weight over your legs when standing, and maintain a light touch on the handlebars.

| Sequence for Workout 60: Knock Your Socks Off | | | | |
|---|---|---|---|---|
| Elapsed Time (min.) | Workout Plan | Heart Zone | Your Heart Rate (bpm) | Interval Time (min.) |
| 0–5 | Easy-pedal warm-up | 2 | _____ | 5 |
| 5–10 | Increase HR to bottom of Z3 | 3 | _____ | 5 |
| 10–16 | 30 sec. at 10 bpm below anaerobic threshold (AT), choice, followed by 30 sec. easy pedal (rec). Repeat a total of 6 times | | _____ | 6 |
| 16–18 | 2 min. easy pedal (rec) | 2 | _____ | 2 |
| 18–19 | 1 min. all-out effort to AT, your choice | | _____ | 1 |
| 19–25 | 15 sec. at AT followed by a 10 beat (rec). Repeat by increasing HR to AT, hold for 15 sec. followed by a 10 beat (rec). Continue this interval for a total of 6 min. | | _____ | 6 |
| 25–27 | 2 min. easy pedal (rec) | 2 | _____ | 2 |
| 27–28 | 1 min. all-out effort to AT | | _____ | 1 |
| 28–30 | Sustain AT heart rate for 2 min., choice | | _____ | 2 |
| 30–36 | From AT heart rate, sprint 10 sec. then (rec) 10 beats, (R) as needed. Repeat 10 sec. sprint and 10 beat (rec) interval for a total of 6 min. | | _____ | 6 |
| 36–38 | 2 min. easy pedal (rec) | 2 | _____ | 2 |
| 38–41 | Increase HR to 75% (midpoint of Z3) with a cadence of 75 rpm and sustain for 30 sec. followed by 1 min. at 95 rpm. Repeat | 3 | _____ | 3 |
| 41–42 | Easy pedal (rec) | 2 | _____ | 1 |
| 42–48 | Increase HR to 75%–80%, standing, comfortable cadence for 5 min. followed by 1 min. at high cadence | 3–4 | _____ | 6 |
| 48–49 | 1 min. easy pedal (rec) | 2 | _____ | 1 |
| 49–53 | Every 30 sec. sprint 15 sec. for a total of 4 min., choice of (R) | 4 | _____ | 4 |
| 53–60 | Easy-pedal warm-down | 2 | _____ | 7 |

# Outdoor Training and Rides

## Workout 61: Doublemint

Double your pleasure, double your fun—that's what this ride is about. You decide from the following list what you will "double" during your ride, then go out and try to do it!

Double:

- Resting HR: Use this number "doubled" to warm up in for 15 to 20 minutes, as long as it's no more than 70 percent of maximum heart rate.
- Duration of the ride (if you normally ride 30 minutes, double it to 60, and so on).
- Ride with twice as many friends as usual.
- Cadence on hills: Instead of 60 rpm, try spinning your way up at 120 rpm.
- Stand twice as long as you sit on hills, or sit twice as long as you stand.
- Pick a ride that has twice as many hills as you normally do.
- Drink water twice as often as is normal for you.
- Hold 60 rpm at 60 percent of maximum heart rate for 6 minutes (6's). Try doubling the minutes, try doubling the rpm, or both.
- Hold 70 rpm at 70 percent of maximum heart rate for 7 minutes (7's). Try doubling the minutes, try doubling the rpm, or both.
- Hold 80 rpm at 80 percent of maximum heart rate for 8 minutes (8's). Try doubling the minutes (not for beginners).
- Hold 90 rpm at 90 percent of maximum heart rate for 9 minutes (9's). Try doubling the minutes (not for beginners).
- Maintain 85 to 90 percent effort in the biggest gear you can for 2 minutes, recover for 2 minutes, then double the minutes and recovery (4 and 4), then double the minutes again (8 and 8).
- Instead of 5 power starts, do 10.
- Instead of 5 spin ups, do 10.
- Spend twice as much time in zone 3 as in all the other zones combined.
- Do 30-second sprints with 1-minute recoveries. Double it to 1-minute sprints, 2-minute recoveries. Double it to 2-minute sprints, 4-minute recoveries. Continue doubling it as many times as you can.
- Find a "doubles" partner.
- Make your rest/recovery time twice as much as your effort or work interval time.

If you do all of these, you can afford to make two bakery stops as opposed to one. The idea is to be creative. Come up with your own "doubles" and challenge yourself.

## Workout 62: S-Squared

The goal in this workout is to improve your speed and your shifting at the same time. Your heart rate should range between zone 2 and zone 4 depending on how many shifts you make and how long you go.

Pick a section of road where you can pedal easily in your big chainring and your easiest gear in back. Jump or accelerate quickly. Shift to a harder gear every 50 to 100 yards as you begin to spin out the gear. Aim for two to three shifts without losing speed. Finish in your hardest gear, then recover to the bottom of zone 2. Repeat four times during a ride to build sprint endurance as well as shifting technique.

**Ride Snapshot**

> 20–30 min. warm-up
> Big chainring, easiest gearing in back, accelerate, shift to harder gear every 50 to 100 yards finishing in hardest gear, zone 4, (rec) bottom of zone 2. Repeat a total of 4 times
> Continue ride

## Workout 63: The Spoke 'n' Word

As the spokes spin faster, the words become fewer! The temptation is to do this interval set at too high an intensity in the beginning by using hard gears. Pick easier gearing and think of this as a long, steady climb during which there will be minimum talking and maximum focusing. This interval set is between 20 and 30 minutes, and you can repeat the set twice. Heart rate will range between zone 2 and zone 4 depending on gearing.

Warm up for 15 to 30 minutes and begin the interval set at approximately 90 rpm. Use the same gear for both the work interval and the rest interval. Use the small chainring on the front and your choice on the back. Increase rpm to 100 for 1 minute, then rest for 1 minute by decreasing rpm to 90. Repeat interval 10 to 15 times. You may choose to use a harder gear and increase rpm from 100 to 110. The work and rest intervals may also change to 2 minutes each.

**Ride Snapshot**

> 15–30 min. warm-up
> 90 rpm,1 min., small chainring, choice of gearing in back, 100 rpm, 1 min., same gearing, (rec) 1 min. Repeat a total of 10–15 times
> Warm down or continue ride

## Workout 64: Over the Hill

Some say life doesn't begin until you hit forty. That may be true, but there are certainly some subtle body changes due in part to gravity and lifestyle that begin to happen in the late thirties.

Notice the fine lines around the eyes, dry skin (drink more water), sagging muscles, and "cottage cheese" flesh, to mention a few. Less muscle means less strength and range of motion, and flexibility decreases. By the time a sedentary individual hits sixty-five, as much as 30 percent of the person's muscle mass is gone along with a decrease in bone density. All this adds up to a greater risk of injury. The key is to stay active, ride your bike, climb those

**Ride Snapshot**

> 20–30 min. warm-up
> 5–15 min., biggest gear @ 50 rpm and heart rate @ 75 percent
> 5-min. recovery
> Repeat one or two more times

hills, and don't be shy about "pumping some iron" in the weight room. These strength-building intervals can be tucked into your ride any time after a 20- to 30-minute warm-up.

A steady 5 percent, 3-mile grade works the best. Push the heaviest or biggest gear you can for 5 to 15 minutes at an rpm of 50 and a heart rate of about 75 percent (midpoint of zone 3). Rest and recover for 5 minutes with easy pedaling and repeat one or two more times.

Remember, one of the biggest differences noticed as people age is the amount of time it takes to recover from intense training. World Mountain Biking Champion Ned Overend put it this way: "Before, I'd do hill repeats and beat myself up until I was ragged and then recover in a few days. Now, I make sure I stop doing intervals when I know I still have one good one in me."

*Riding with both your emotional and physical heart leads to improved performance.*

# 11

# The Weight Management Program for Cyclists

*It took a year, but it lasted a lifetime. Fran Scofield discovered that her bike was one of the best fat-burning machines ever built. She discovered this about her 15-speed as the centerpiece of a new weight-management exercise program. She rode with a new mission—and she enjoyed it more.*

*She e-mailed me to say that the first year she lost twenty-three pounds. Rather than a weight-loss goal in pounds, she set a bike goal: to ride a metric century using her monitor. To accomplish this, Fran followed a training program developed around her Fat$_{Max}$, or her maximal fat-oxidation heart rate. She accomplished that ride and discovered a new Fran, a woman who loved the outdoors and loved her bicycle.*

*The second year Fran set a new weight-management goal: to get stronger and to go faster on her bike. Her goal was to complete a 100-mile charity bike ride at the same average heart rate she had ridden the year before but to go thirty-eight additional miles, the difference between a metric century and a mile century. She needed to be fitter to accomplish this, and she accomplished it by training in higher zones for more time in a progressive manner.*

*Fran shifted her body composition by adding muscle strength and dropping fat weight, and she crossed the finish line again as a strong rider. That is because any person who starts riding in the heart zones program is not the same as the one who finishes it. Training, that process of setting goals, developing a program, and executing on it, is a powerful, powerful process. Fran learned that if you focus on getting fit or fitter on the bike rather than focus on the fat, you usually lose weight, gain muscle, and find the joy of riding.*

—SALLY EDWARDS

The preceding chapters led you through a ten-step process for getting fitter on your bike with your heart rate monitor. Of course, getting fitter usually means shedding some unwanted pounds, but fitness is the emphasis in the ten steps. Nevertheless, many riders still tell us that their focus is to lose weight and that if getting fitter occurs too, all the better. For this reason, we have included this chapter to address specifically a weight management program that can work for you.

A heart rate monitor is first and foremost a fat monitor. Put a bike and a heart rate monitor together, add to them a specific fat-burning cycling program, and you are equipped with the tools and the motivation it takes to be successful in losing weight and gaining muscle. Notice the three tools you need to start a weight-management program: a fat burning program, a monitor, and a bike you love. The first step in most weight management programs is to begin the process by making some changes. After all, if you keep doing things the same way, you are guaranteed to get the same results. The first step to most changes is the "learning" step. We begin there.

Weight management is a complex process. Success in gaining, losing, or maintaining weight is dependent on a combination of emotional, physical, and mental factors. One key to managing these factors is to learn the process of change and feed it with a heavy dose of positive motivation. The cycling fat-burning program discussed here is based on teaching your body to expand your individual fat-burning range and to improve your $Fat_{Max}$. Here are two important definitions:

The *fat-burning range* is a range of heartbeats, the exercise intensity, that is based on your personal physiology and that burns the most fat as a source of calories when you ride your bike.

The *$Fat_{Max}$* is that specific riding intensity at which you burn the most fat calories per minute. This is also the top (ceiling) of your fat-burning range and your highest fat-burning rate. It is not the highest total burn rate but is the highest for burning fat. Exercise scientists like to call this the peak fat oxidation rate.

It is important to remember that fueling your body in accordance with your individual energy needs is essential. Weight gain or loss is not simple. In fact, if you have tried to follow the equilibrium equation used by many weight-loss advisers and exercise scientists, which states "a calorie in equals a calorie out," you may have learned quickly that your physiology, and that of many others, did not follow the equation. That is why calorie-counting diets so often fail. Human physiology simply does not respond to this seemingly logical energy-in-equals-energy-out equation. There are many reasons for this fact. For most people, the equation doesn't balance because of emotional, chemical, and environmental human responses to the weight-loss process. In addition, there are strong emotional issues around food and exercise that alter our behaviors and activities.

The first step of the $Fat_{Max}$ program is to calculate two different factors: (1) your fat-burning range and (2) your $Fat_{Max}$ or the range of heartbeats, the different exercise intensities, and the top heart rate number that is specific to your current fitness level.

## FAT IS BURNED IN EVERY HEART ZONE

Because there are many myths about fat burning, there are plenty of commercial reasons to try to sell the false promises of weight-loss programs and weight-gain gimmicks. This niche market makes a lot of money for people, and it's a huge multibillion-dollar business that preys on people's naivete. You should approach your $Fat_{Max}$ program with some solid facts about how fat is burned:

- Fat burns in each of the five heart zones.
- Fat burns in a different percentage in each zone.
- Fat burns in a different amount in each zone.
- Fat burns as a percentage of the total calories burned in each zone.
- More total fat burns in the higher zones.
- Fat burns as a "fat burn rate" based on the number of calories of fat per minute used.
- Fat burns only when oxygen is present.
- Additional fat does not burn once you become "anaerobic," or out of the aerobic training zones.
- To burn more fat, you must increase your anaerobic threshold and thus increase the fat-burning range.
- Fat does not burn in a "zone" but in a constantly changing "range" based on your current sport-specific fitness level.
- To enlarge your fat-burning range, you must increase your $Fat_{Max}$.
- Increasing your "fat-burning capacity" increases the amount of fat burned.
- The fitter you are, the more fat you burn.
- Fit people burn more fat than unfit people.
- Fat people can become fit.

## PERCENTAGE OF FAT BURNING IN THE FIVE HEART ZONES

As a quick review, the Heart Zones Training chart shows the five heart zones and their corresponding percentage of your individual and sport-specific maximum heart rate.

# Heart Zones Cycling

## Maximum Heart Rate

| TRAINING ZONES (% MAXIMUM HEART RATE) | FUEL BURNING | 150 | 155 | 160 | 165 | 170 | 175 | 180 | 185 | 190 | 195 | 200 | 205 | 210 | 215 | 220 |
|---|---|---|---|---|---|---|---|---|---|---|---|---|---|---|---|---|
| **Zone 5** Red-Line Zone 90%–100% Max HR | | 150 ◇ 135 | 155 ◇ 140 | 160 ◇ 144 | 165 ◇ 149 | 170 ◇ 153 | 175 ◇ 158 | 180 ◇ 162 | 185 ◇ 167 | 190 ◇ 171 | 195 ◇ 176 | 200 ◇ 180 | 205 ◇ 185 | 210 ◇ 189 | 215 ◇ 194 | 220 ◇ 198 |
| **Zone 4** Threshold Zone 80%–90% Max HR | CARBOHYDRATE BURNING | 135 ◇ 120 | 140 ◇ 124 | 144 ◇ 128 | 149 ◇ 132 | 153 ◇ 136 | 158 ◇ 140 | 162 ◇ 144 | 167 ◇ 148 | 171 ◇ 152 | 176 ◇ 156 | 180 ◇ 160 | 185 ◇ 164 | 189 ◇ 168 | 194 ◇ 172 | 198 ◇ 176 |
| **Zone 3** Aerobic Zone 70%–80% Max HR | | 120 ◇ 105 | 124 ◇ 109 | 128 ◇ 112 | 132 ◇ 116 | 136 ◇ 119 | 140 ◇ 123 | 144 ◇ 126 | 148 ◇ 130 | 152 ◇ 133 | 156 ◇ 137 | 160 ◇ 140 | 164 ◇ 144 | 168 ◇ 147 | 172 ◇ 151 | 176 ◇ 154 |
| **Zone 2** Temperate Zone 60%–70% Max HR | FAT BURNING | 105 ◇ 90 | 109 ◇ 93 | 112 ◇ 96 | 116 ◇ 99 | 119 ◇ 102 | 123 ◇ 105 | 126 ◇ 108 | 130 ◇ 111 | 133 ◇ 114 | 137 ◇ 117 | 140 ◇ 120 | 144 ◇ 123 | 147 ◇ 126 | 151 ◇ 129 | 154 ◇ 132 |
| **Zone 1** Healthy Heart Zone 50%–60% Max HR | | 90 ◇ 75 | 93 ◇ 78 | 96 ◇ 80 | 99 ◇ 83 | 102 ◇ 85 | 105 ◇ 88 | 108 ◇ 90 | 111 ◇ 93 | 114 ◇ 95 | 117 ◇ 98 | 120 ◇ 100 | 123 ◇ 103 | 126 ◇ 105 | 129 ◇ 108 | 132 ◇ 110 |

Zone 1, the Healthy Heart Zone, is easy and light intensity. Note that in the column Fuel Burning, approximately 85 percent of the calories used are fat and about 15 percent are glycogen (also known as carbohydrates). Within this zone, the blend of fuel burned when you ride your bike is a ratio of 85 percent fat to 15 percent carbohydrates. However, the total amount of fat burned is extremely low. A fit male rider burns 2–6 total calories per minute riding in this zone.

Zone 2, the Temperate Zone, falls within 60–70 percent of your maximum heart rate. It is a moderate-intensity zone that offers pain-free training. The amounts of fat and glycogen change to a different ratio—approximately 75 percent fat to 25 percent glycogen. As exercise intensity increases, the ratio of fuels metabolized shifts as a percentage but not as a total amount away from fat. This pattern continues through to the highest exercise intensity, zone 5, the Red-Line Zone. A fit male rider burns 5–8 total calories per minute riding in this zone.

Zone 3, the Aerobic Zone, falls within 70–80 percent of your maximum heart rate. It is the beginning of the more intense exercise zones, the performance zones. Since the amounts of fat and glycogen change to a different ratio depending on how fit you are, the fitter you get, the more fat you will burn. In zone 3 the ratio is approximately 50 percent fat to 50 percent carbohydrate or glycogen. A fit male rider burns 7–12 total calories per minute riding in this zone.

Zone 4, the Threshold Zone, falls within 80–90 percent of your maximum heart rate. Exercise here is hotter and higher and more intense. It is called the "threshold" zone because for most fit people, your anaerobic threshold, the top of your fat-burning range, lies within its ceiling and floor. The amounts of fat and glycogen change to a different ratio, approximately 25 percent fat to 75 percent carbohydrate. Your anaerobic threshold heart rate number is the same as your $Fat_{Max}$ heart rate. Most fit folks have a $Fat_{Max}$ somewhere within this heart zone. A fit male rider burns 10–15 total calories per minute riding in this zone.

Zone 5, the Red-Line Zone, falls within 90–100 percent of your maximum heart rate. It is the top of the performance-training zone, where exercise is hot, hard, and the highest intensity. The most fat and the most glycogen in total calories, not percentages, are burned in this zone. The ratio is approximately 10 percent fat to 90 percent glycogen. A fit male rider burns 15–20 total calories per minute riding in this zone.

What is significant to know is that the Fuel Burning column in the Heart Zones chart is cumulative. That is, the amount of calories contributed by fat and carbohydrate is the sum of the entire vertical column, not just the horizontal representation. This is significant because fat, protein, and carbohydrates are burned in all zones but in different ratios and different total amounts as exercise intensity or riding effort changes.

## UNDERSTANDING THE FAT-BURNING RANGE

The fat-burning range is the exercise intensity, measured by heart rate, where fat is used effectively as a source of fuel. Cyclists commonly misunderstand the nature of the fat-burning range. The source of confusion centers around three words—fat, burning, and range—and comes from the disparate information about them.

There are two basic and differentiating concepts about burning fat in the heart zones:

1. The *percentage* (%) of fat burned as the source of fuel during physical activity

2. The total *amount* of fat (calories) burned during physical activity

These two concepts are quite different. In low-intensity physical activity, a higher percentage of fat calories is burned as a source of fuel, but—and this is important—fewer total fat calories are burned. The chart below shows in more detail the fat utilization as both a percentage and total calories burned in each and the five different heart zones:

| Percentage (%) of Fuels and Number of Calories Burned during Exercise | | | | | |
|---|---|---|---|---|---|
| Zone Number | Percentage of Fat | Percentage of Carbohydrates | Percentage of Protein | Calories Burned in 30 Minutes of Cycling* | Calories Burned per Minute* |
| 5 | 10–15 | 85–90 | Approx. 5 | 450–600 | 15–20 |
| 4 | 10–20 | 80–90 | Approx. 5 | >450 | 10–15 |
| 3 | 40–60 | 50–85 | Approx. 5 | >330 | 7–12 |
| 2 | 50–70 | 25–50 | Approx. 5 | >240 | 5–8 |
| 1 | 70–85 | 10–25 | Approx. 5 | >180 | 4–6 |

\* This is only an estimate. People burn fat, carbohydrates, protein, and total calories based on their individual physiology, body composition, current fitness level, current diet, and more.

Within each heart zone, you use a different proportion of fuels when you ride. The three basic sources of caloric energy are used: fats, proteins, and carbohydrates. The amount oxidized of these three nutrients varies depending on many conditions, but the primary factors are as follows:

• Balance of fuels in your diet

• Timing of last meal

• Exercise intensity of the physical activity

• Your current fitness level by sport

• How much you eat during the workout

- To a lesser extent, the amount of alcohol in your diet
- Your gender
- Total number of calories eaten daily
- Genetic makeup
- Environmental factors
- Past training experience
- Amount and kind of physical and emotional stress

When any of these factors change, the ratio of fuels burned changes. This is an important concept. When you make a change, or a shift, in any of the factors, your body shifts its metabolic response. That is why the percentages of fat, carbohydrates, and protein vary widely and are given as individual ranges and not absolute percentages. The amount of fat and carbohydrates you use when you ride depends on your nutrient intake, timing of the last meal, exercise intensity (heart zone), fitness level, and the type and quantity of food you eat during the exercise. As you now know, fat burning is dependent on you and your physiology.

As an example, the previous table shows that as exercise intensity increases from zone 1 to the highest zones, the ratio of nutrients that are burned or oxidized changes. In the low heart zones, fat is burned as the primary source of fuels but in low quantities. In the high heart zones, carbohydrates are burned as the main source of fuels. Likewise, as you train in higher heart zones, more total calories per minute are burned. Note that in zone 1, approximately 180 calories are burned during this thirty-minute period. For the same thirty minutes in Zone 4, approximately 430 calories are burned. Which would you prefer to burn during thirty minutes of riding—180 calories or 430 calories?

As you ride your bike faster, your exercise intensity increases and so does the number of calories burned per minute. This is called the "burn rate," and it is measured in calories used per minute (Butterfield 1994). The burn rate of one rider is different from that of another rider, depending on the individual rider's current physiology.

There is a wide range of fuel-utilization differences among individuals. This is known as "fat-burning capacity," or a person's ability to use fat as a source of fuel. This difference in fat-burning capacity is based on each individual's unique physiology, fitness levels, dietary habits, and frequency and time of eating. Because of these variables, it is possible only to approximate the energy percentages in each of the heart zones. In laboratory testing, an individual's burn rate and percentage of nutrient contribution can be accurately measured.

## Understanding the Burn Rate Formula

There are three parts to how many calories you burn per minute (calories/minute) or per day (total daily energy expenditure [EE]). Let's say that the total number of calories you burn per day averages about 2,000. However, as you eat, sleep, ride your bike, etc., you burn calories at a different burn rate, and this rate will always depend on the following:

1. Your current activity level
2. Your current metabolic rate
3. Your current food metabolism rate

The first component, your current activity level, is based on the intensity level of the activity throughout your day. For most of us, this comprises about 15–30 percent of our daily calories expended. Your current metabolic rate, the second component, is the total caloric cost to keep your body working, whether you are awake or asleep. For most, the metabolic rate consists of our sleeping metabolism plus our basal metabolism plus our

## YOUR BURN RATE

Your burn rate is the total number of calories burned per minute. It is the caloric cost per minute at each moment, whether your are active or stationary. Your personal burn rate is determined by a formula that accounts for your total energy expenditure (EE):

Burn rate (total daily energy expenditure) =
Metabolic rate (MR) + EE$_{\text{activity – duration, intensity, and type of movement}}$
+ Food metabolism (calories expended to digest protein, fat, and carbohydrates)

In this formula, food metabolism is the caloric cost to digest nutrients that you eat, or dietary-induced thermogenesis.

The more you weigh, the higher your burn rate compared with that of a lighter-weight cyclist performing the same physical movement. The heavier you are, the more mass there is for you to move. For example, a person whose weight fluctuates between 130 and 160 pounds has two different burn rates. At 130 pounds and average fitness level, the person can burn approximately 5 kcal per minute in brisk walking, compared with 8 kcal at the higher weight. If this person increases exercise intensity into zone 3 by jogging, the burn rates would increase to approximately 10 kcal and 13 kcal respectively. This principle applies whether you are a cyclist, a runner, or anyone who does physical activity of any sort.

arousal metabolism. The caloric cost of being alive is approximately 60–75 percent of our daily energy expenditure. Finally, there is the caloric cost of your food metabolism. This is the number of calories burned to digest food, called "dietary-induced thermogenesis." For most individuals, the caloric cost of digesting, absorbing, and assimilating food nutrients plus their effect on our system is about 10 percent of our total daily energy expenditure.

When you add these three calorie-burning components together, the sum is your total daily energy expenditure (EE). Several factors affect your total daily energy expenditure, such as the environment, the climate, and pregnancy. Changes in any one of the three principal components results in changes in the "energy out" side of the caloric balancing act that your body tries to stabilize (your "set point"). It is important to recognize that, by far, the most profound effect on your energy expenditure is your current activity level. Increase your activity and you dramatically shift the energy-balancing equation in favor of the calories out. You can nearly double your total daily caloric output with three or four hours of hard riding.

The type or mode of exercise is a factor in determining your burn rate. Physical activity that includes larger muscles and recruits more total muscles results in a higher burn rate. Cross-country skiing, for example, has a higher burn rate than bicycling. As a rule, activities that require you to support your body weight have higher burn rates than those like cycling or swimming in which body weight is supported by the nature of the sport.

The chart shows some common burn rates (caloric costs) for different activities:

| Calories Burned per Minute | | | | | | |
|---|---|---|---|---|---|---|
| | | Body Weight | | | | |
| Activity* | Burn Rate per Minute** | 110 Pounds | 130 Pounds | 150 Pounds | 170 Pounds | 190 Pounds |
| Swimming | 0.156 | 7.8 | 9.2 | 10.6 | 12.0 | 13.4 |
| Cycling | 0.169 | 8.5 | 10.0 | 11.5 | 13.0 | 14.5 |
| Running | 0.193 | 9.7 | 11.4 | 13.1 | 14.9 | 16.6 |
| Basketball | 0.138 | 6.9 | 8.1 | 9.4 | 10.6 | 11.9 |
| Aerobic Dancing | 0.135 | 6.7 | 7.9 | 9.2 | 10.4 | 11.6 |

**Source:** Data from Bannister and Brown 1968.
* All activities are set at approximately 70%–80% maximum heart rate, zone 3.
** Kcal per minute per pound of body weight.

The higher the burn rate, the more total calories expended. There are different ways to increase your burn rate. One way is to shift your body composition to higher muscle mass. Body composition is the ratio of lean mass (also known as fat-free mass) to fat mass (adipose tissue). Body composition is usually expressed as a percentage of total body weight. For example, if a person currently has 30 percent fat mass, the reciprocal of this number, 70 percent, is the fat-free or lean body percentage. Increasing fat-free mass makes metabolic rates increase and burn rates go even higher.

## TOTAL BURN RATES AND FAT BURN RATE

The question Sally Reed is most frequently asked when she speaks about how to increase your fat-burning range is "In what zone do I burn the most fat?" This is an important question. The answer is always the same, and as a tease, she first answers the question with an explanation and then with the two words that you should always use when you are asked the question: What is the *ideal zone* for fat burning?

The heart zones that burn the most fat are different for each rider. Here are a few fat-burning facts:

- The total caloric burn rate is as important as the ratio of fuels.
- No *additional* fat is burned when exercising above the $Fat_{Max}$.
- Oxygen and glucose must be present for *additional* fat to burn.
- You burn different amounts of fat from one activity to another.
- Increasing your fat-burning capacity, or your ability to burn a higher percentage of fat, by cycling is key to your weight-loss goals.
- To increase your $Fat_{Max}$, riding at or around it is essential.

It is misleading to suggest that because the percentage of fat burned is higher in low zones, that they are better zones for fat burning. At low riding speeds and low heart rates, fat is burned at the highest percentage, but more importantly it is burned in the smallest amounts. That is because there is an inverse relationship between total calories and percentage of calories used:

High intensity → Lower fat percentage
High intensity → Higher total amount of fat burned

Low intensity → Higher fat percentage
Low intensity → Lower total amount of fat burned

Some cyclists and journalists believe that it is better to do "fat-burning exercises of low intensity" than to ride at optimum fat-burning rates. This statement is misleading because the higher the heart zone, the higher the energy expenditure or the higher the burn rate.

The rate you burn or metabolize the greatest energy from fat as the fuel source is dependent in part on how bike-fit you are. The fitter you are when you ride, the more energy you can burn from fat metabolism. The less bike-fit you are, the less fat you burn, because fat-burning is activity-specific. If you are very bike-fit but less run-fit, you burn more fat at the same heart rate biking than running.

For fat to burn, oxygen must be present. The highest fat-burning rate is the one at the top of the oxygen-sufficient zone, or that point at or below the anaerobic threshold heart rate—your $Fat_{Max}$. The fat-burning range starts at the beginning of the first benefits from aerobic activity, generally considered to be 55 percent of maximum heart rate. The ceiling (top) of the fat-burning range is at the point of anaerobic threshold. When the anaerobic threshold or $Fat_{Max}$ is reached, no additional fat is metabolized. Above your $Fat_{Max}$, the same amount of fat is burned, and the balance of the calories comes from other nutrient sources. That is, there is no additional fat burned because oxygen is limited above the anaerobic threshold heart rate and oxygen utilization must increase to increase fat oxidation.

You now have enough information to answer the most frequently asked question about fat burning: "At what heart rate do I burn the most fat?"

The short answer is "It depends." It depends on your $Fat_{Max}$ heart rate. If you ride to raise this heart rate, you'll burn more fat.

How do you increase your $Fat_{Max}$ heart rate and move it as close as you can to your maximum heart rate? That's the essential point here. And that's what the fat-burning riding program is designed to do: to get you fitter and fitter. The fitter you are, the larger your fat-burning range is.

## UNDERSTANDING YOUR FAT$_{MAX}$

Exercise scientists love to be precise in their language, which is important in their research and writing. One group explained the process of fat oxidation as follows: "Shifts in energy substrate mobilization and utilization occur as exercise intensity increase. There is a progressive increase in the relative contribution of carbohydrate to energy expenditure and a corresponding decrease in the relative contribution of fat oxidation to energy expenditure" (Achten 2002). In other words, as you ride your bike in higher and higher heart zones, the fuels you burn change, with more carbohydrates burned as a percentage of the calories burned at higher intensities. As you ride your bike even harder, you eventually reach an intensity level that burns the most fat per minute. This is known as the maximal fat-oxidation heart rate, or $Fat_{Max}$. But at what heart rate do you reach this maximal rate of burning fat?

Generally, the highest rate of fat burning is found at moderate exercise intensity ranges depending on how fit you are. Your goal is to increase your bike-fitness level by riding your bike smarter in the heart zones. Increasing the number of total calories expended per day and increasing your ability to burn more fat will result in improved fax oxidation, or fat-burning capacity.

There is a silver lining in improving your fat-burning capacity. You get an added benefit: Fat burning increases after you stop exercising the fitter you are. You are a better fat-burning machine the fitter you get, even when you are just sitting in a chair doing little to no activity. Exercise scientists say it this way: Your ability to oxidize fatty acids is directly related to your improvement in fitness performance as a result of your improved aerobic capacity. It is now time to learn how to enlarge your fat-burning range.

## ENLARGING YOUR FAT-BURNING RANGE

By definition, the fat-burning range for you is the exercise intensity between two different metabolic thresholds: your aerobic threshold ($T_1$) and your anaerobic threshold heart rate ($T_2$). $T_2$ is the important heart rate number because you must cross it to reach a major change in metabolic energy. By expanding the fat-burning range, you burn more fat and increase your $Fat_{Max}$, your $T_2$ heart rate.

The aerobic threshold, $T_1$, is that percent of your maximum heart rate (on average, 55 percent) where aerobic benefits first start to occur. The $Fat_{Max}$, $T_2$, is that percent of your maximum heart rate where anaerobic metabolism and its benefits occur. By raising the ceiling of your fat-burning range, you enlarge it.

What has been missing in weight-management programs for most people is an easy and inexpensive tool to use to measure these two thresholds, $T_1$ and $T_2$. A simple protocol using a heart rate monitor can set both aerobic and anaerobic threshold heart rate values. For an extremely sedentary person, the anaerobic threshold may be as low as 60–70 percent of cycling maximum heart rate. For extremely fit and competitive riders, the top of the fat-burning range may be as high as 95 percent of maximum heart rate. The greater the range of heartbeats between the $T_1$ and $T_2$, the more total fat burned.

For most people who want to lose body fat and at the same time lose body weight from riding, the best way to expand the fat-burning range is to raise the $T_2$ heart rate number. First, determine your two threshold numbers:

- Measure your aerobic threshold floor, $T_1$ (55 percent maximum heart rate)
- Measure your $Fat_{Max}$, $T_2$ (up to 95 percent maximum heart rate)

Your two threshold heart rate numbers delineate your fat-burning range, and riding within them results in increased fat and weight losses. By riding in the fat-burning range, you use the highest percentage and total amount of fat, both at rest and during training. When you increase your exercise in the fat-burning range, your energy equation shifts, and this shift is the key to weight management.

## SETTING YOUR FAT-BURNING RANGE

The fat-burning range is a span of heartbeats in which fat is used as a primary source of fuel for riding. The fat-burning range is metabolically determined. The top, $T_2$, and bottom, $T_1$, of the fat-burning range are specific heart rate numbers that you can measure. Quantifying your fat-burning range is accomplished by measuring these two metabolic thresholds. The bottom of the range is your aerobic threshold, which is a fixed number, and the top of the range is your current anaerobic threshold heart rate number, which changes with your fitness level.

The bottom of the fat-burning range is considered by most exercise scientists to be that minimum degree of exercise intensity where oxygen-consumption improvements first occur. This is generally measured at around 55 percent maximum heart rate. At this extremely low-intensity exercise heart rate, the burn rate measured in calories per minute is minimal, from 2–6 calories per minute. The metabolic bottom of the fat-burning range is the first point where cardiovascular fitness improvement (oxygen capacity) can be measured.

$T_1$ can be measured using a heart rate monitor and performing the first of two tests in this chapter. The first test takes 2–4 minutes and is a maximum heart rate, "all-out effort" test that requires lower levels of exertion than the second type, the "true maximum test." Using low-intensity exercise to estimate maximum heart rate is an easy way to set the bottom of the fat-burning range in heartbeats per minute, but those of you given clearance by a medical professional will find more accuracy in the true maximum test.

A maximum heart rate test is a strenuous workout or ride. Your job is to get the highest number you can register on your heart rate monitor. This number is to be used as or near your maximum heart rate. If you think you could have ridden harder and extracted a higher heart rate number, then add 5–10 bpm to the highest number you saw on your monitor during your ride.

For this test, you will need a heart rate monitor, a stopwatch (or bike monitor or cycle computer), and a 1- to 2-mile stretch of road with a slight 5-degree uphill at the end.

## Instructions for Setting the Bottom of Your Cycling Fat-Burning Range, $T_1$

- Warm up adequately using your monitor. For most people, the warm-up should be about 10 percent of your total riding time, and your heart rate toward the end of the warm-up should reach into zone 2 or until you are comfortable.
- Find a flat 1- to 2-mile stretch of road with a slight uphill for the final 100–300 yards.
- Start at 130 bpm on your monitor and then begin the test by gradually increasing your speed such that every 15 seconds your heart rate increases 5 bpm.
- When you can no longer increase your heart rate in a 15-second interval and you feel exhausted, the test is over.
- Slow and cool down.
- Use the highest number you saw on your monitor as your "tested cycling" maximum heart rate.
- Use the following chart to determine the midpoint of zone 1, which is your cycling $T_1$.

| An Unfit Person with a Shrunken Fat-Burning Range | |
|---|---|
| **Zone Number** | **Percent Max HR** |
| 5 | 90–100 |
| 4 | 80–90 |
| 3 | 70–80 |
| 2  $T_2$ ↑ CEILING anaerobic threshold | 60–70 |
| 1  $T_1$ ↕ FLOOR aerobic threshold | 50–60 |

| A Fit Person with an Enlarged Fat-Burning Range | |
|---|---|
| **Zone Number** | **Percent Max HR** |
| 5 | 90–100 |
| 4  $T_2$ ↑ CEILING anaerobic threshold | 80–90 |
| 3 | 70–80 |
| 2 | 60–70 |
| 1  $T_1$ ↕ FLOOR aerobic threshold | 50–60 |

## Options

- Invite a friend to join you, someone who is slightly faster to ride with you when you do this assessment. See if the effect of competition and cooperation between both riders will result in a higher number on your monitor.
- You can perform the same ride on an indoor cycle. Since motivation is key to reaching your highest number on your monitor, someone inspiring you or riding with you can help you reach for your maximum heart rate.

## Instructions for Setting the Top of Your Fat-Burning Range, $T_2$

This assessment is very similar to the Anaerobic Threshold Ride described in Chapter 5; we're repeating it here to save you the trouble of searching for it.

The intensity level of this ride is high, because you ride up to and sometimes beyond your anaerobic threshold, until you reach a state where the specific riding muscles have an insufficient amount of oxygen for comfortable riding. This is the riding intensity or point called the anaerobic threshold heart rate, or $Fat_{Max}$.

- Warm up adequately. Select a percentage of your estimated maximum heart rate, or a perceived exertion rate on a scale of 1 to 10 that would measure a 7, and continuously maintain this speed or pace for 20 minutes.

- After you have held the highest sustainable heart rate for 20 minutes, quickly slow for 2–4 minutes but continue to spin. This is your "active" recovery time between the two sets.

- Again, increase your pace or effort until you reach the same high heart rate number that you rode for the first twenty minutes, and continue to hold it for a second 20 minutes.

- After completing the second 20 minutes, ask yourself, "Could I have ridden harder and held a higher heart rate number?"

- If the answer is "no," record this heart rate number in your logbook as your estimated anaerobic threshold heart rate, or the top of your fat-burning range. This heart rate number is your $Fat_{Max}$, or $T_2$.

- If you answered "yes," that you could have held or sustained a higher number, then rest for 2 to 10 days and retake the test to determine the top of your fat-burning range.

The highest heart rate you can sustain for two 20-minute rides with a brief rest between is your best estimate of current bicycling $Fat_{Max}$.

## DESIGNING A FAT-BURNING PROGRAM THAT FITS YOU—THE "11TH STEP"

Congratulations. You now know your fat-burning range, a great deal about what it means, and why it's important for weight loss to train within its top and bottom parameters. The last piece missing is a program that helps you use your bike with your monitor to achieve success.

After thirty years of training, we know that the best path to success is to develop a step-by-step, sequential program to achieve a goal, an intrinsic goal that is buried deep in your heart. If you are committed and determined to reach a weight goal, you must set one. The American

College of Sports Medicine recommends that you start by setting that goal at 5–10 percent of your current body weight—and no more than this, at first. We agree with that recommendation.

If your current dry weight is 200 pounds, your weight-loss goal should be 10–20 pounds. After you achieve this weight goal, hold it and stabilize your physiology. That is, once you have accomplished this success, maintain that weight for a period of 1–4 weeks. If you want to lose more weight, do it after you have stabilized or allowed your body to reestablish its set point at that new weight before you set a new goal.

You have just finished the first three steps of the basic Heart Zones ten steps:

1. Determine your maximum heart rate.

2. Set your 5 zones.

3. Write down your weight-management goals.

For weight loss, you now add one additional step to your riding plan; you need to determine your $T_1$ and $T_2$. Use the two workout rides previously described to set these key metabolic thresholds. They mark the bottom and top of your fat-burning range and the range you will maintain for your weight-loss riding program.

4. Determine your fat-burning range.

Next, finish the remainder of the steps in the $Fat_{Max}$ program.

5. Determine how fit you currently are on the training wheel.

6. Determine how much riding time you have.

7. Put your riding time into your fat-burning range.

8. Write a weekly riding program.

9. Do the rides.

10. Monitor by measuring your improvement.

11. Ride to raise your $Fat_{Max}$ and to focus on fitness, not on fatness.

## FAT-BURNING RIDE GUIDE

You probably would like some different types of rides to fit your new fat-burning program. Any ride or workout in this book that stays within your fat-burning range will work perfectly for your new program. Workouts that are especially good for riding in your fat-burning range include those like Talk Is Cheap (Chapter 8) and Change of Heart (Chapter 6), and workouts that are below your $Fat_{Max}$.

Here are a couple of rules to follow when you are riding within your fat-burning range:

- Train weekly with one interval training session a week that includes a brief time above your $Fat_{Max}$. This results in helping to push up your $Fat_{Max}$, your $T_2$ number.
- Weekly training should include one or two sessions of "at-about-around" training. This is where you ride within a range of 10 beats on either side of your anaerobic threshold. For example, if your anaerobic threshold is 145 bpm, do a session where you stay in the range of 135–155 bpm and the average is 145 bpm.

Remember that at least 60–90 percent of your riding time should be aerobic training, because oxygen must be present for fat to burn.

## THE FAT-BURNING TRANSITION

Lifelong learning is a process that we all should instill in ourselves at any age. Being smart by using modern science combined with tools such as our bicycle and heart rate monitor, and using our natural instincts and the data from sources such as our monitors, are central elements in establishing lifetime health and fitness skills. With the application of data, tools, and information, you have a greater chance of being successful in accomplishing your weight-loss or weight-gain goals. Change is our charge as human beings, and here's a review of some of the things you can do to support the transition from old to new ways of riding:

- By using the heart rate monitor, you can determine your best intensity levels for burning fat, called the fat-burning range. The fat-burning range is the heartbeat space between aerobic threshold ($T_1$) and $Fat_{Max}$, or anaerobic threshold ($T_2$).
- The bottom of the fat-burning range is the same for everyone, 55 percent of maximum heart rate. The only way to enlarge the fat-burning range is to increase the top of it, or the anaerobic threshold.
- When you are extremely bike-fit, your fat-burning range is enormous, as large as 55–95 percent of your maximum heart rate. When you are unfit, the fat-burning range is narrow. This means that when you are unfit, you don't burn any *additional* fat when exercising above $T_2$, which may be as low as 70 percent of your maximum heart rate.
- The ratio of fat to carbohydrates burned during exercise depends on a number of factors, including dietary composition, the timing of eating and exercising, fitness level, riding intensity, and food intake during the workout.

- The number of calories burned per minute of riding determines the burn rate during your riding time. The higher the burn rate, the higher the number of calories burned. To achieve effective ride training that results in weight loss, it is best to train progressively toward the top of the fat-burning range. This results in more total calories burned as well as the highest number of fat calories burned.
- The type of activity a person does affects burn rate. Choosing activities that use large muscle groups and that require you to support your body weight results in the highest total energy expenditure (EE).
- People with a higher percentage of fat-free mass have a higher burn rate because their metabolic rates (MR) are higher. The higher the burn rate, the more total calories expended at rest. The formula for determining your daily rate of caloric expenditure includes three factors:

Burn rate (total daily energy expenditure) =

MR + EE$_{\text{activity – duration, intensity, and type of movement}}$
    + Food metabolism (calories expended to digest protein, fat, and carbohydrates)

- By changing any of the variables in this formula, you cause energy shifting to occur. For a weight-loss program to be successful, energy shifting is essential such that it results in a change in the energy-intake-energy-output equation. One of the best ways to lose weight is to increase your burn rate by exercising within your individual fat-burning range.

Remember Fran Scofield, the rider who followed the ten-step program to finish her first metric century and lost twenty-three pounds that first year? She was successful because she focused all of her weight-loss energy and attention on her goal of riding the century, not on losing weight. The weight came off when she shifted her attention away from the bathroom scales or her fancy new body-fat scale and focused it on that weekend in June when she would be lining up with 5,000 other women at the start of California's Cinderella Classic. She was a different woman when she rode across that finish line loving her bike, riding within her heart zones, and smiling as she found the cyclist inside herself. That is, in large part, the joy of riding.

## REFERENCES

Achten, Juul, et al. Determination of the Exercise Intensity That Elicits Maximal Fat Oxidation. *Medicine and Science in Sports and Exercise*, vol. 34, no. 1 (January 2002).

Bannister, E. W., and S. R. Brown. The Relative Energy Requirements of Physical Activity. In H. B. Falls, ed., *Exercise Physiology*. New York: Academic Press, 1968.

Butterfield, Gail. Hershey Food Corporation. Topics in Nutrition and Food Safety. *Fueling Activity* (Fall 1994): p. 6.

# A

# Heart Zones Cycling Indoor Workouts

| Workout | Percent Maximum Heart Rate | | | HZT Points | Total Minutes | Chapter |
| --- | --- | --- | --- | --- | --- | --- |
| | 50%–70% Healthy Heart | 60%–80% Fitness | 60%–90% Performance | | | |
| Change of Heart | X | | | 70 | 35 | 6 |
| Crisscross Z1 and Z2 | X | | | 30 | 20 | 3 |
| Recovery Intervals | X | | | 64 | 30 | 5 |
| Five-by-Two | X | | | 69 | 33 | 4 |
| Rock Bottom | X | | | 98 | 40 | 9 |
| Peekaboo | X | X | | 84 | 30 | 7 |
| Talk Is Cheap | X | X | | 122 | 45 | 8 |
| Lancelot | X | X | | 159 | 56 | 10 |
| Heartbeat | | X | | 149 | 50 | 5 |
| Ladder to Success | | X | | 140 | 60 | 8 |
| 30-Beat Interval | | X | | 62 | 30 | 3 |
| A Positive Spin | | X | | 151 | 52 | 10 |
| Fast Lane | | X | | 156 | 55 | 9 |
| Crisscross Z2 and Z3 | | X | | 110 | 45 | 4 |
| Winner's Circle | | X | | 165 | 55 | 7 |
| The Zipper | | X | X | 154 | 50 | 8 |
| Tailwind | | X | X | 209 | 60 | 4 |
| Afterburner | | X | X | 181 | 53 | 6 |
| Seattle Ridge | | | X | 224 | 60 | 9 |
| Spentervals | | | X | 187 | 55 | 6 |
| At, About, Around | | | X | 233 | 60 | 7 |
| Happy Feet | | | X | 219 | 62 | 10 |
| Pumped | | | X | 194 | 58 | 9 |
| Two-by-Twenty | | | X | 242 | 65 | 5 |
| Top Spin | | | X | 194 | 60 | 3 |
| Allez! Allez! | | | X | 215 | 65 | 3 |
| Escalator | | | X | 181 | 55 | 5 |
| La Bicicletta | | | X | 199 | 60 | 4 |
| Red Light, Green Light | | | X | 172 | 54 | 6 |
| Sitting Bull | | | X | 200 | 60 | 7 |
| Salty Dog | | | X | 232 | 70 | 8 |
| Knock Your Socks Off | | | X | 195 | 60 | 10 |

# B

## Heart Zones Cycling Outdoor Workouts

| | Percent Maximum Heart Rate | | | |
| Workout | 50%–70% Healthy Heart | 60%–80% Fitness | 60%–90% Performance | Chapter |
|---|---|---|---|---|
| The Observation Trip | X | X | | 4 |
| Steady-State Pace Ride | X | X | | 4 |
| Noodling | X | | | 6 |
| Doublemint | X | X | X | 10 |
| Steady Eddie | X | X | | 7 |
| Aerobic Time Trial | X | X | | 5 |
| Crisscross Zone 3 | | X | | 3 |
| Saturday Night Fever | | X | | 8 |
| The Recovery Interval Ride | | X | X | 4 |
| SOS | | X | X | 9 |
| Cruisin' | | X | X | 6 |
| Paceline Ride | | X | X | 6 |
| The Pyramid Scheme | | X | X | 6 |
| Five-by-Five | | X | X | 8 |
| Need for Speed | | X | X | 7 |
| The Heat Is On | | X | X | 4 |
| S-Squared | | X | X | 10 |
| The Spoke 'n' Word | | X | X | 10 |
| Rock 'n' Roll | | X | X | 8 |
| Distance Improvement Ride | | X | X | 5 |
| The Biggest Number | | X | | 3 |
| The All-Out Trip | | X | | 3 |
| Maximum Heart Rate Hill Sprints | | X | | 3 |
| The All-out Time Trial | | | X | 5 |
| Anaerobic Threshold Ride | | | X | 5 |
| Sign Here, Press Hard | | | X | 9 |
| Hill Sprints | | | X | 9 |
| Spitfire | | | X | 7 |
| Head for the Hills | | | X | 7 |
| Hill-Billy | | | X | 8 |
| Snookie | | | X | 9 |
| Over the Hill | | X | | 10 |

# C

# Heart Zones Training Point System

The heart zones training point system is one of the first methods created through which an athlete, coach, or trainer can quantify workload. By using a heart rate monitor, it is now relatively easy to measure individual training load.

The HZT point system uses the quantification of *frequency* (F) as the number of workouts per week, *intensity* (I) as measured by numerical heart zones, and *time* (T) in each zone to determine daily, weekly, and monthly points.

Heart zones have weight. The higher the heart zone, the heavier the exercise stress. To determine your weekly HZT points or training load, simply multiply the number of workouts per week (frequency) times the number of the zone (intensity) times the number of minutes (time).

F x I x T = Training load
Example: 6 workouts x zone 3 x 30 minutes = 540 HZT points

What is the maximum number of HZT points? What is a healthy number of points? What is the ideal number of points? There's no set answer to these questions because the system is totally individualistic. Each person has an individual workload threshold or a quantifiable amount of exercise he or she can sustain. HZT points may range from 200 points a week to more than 6,000. Higher points don't mean you are a better athlete, or faster or fitter, but that your tolerance of exercise quantity is higher. Workload thresholds vary greatly among individuals. For example, Sally Edwards averaged 3,000 HZT points a week while training for her fifteenth Ironman race; this was the training load that optimized her physiology.

Athletes can use HZT points to predict when they will be at their peak performance level or when they are training to the point of injury or overtraining. By calculating training load accurately, you will get better results with your training. Train at different weekly point levels to determine just how much, how hard, and how long you as an individual can train to optimize your physiology. With your bike, your monitor, and your Heart Zones program, you can get fitter and faster, plus reduce your amount of fat.

# D
# Synopsis of ACSM Report

The combination of frequency, intensity, and duration of chronic exercise has been found to be effective for producing a training effect. The interaction of these factors provides the overload stimulus. In general, the lower the stimulus the lower the training effect, and the greater the stimulus the greater the effect. As a result of specificity of training and the need for maintaining muscular strength and endurance and flexibility of the major muscle groups, a well-rounded training program including aerobic and resistance training and flexibility exercises is recommended. Although age in itself is not a limiting factor to exercise training, a more gradual approach in applying the prescription at older ages seems prudent. It has also been shown that aerobic endurance training of fewer than two days a week at less than 40–50 percent of $VO_2$, and less than 10 minutes, is generally not a sufficient stimulus for developing and maintaining fitness in healthy adults. Even so, many health benefits from physical activity can be achieved at lower intensities of exercise if frequency and duration of training are increased appropriately. In this regard, physical activity can be accumulated through the day in shorter bouts of 10-minute durations.

In the interpretation of this position, it must be recognized that the recommendations should be used in the context of participants' needs, goals, and initial abilities. In this regard, a sliding scale as to the amount of time allotted and intensity of effort should be carefully gauged for the cardiorespiratory, muscular strength and endurance, and flexibility components of the program. An appropriate warm-up and cool-down period that would include flexibility exercise is also recommended. The important factor is to design a program for the individual to provide the proper amount of physical activity to attain maximal benefit at the lowest risk. Emphasis should be placed on factors that result in permanent lifestyle change and encourage a lifetime of physical activity.

**Source:** *Summary of "The Recommended Quantity and Quality of Exercise for Developing and Maintaining Cardiorespiratory and Muscular Fitness and Flexibility in Healthy Adults,"* Medicine and Science in Sports and Exercise, *vol. 30, no. 6, June 1998.*

*This pronouncement was written for the American College of Sports Medicine by Michael L. Pollock, Ph.D., FACSM, Glenn A. Gaesser, Ph.D., FACSM, Janus D. Butcher, M.D., FACSM, Jean-Pierre Despres, Ph.D., Rod K. Dishman, Ph.D., FACSM, Barry A. Franklin, Ph.D., FACSM, and Carol Ewing Garber, Ph.D., FACSM.*

# E

# Indoor Trainers, Studio Bikes, and Cycling Computers

## INDOOR TRAINING

Cycling indoors can be fun and motivating when your workouts have a purpose and a plan. Indoor cycling is one of the most time-efficient and inexpensive ways to train during the winter months or off-season. Some cyclists train throughout the year using indoor training to work on specific aspects of their cycling fitness. Rarely is the regime boring when you have the cycling tools: a good bike and an HRM.

Sitting on a bike and sweating for 60 minutes for no apparent reason is not "training." In contrast, riding with a specific purpose and goal in mind is.

How do you stick with an indoor training program? Start by calling your exercise "training." Set some goals, individualize your workouts using a heart rate monitor, and write a training program.

Indoor training is important unless you live in a land where the sun shines twenty-four hours a day and snow, ice, and rain are not in the local weather forecaster's vocabulary. The question is not whether to train indoors but how, where, and on what. The "how" is what Heart Zones Cycling using a heart rate monitor is all about: training most efficiently and effectively indoors or out. The "where" is your choice of a health club setting or investment in home equipment. The "what" is the type of training equipment you'll use.

In a health club, you have the advantage of training on various kinds of equipment and with others in a group exercise format such as studio or indoor cycling. If you haven't tried indoor cycling or a spin-bike class, do it. Bring your heart rate monitor so you can measure the intensity level and adapt the class to meet your goals. Classes can be lots of fun, and some people find they work harder when someone is coaching them through a workout. Many people like to share the fun and sweat with a friend or group.

Training at home may require more discipline, but the advantages are that you can use your own bicycle on an indoor trainer, save some time by not commuting to a facility, and pick the ride not the coach.

## Types of Trainers

Trainers come in several types: a conventional trainer where you mount your bike after taking off the front wheel, a trackstand trainer where your rear wheel is cradled and your front wheel is left on, or rollers. Which you use is a matter of personal choice. Ask your local bike shop to recommend one, and if possible, try one before buying.

On an indoor trainer, resistance devices can be either fan, magnetic, roller wheels, or fluid. Resistance fans are typically cheaper and noisier. Magnetic-type devices usually offer more resistance for very strong riders but aren't necessarily better. Rollers improve your balance and pedaling technique.

Sally Reed trains and teaches on a studio bike, or what some call a spin bike. Although the bike is designed to fit a wide range of body type and size, it's difficult to get a good fit if you are short (under 5 feet 2 inches) or very tall (over 6 feet 5 inches). The flywheel on the bike weighs between 30 and 50 pounds, and the resistance is usually a belt or pads that apply pressure to the flywheel. These bikes are fun but are strictly "fixed gear," meaning the pedals

| Indoor Trainers | | |
|---|---|---|
| **Trainer** | **Price** | **Phone/Website** |
| Blackburn TrackStand Defender | $230 | 800-456-2355 www.blackburndesign.com |
| Performance Travel Trac 2000 | $220 | 800-727-2453 www.performancebike.com |
| CycleOps Fluid+ | $299 | 212-924-6724 www.cycle-ops.com |
| Cateye CS1000 Cyclosimulator | $350 | 800-522-8393 www.cateye.com |
| Elite Volare Fluid Drive | $260 | 360-692-6540 www.elite-it.com |
| Minoura MagTurbo ERGO-10 | $130 | 800-601-9592 www.minoura.co.jp |
| Tacx Cycleforce Excel | $659 | 847-465-8200 www.tacx.nl |
| Kreitler Wind Trainer | $350–$375 | 800-333-5782 www.kreitler.com |
| RacerMate CompuTrainer | $1,000–$2,000 | 800-522-3610 www.computrainer.com |
| QuickStand C-Force | $279 | 800-727-9377 www.biketrainer.com |

**Note:** The use of rollers, a type of indoor trainer, is not recommended for beginning cyclists. It is an excellent training tool for advanced cyclists because it requires advanced skills.

| Studio Bicycles | | |
|---|---|---|
| **Spin Bike** | **Price** | **Phone/Website/Address** |
| Reebok | $600–$800 | Reebok CCS Fitness<br>800-344-0444; www.ccsfitness.com |
| Schwinn | $600–$1000 | Direct Focus<br>800-688-9991; www.directfocusinc.com |
| Keiser | $600–$800 | Keiser Corporation<br>800-888-7009; www.keiser.com |
| Star Trac V-Bike | $600–$800 | Star Trac by Unisen Inc.<br>800-228-6635; www.startrac.com |
| Greg LeMond Revmaster | $700–$900 | LeMond Fitness<br>818-762-5248; www.pelotonfitness.com |

go around with the flywheel and thus offer no coasting—only spin. To date, studio bikes lack fancy gadgets or gears; a resistance knob or lever adjusts the resistance on them.

If you're considering a spin bike, you can contact one or more of the more popular studio-bike companies. Take a class or try one out before making a commitment to purchase one. Plan to spend between $600 and $900 to purchase a new bike. Check with local athletic clubs for old bikes for sale; you can sometimes find these for between $200 and $400. Again, ride them first to make sure they haven't been ridden into the ground.

| Cycling Computers |
|---|
| Avocet USA, Inc.<br>www.avocet.com |
| Campagnolo USA, Inc.<br>www.campagnolo.com |
| Cat Eye<br>www.cateye.com |
| Planet Bike<br>www.planetbike.com |
| Polar<br>www.polarusa.com |
| Shimano Bicycle Components<br>www.shimano.com |
| Sigma Sport, USA<br>www.sigmasport.com |
| Specialized Bicycle Components<br>www.specialized.com |
| Topeak<br>www.topeak.com |
| Vetta USA Limited<br>www.vetta.com |

# F

# Workout Abbreviations and Terms

| Abbreviation or Term | Definition |
|---|---|
| (%) | Percentage of maximum heart rate. |
| (a number) | For example, (8) means 80 rpm or a count of 8 revolutions in 6 seconds. |
| Active recovery | Easy, slow pedaling with little or no resistance (easy gearing). |
| AT | Anaerobic threshold. The heart rate number at which your body is producing more lactic acid than can be metabolized; also known as the lactate threshold or crossover point. |
| AT HR | Riding at, about, or around your estimated anaerobic threshold. Typically the highest heart rate number you can sustain for an extended period of time. |
| Bottom | The lowest heart rate number or percentage in each zone. Also known as the floor of the heart zone. |
| Choice | You decide "how" to change the intensity based upon your goals. You may choose resistance, gearing, cadence, a standing position, a seated position, or any combination. |
| Easy pedal | No resistance, easy gear, low rpm. |
| HR | Heart rate, usually expressed in bpm. |
| ILT | Isolated-leg training. |
| Interval | Alternating periods of higher intensity with periods of lower intensity or recovery time. |
| Max HR | Maximum heart rate, usually expressed in beats per minute (bpm). |
| Midpoint | Halfway between the bottom and top of a heart zone. Usually expressed as a heart rate number or as a percentage. |
| Peak heart rate | The highest heart rate number during a workout period. |
| (R) | Resistance or gearing. |
| (Rec) | Recovery or decrease in intensity. |
| RHR | Recovery heart rate, usually expressed in bpm. |
| rpm | "Pedal" revolutions per minute. Also known as cadence. To determine rpm or cadence, count the number of pedal revolutions in 6 seconds and multiply by 100. |
| Timed recovery | During recovery, count the number of heartbeats dropped in a period of time. |
| Top | The highest heart rate number or percentage in each zone. Also known as the ceiling of the heart zone. |
| TTHR | Talk-threshold heart rate. A narrow range of heartbeats in which you can still talk but you don't want to exert yourself any harder. |
| Work-recovery | Together, an interval consisting of an exercise bout or time period followed by a rest or recovery period. |
| Z1, Z2, etc. | Zone 1, zone 2, etc. |

# Glossary

**Adaptation:** The process of physiological change that occurs when the body responds to the stresses of training loads.

**Aerobic capacity:** The ability of the body to remove oxygen from the air and transfer it through the lungs and blood to the working muscles.

**Aerobic:** With or in the presence of oxygen; an exercise program at an intensity low enough to keep you and your muscles from running out of oxygen.

**Ambient heart rate:** The number of beats per minute your heart contracts when you are awake but in a sedentary and stationary position.

**Anaerobic threshold:** The point at which your body is producing more lactic acid than can be metabolized; also known as the lactate threshold.

**Anaerobic:** Without oxygen; exercise characterized by short-spurt, high-intensity activities during which the muscles briefly operate at an oxygen deficit.

**Average heart rate:** The mean heart rate during an exercise period.

**Base:** A training term for the fitness level required to exercise for a relatively extended duration without tiring.

**Bonk:** A point of fatigue in which necessary fuels are spent and an individual is limited in his or her ability to continue to maintain an exercise intensity. Also known as hitting the wall.

**Bottom of the zone:** The floor, or lower limit, of a heart zone.

**Cadence:** The tempo or the beat of the movement measured in revolutions per minute.

**Carbohydrates:** Organic compounds that, when broken down, become a main energy source for muscular work.

**Cardiac cycle:** The period of time between two consecutive heartbeats.

**Cardiac drift:** The rise in heart rate during exercise that occurs as a result of loss of blood volume principally from dehydration. Also known as cardiovascular drift.

**Cardiac output:** The amount or volume of blood pumped by the heart per minute. Cardiac output is equal to heart rate times stroke volume.

**Cardiac:** Pertaining to the heart.

**Crossover point:** The heart rate where your metabolism shifts fuels, such as from burning fats to carbohydrates. This is the same as $Fat_{Max}$.

**Easy pedal:** An easy cadence with easy resistance.

**Endorphins:** Natural chemicals similar to opiates released into the bloodstream by the brain that result in the feeling of happiness from training.

**Exercise heart rate:** The number of beats per minute you are experiencing during a workout.

**Fat$_{Max}$:** Maximal fat oxidation heart rate number.

**Fats:** Concentrated sources of energy for muscular work. They are compounds containing glycerol and fatty acids and may be saturated or unsaturated.

**Functional capacity:** The ability to do normal daily activities, especially work. Also known as fitness capacity.

**Gas analyzer:** A device that measures the volume, concentration, and content of inspired and expired atmospheric air.

**Heart rate function:** The different features that a heart rate monitor provides, such as time of day, training zones, stopwatch, and others.

**Heart rate monitor:** An electronic device that measures and displays the electrical activity of the heart.

**Heart rate:** The number of beats or contraction cycles your heart makes per minute, measured by the electrical impulses emitted by the heart during this process.

**Heart zones:** A range of heartbeats, usually 10 percent of your individual maximum sport-specific heart rate. There are 5 different heart zones.

**Intensity:** The degree of energy, difficulty, or strength, as relates to a workout.

**Interrecovery:** A way of doing intervals such that recovery is between workout sessions, usually between workout days.

**Interval:** The duration of a given intensity of training. Used in training to mean a set of stress and recovery sessions.

**Intrarecovery:** A way of doing intervals such that recovery is within one workout session rather than between workouts.

**Karvonen formula:** An arithmetical formula to determine maximum heart rate based on using both the maximum and the resting heart rates to establish training zones.

**Lactate analyzer:** A monitoring device that measures blood lactate levels.

**Lactic acid:** Product of the body's metabolic processes that is created in all of the heart rate zones and is shuttled away from the skeletal muscles to different parts of the body where it is oxidized.

**Limits:** The dividing lines of a heart zone—the top of a limit is the ceiling, and the bottom of a limit is its floor.

**Maximum heart rate (max HR):** The greatest number of beats per minute possible for your heart. This number is highly individualized and varies with fitness, age, gender, and other factors.

**Metabolism:** The chemical changes in the body's cells by which energy is provided for vital processes.

**Mitochondria:** Strings of carrier molecules within the cell; they act like tiny energy factories, taking fuel and uniting it with oxygen for muscular combustion in muscles.

**Overreaching:** Training that results in negative muscle fatigue, such as injury or prolonged fatigue.

**Overtraining:** Training too hard, to the point of stress or injury.

**Oxygen consumption:** The amount of oxygen utilized by the body during exercise. Maximum oxygen consumption is aerobic power or cardiorespiratory endurance capacity.

**Palpate:** Applying touch to feel for a medical diagnosis, as in palpating an artery in order to manually count heart rate.

**Peak heart rate:** The highest heart rate number reached during any one workout period.

**Periodization:** Varying the amount of training load over time to prevent monotony and over-training yet produce a positive training effect.

**Pickups:** A type of training that includes several quick bursts of speed.

**Pulse:** The regular throbbing felt in the arteries. Caused by the contractions of the heart. This is not the same as electrically measured heart rate.

**Recovery heart rate:** The difference in the heart rate after a set postexercise rest interval such as 2 minutes.

**Red-lining:** Spending time doing high-intensity, hot training sessions mostly in heart zone 5.

**Repeats:** Repetition of the same set of exercises or training events.

**Resting heart rate:** The number of heartbeats per minute when the body is at complete rest, usually determined upon waking but before arising.

**RPE:** Rate of perceived exertion. A way of assigning a numerical value based on the perception of the effort.

**Rpm:** Revolutions per minute.

**Spin (and spinning):** Fast cadence; high rpm of your pedal stroke.

**Steady-state:** A heart rate or training rate that is submaximal and maintained at a constant intensity, speed, or rate of work.

**Strength:** The maximum force or tension that a muscle can produce against resistance.

**Superspin:** Training at an rpm above 120.

**$T_1$:** Threshold where aerobic benefits first occur; measured as 55 percent of your sport-specific maximum heart rate.

**$T_2$:** Threshold where you cross over your anaerobic threshold, or your $Fat_{Max}$.

**Target heart rate:** A heart zone that is variable and set for the specific workout.

**Tempo:** The cadence or the speed of the revolutions per minute.

**Threshold heart rate:** The heart rate number at a crossover point between aerobic and anaerobic metabolism. Also known as $Fat_{Max}$.

**Time trial:** A way of training or racing that is done solo.

**Top of the zone:** The ceiling, or upper limit, of a heart zone.

**Training effect:** The response to the level of fitness or functional capacity as a result of a dosage of exercise.

**Training load:** The total amount of exercise as determined by frequency, intensity, time, and mode of the exercise experience.

**Training volume:** The amount of time and frequency or time and distance of a workout or series of workouts.

**Training:** Any sustained exercise—cardiovascular, resistance, or a combination of the two—done at a heart rate or intensity level sufficient to result in metabolic adaptation in the muscles involved. The commonly accepted lower threshold, or floor, for cardio training is considered to be 50 percent of maximum heart rate.

**Triglycerides:** The chemical name for the fat stored in the body; most of the fat in foods is also triglycerides.

**$VO_2$ max:** The maximum volume of oxygen that the body can utilize, regardless of intensity increases; it is synonymous with "maximum oxygen consumption" and "maximum oxygen uptake."

**Zone size:** The dimensions of a heart zone. All heart zones have a size of 10 percent of the maximum heart rate.

**Zone weight:** The mathematical value of a zone that is used to determine training load. For example, the Aerobic Zone is zone number 3, or a zone weight of 3.

# Index

# About the Authors

**Sally Edwards** has been training and racing for more than thirty years. She has set world records and won races ranging from a mile in length to Ironman distance. Starting as a runner, Edwards won the Western States 100 Miler and ran in the Olympic Marathon trials, then she transitioned into a professional triathlete and an adventure racer. For the past decade, she has been the national spokesperson for the Danskin Women's Triathlon Series, finishing more than eighty of the

events, frequently as the volunteer "final finisher" so that no other woman has to finish last.

She has founded several successful businesses and taken each of them to a national level. Currently, Edwards is the CEO of Heart Zones, a multifaceted business that develops educational and training programs using the technology of a heart rate monitor. She is a professional speaker who gives presentations on both fitness and success in life to audiences around the world.

Edwards equally divides her home life between Seattle, Washington, and Sacramento, California.

**Sally Reed,** M.A., is the athletic director of the prestigious Bellevue Club in Bellevue, Washington, and a competitive triathlete, endurance cyclist, and former world-class skier. More importantly, in 1997, she created the Heart Zones Cycling training system. After attending one heart zones training seminar, she designed, wrote, and started teaching the first Heart Zones Cycling programs that are the basis of this book.

For the past three years, she has traveled around the country writing, speaking, certifying, and teaching seminars, workshops, camps, and programs on Heart Zones Cycling. She has written more than a hundred workouts using a heart rate monitor on a bike as well as a manual for cycling coaches and instructors to become certified.

Reed lives with her husband, Scott, in Issaquah, Washington.

# Reach Your Cycling Fitness Goals with This Powerful Heart Zones™ Combination!

Whether you're a beginner or advanced cyclist, mountain biker, roadie, studio bike rider, or triathlete, let experts Sally Edwards and Sally Reed help you reach your training and fitness goals by incorporating the five heart zones training systems into your workout.

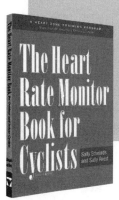

**The Heart Rate Monitor Book for Cyclists, 2nd Edition**
*by Sally Edwards and Sally Reed*
New workouts with charts and tables help cyclists of all levels ride smart and stay fit while training both indoors and outdoors using a heart rate monitor. Plus a new chapter on weight loss provides essential information on burning fat and gaining muscle. Edwards and Reed use the five heart zones to show you how to strengthen the heart and maximize your training and fitness. New, easy-to-use 7" x 10" size. Paperback. 256 pp. **VP-MN2 $17.95**

**The Heart Rate Monitor Workbook for Indoor Cyclists**
*by Sally Edwards and Sally Reed*
A full range of indoor training rides, divided into three different categories: training to improve your health, training for fitness, and training to enhance your performance. Each workout consists of an overview and detailed description of the workout; a profile that provides a visual snapshot of the ride; and a detailed stats and tips table that shows the total number of heart zones training points earned, the total minutes spent in each of the five heart zones, and the estimated calories burned during the workout. Includes 50 different workouts! Paperback.
8 1/2" x 11". 144 pp. **VP-HRW $14.95**

800/234-8356 • Fax: 303/444-6788 • E-mail: velo@insideinc.com • Web: VELOGEAR.COM
Shops and distributors call 800/811-4210, ext.169. VeloPress books are also available from your favorite bike shop or bookstore.